GW00640879

Programming with C
An Introduction

Programming with C

An Introduction

Alex Siday

University of Teesside

Edward Arnold

A member of the Hodder Headline Group

LONDON   NEW YORK   SYDNEY   AUCKLAND

First published in Great Britain in 1995 by
Edward Arnold, a division of Hodder Headline PLC,
338 Euston Road, London NW1 3BH

Distributed in the USA by
Routledge, Chapman and Hall Inc.
29 West 35th Street, New York, NY 10001

British Library Cataloguing in Publication Data
A catalogue record for this book is available from the British Library

ISBN 0 340 60035 7

1 2 3 4 5   95 96 97 98 99

Typeset in Times by GreenGate Publishing Services, Tonbridge, Kent
Printed and bound in Great Britain by J.W. Arrowsmith Ltd., Bristol

Contents

Preface

The purpose of this text is to develop in the reader an understanding of how programs are put together and some skill at designing, implementing and testing them. The best way to learn about programming is to do it. Write and run programs.

We will be using C as our programming language and its various features will be introduced when they are needed. Programming issues will be examined first and where they require specific language features these will then be presented. The reader should keep in mind the distinction between programming and programming languages. A good programmer is almost certainly a good programmer whatever the language and once you have developed some programming skills through using C it should be relatively easy to employ those skills using other languages.

In choosing C we are trying to achieve two things. First we want to use it as the language through which programming ideas are expressed. Second we want the reader to gain some knowledge of what is currently perhaps the most widely used programming language.

This is a compromise in that although C is widely used it presents problems for anyone new to programming which other languages do not. Pascal has always been viewed as the preferred choice for a first programming language and undoubtedly from a language standpoint it has advantages. A considerable amount of effort has to be put into mastering any language and the view taken here is that effort far outweighs the difference in difficulty between C and other possibilities. Further there is no reason why the extra difficulties encountered with C cannot be satisfactorily dealt with. Very large numbers of people initially exposed to Pascal find that they have to learn C. Why not then start with C?

Knowing how to program and knowing a programming language are quite separate. The reader should work at writing good programs and not those that simply demonstrate an understanding of C's more obscure features.

From time to time a feature of C will be introduced but not fully explained, this being left until later. This is because, although the feature is needed at the stage it is introduced, and although its effect is easy to understand, how it achieves that effect will not be apparent until more of the language has been covered. Dealing with language features fully as they are encountered would distort the objectives of this book which is principally about programming. The reader is asked to make a small act of faith in the expectation that all will be clear at a later stage.

Appendix 1 covers all of the language features that are made use of throughout the text and the reader may find it worth referencing from time to time. Although all the important features are described its coverage of C is not in any sense complete.

C along with many other programming languages is profoundly influenced by conventional computer design and **Chapter 1** covers those hardware features that should be reasonably well understood to use C effectively. In particular it deals with the way values such as integers and characters are represented in memory and the way memory is organised. This should ensure a good understanding of the way **type** is supported in C and the role of **pointers**.

Chapter 1 also covers some aspects of the software systems that programs are developed and run on. It is necessary to know in principle what text editors, compilers and linkers do in order to understand how to go about writing and running programs.

The text identifies two levels of design and two ways in which designs are written down. **Chapter 2** looks at the design of small programs using **pseudo-code** to express these designs. Later chapters deal with the problem of designing larger programs where **module structure charts** are employed.

Errors occur in programs for many reasons. One of these is that programs have not been thought through carefully enough. Time spent attempting to ensure that a program's pseudo-code design is reasonably sound is saved many times over at the program implementation stage. Programming is a non-trivial activity demanding care and clear thinking. **Chapter 2** also looks at ways of analysing a program's behaviour at the pseudo-code level. Such analysis should not only identify potential errors it should also suggest simplifications to a design. The simplest solution to a programming problem should be sought. Initial designs are almost invariably over-complex. Carrying this unnecessary complexity through to implementation is clearly undesirable.

Chapter 3 uses two very simple programming tasks to explain the structure of C programs, the declaration of scalar variables, C expressions, iteration, conditional statements, the role of the C library and library functions. One of these is a development of a pseudo-code design given in **Chapter 2**.

Chapter 4 covers the nature and role of program specifications, techniques for moving from a specification to a program design, modular structure and the use of **module structure charts.** A notation for writing down such charts is presented using as an example the design and implementation of a program to evaluate simple arithmetic expressions. This example is also used to show how programs can be developed through a process of **step-wise enrichment**.

Chapters 5 and **6** deal mainly with language issues. **Chapter 5** covers functions, parameters, pointers, extent, scope and linkage. **Chapter 6** starts with the problem of how a telephone directory might be organised with the objective of writing a computerised directory facility. In order to do this arrays, structures and files are needed and this chapter concentrates on their presentation.

Chapter 7 presents the design and implementation of the computerised directory program from a design expressed in the form of a number of structure charts through to the C program itself. In implementing the program alternative ways of representing the directory are examined.

Chapter 8 describes a simple machine architecture along with its instruction set and a corresponding assembler language . This is used as the basis of a case study in software development. The design of an assembler/interpreter system is presented again in terms of structure charts and the functions needed to implement the assembler/interpreter are described. The code for the assembler/interpreter is provided in **Appendix 2.**

A number of areas of computer science have been brought together in this text in the belief that their understanding is important to good programming. The reader will find much of the material straightforward but some of it not so. For example, **Chapter 2** touches on ideas that are normally given a rather formal treatment in the context of program correctness and may take a little effort to appreciate. They have been included to illustrate how one might justify that a program design will work. (Good programmers attempt to find such justifications, poor programmers do not.) **Chapter 8** in particular may prove demanding. It illustrates how a medium scale application is put together and the reader will need to take time to absorb the ideas covered in the chapter.

Wherever possible the reader should get working both the programs given in the test and also those asked for in the exercises at the end of each chapter. The value of practical work in this area of study cannot be over emphasised.

I would like to acknowledge the help given to me by Peter Crane, a colleague here at Teesside, whose careful reading of the text identified numerous errors and lead to a number of improvements in its content and organisation.

Alex Siday

1

The computer
– a programmer's perspective

1.1 Computers and programs

Before making any attempt at writing programs we need to look at what programs are and to do that we need to understand what in principle a computer is. Put at its simplest, a computer is a device for manipulating **data.**

For example we could program a computer to act as a telephone directory. It would hold the directory and if we wanted to find someone's telephone number we would type the person's name in at the keyboard with the computer responding by displaying his number on the screen. The collection of names and numbers held and searched by the computer, the name typed in at the keyboard and the number displayed on the screen are all examples of **data values**. If we type in **Adams E** at the keyboard, **Adams E** is an example of a data value – it is presumably the name of someone. If the computer responded with **1937** (a four digit telephone number) again we have an example of a data value – the telephone number of that person.

This example illustrates an important property of data. We can classify data into different **types** of data. A telephone number is not really the same type of value as a name that appears in a telephone directory. Part of a programmer's job is the identify the various types of data that a particular application may need to manipulate and find ways of **representing** that data within the program.

Data representation will be dealt with more fully later. Here it is enough to be aware that we are using a four digit sequence to represent telephone numbers and that these are not numbers in the conventional sense. For instance it is meaningless to add two telephone numbers together because the resultant value cannot be given a sensible interpretation.

The same four digit sequence **1937** can represent many other types of data value. For example it might represent a date or the number of people working for a particular company. The sort of operations that we can sensibly apply to such values are related to the type of value we are dealing with and not the way the value is represented. Adding two telephone numbers makes no sense and nor does comparing them for anything other than equality. What does it mean to say that the telephone number **1937** is less than the telephone number **1988**? If these digit sequences represent dates then it does become sensible to make such comparisons.

The year **1937** came before **1988**. Adding dates gives nothing useful, but if the two digit sequences represent the number of hourly paid workers and monthly paid workers in a company addition is meaningful, since it gives the number of company employees.

Computers are able to operate on words – the text of this book has been prepared using a computer, sound and even pictures. The nature of the processing carried out by computers is also very varied and it is this flexibility of use that has allowed the computer to be used in such diverse roles as calculating gas bills and controlling the flight of 'fly-by-wire' airplanes.

1.2 A simplified view of personal computer hardware

Although there are many types of computers, personal computers by far outnumber the other types so we will look at the basic organisation of a personal computer. The hardware of such a machine will normally consist of a **keyboard**, a **screen** ,one or more **hard disks**, one or more **floppy disks** and a box containing a variety of electronic components which combine to provide the processing power of the computer which we will refer to as the **processing unit.**

The purpose of each of these components is as follows

- The screen and keyboard provide the means by which the user can communicate directly with the computer. The keyboard allows the user to type in commands, programs and other forms of input such as values to be processed by programs. Responses from the computer to the user will get displayed on the screen. Keyboard input takes the form of sequences of characters (letters, digits and a variety of other characters such as punctuation characters). The output displayed on the screen very often takes the form of sequences of characters but graphical output such as diagrams, pie charts and so forth are also possible.
- Both hard and floppy disks provide a way of preserving data after the machine has been switched off. Data held in the processing unit may get overwritten while the processing unit is running and will cetainly get lost when it is switched off. If it is necessary to preserve data this can be done by putting the data either on the hard disk or on a floppy disk. Although they are physically and in function nothing like audio cassettes they share with audio cassettes the property that data can be stored on them for later use and that this data can be overwritten with different data if it is no longer needed.

We need a way of writing to and reading from disks. Computer systems include **disk drives** for this purpose. Typically a machine will have one hard disk drive and one or more floppy disk drives. These drives carry out the final stages of copying data from a disk or placing data on a disk.

The major differences between hard disks and floppy disks are

(a) hard disks can hold much more data than can floppy disks

(b) copying data from or to a hard disk is normally much faster than with floppy disks

(c) There may be several hard disks attached to a computer. However they will each have a dedicated disk drive and cannot easily be detached from the drive. With floppy disk drives the user is able to insert and remove floppy disks more or less freely.

- The processing unit is made up of a number of interacting electronic components. Among these are included the **main memory, processor** and a number of **controllers.**

Main memory is used as a store to hold both programs and data. The contents of memory are normally only preserved while the computer is switched on. Once the computer is switched off whatever is in memory is lost.

Programs and data held on either a floppy disk or a hard disk can be copied into main memory. Data typed at the keyboard will also get placed in main memory. The movement of data from either a disk or the keyboard into memory is called **input**. Data generated in memory by the processor may get displayed on the monitor screen or get copied to a disk. The copying of data from main memory in this way is called **output**.

The processor carries out the actual data processing under the direction of a **machine code program** held in main memory. Machine code programs are sequences of instructions to the processor directing its behaviour. We will say a little more about the nature of machine code programs later. The program's access to data in main memory is extremely fast in comparison with access to data held on disk. Main memory holds both the program that is determining the behaviour of the processor and any data that the processor is manipulating as directed by the program.

By changing the program in memory the computer can be made to carry out different tasks. The processor is described as **executing** or **running** the program in memory. During even a fairly small period of time (a few hours or a morning) a computer may execute very many different programs,each program being loaded into memory in turn and then executed. Some systems allow several programs to be in memory at the same time, with the processor interleaving the execution of these programs. Which programs get loaded will depend on what use the computer is put to.

The processor also has a limited amount of memory separate from main memory and any data it has been directed to work on is first moved from main memory into this memory. It consists of a collection of specialised units called **registers** and is considerably faster to access than main memory. Note that such registers form an integral part of the processor, whereas main memory does not. The processor carries out its work using these registers bringing data from main memory into registers and copying the values from registers to main memory as determined by the program instructions. If the processor has been directed to add together two numbers these numbers will end up in the registers used for arithmetic before the addition takes place. The instructions that make up the program are also moved one at a time into processor memory in order that the processor can interpret the instruction.

There are normally some processor registers that the programmer can access directly. For example the M68000 processor has eight data registers that can be used by the programmer to hold numeric values. This is not the case for all registers however. The register used to hold the next instruction to be executed, for example, cannot be accessed by the programmer.

When a piece of data is being processed it will perhaps start out on disk, moving first into main memory and then into the processor's memory before the processor actually does anything with it.

Note that we think of a program in memory as an active component operating on a passive component, data, by directing the computer's processor to manipulate the data in some way. Another view is that the program is data that the processor operates on, with the processor being the active component and the program in memory the passive component. It is certainly the case that at times we treat a program as data. In loading a program from disk to main memory it is being treated as such.

Controllers are hardware components designed to support input and output. The keyboard, the screen and the disk drives are all called **devices**. There are many other devices that can be connected to a computer. For example printers are very commonly used with PCs. Data normally flows from a device into memory or from memory to the device. This flow of data has to be managed and this management is shared between the device itself, the processor and the controller which interfaces the device with the rest of the computer system.

Figure 1.1 shows how the components of a typical desk top computer are organised indicating the flow of data between components using arrowed lines. The labels c1, c2, c3 and c4 refer to the screen controller, the hard drive controller, the floppy drive controller and the keyboard controller.

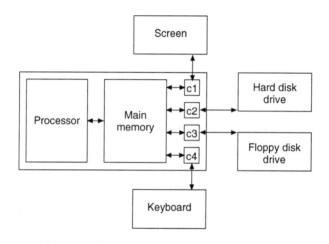

Figure 1.1 *The structure of a simple computer*

1.3 Main memory and its uses

Understanding the principles of how the hardware of a computer works helps the programmer appreciate the scope and limitations of such machines. It also helps in making use of languages like C. Knowing how main memory is organised and used is particularly important. For example the use of pointers in C is often considered 'tricky' but if the relationship between the concept of a pointer and main memory addressing is understood then many of the difficulties associated with pointers disappear.

To get over some of the ideas associated with main memory we will make use of a simple analogy. Figure 1.2 shows a of a sheet of paper on which the digits **0,1,2,**

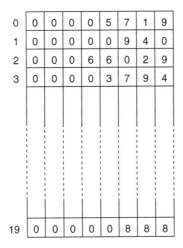

Figure 1.2 *A digit pad*

... **9** can be written. The sheet is made up of 20 lines with each line providing space for exactly eight digits. We will refer to such sheets as digit pads.

In order that we can identify the individual lines that make up a digit pad we will number them starting with the number **0**. Normally we tend to number objects starting with **1**. For example house numbers almost always start at **1**. Programmers, accepting that **0** is as good a number as any, are happy to number from **0**. The purpose of numbering is two fold. It provides a way of labelling things. We know what we mean by line **13** of a digit pad. It also orders. Line **12** appears immediately before line **13**. Line **14** appears immediately after it. We are labelling and ordering whether we start our numbering at **0** or **1**.

We will call the numbers labelling lines **addresses**. The address of the first line of the pad is **0** and the address of the last is **19**.

Let us suppose that digit pads have the property that if we write a digit in one of the eight digit boxes found on a line it overwrites what is there already and that the digit boxes always have a digit written in them. If we could buy such digit pads they would come with perhaps a random set of **160** digits. We give our digit pad this property because computer memory behaves in a similar way.

Let us also suppose that the only things that can be written in digit boxes are digits.

Notice that we have used two ways of describing **0,1,2, ... 9**. We have described them as digits and also as numbers. They are in fact digits – marks on paper – normally used to **represent** numbers.

The number represented by the sequence of digits **102** can also be written down using Roman numerals as in **CII** and using letters as in **one hundred and two**. Whichever way we choose to write the number down it is always the same number. Thus numbers and the way we write them down are different and should be carefully distinguished.

The distinction between a physical representation and what is represented can also be seen by considering the sequence of characters

MIX

This is a physical representation (marks on paper) of something but what does it stand for? Is it the verb 'to blend together' or are the characters to be interpreted as roman numerals giving an entirely different meaning namely the number **1009**? There is no way of telling from the sequence of characters itself. It is the context in which '**MIX**' is found that will determine its meaning. What you see is a physical representation of something. The 'something' may be an abstract idea such as a number or an action such a mixing ingredients. The physical representation may mean different things in different contexts.

What could we use a digit pad for? We could write down our 20 most used telephone numbers and place the pad by our telephone. We would of course have to remember that the doctor's telephone number was say on the first line (at address **0**) our grand aunt Dot's on the second (at address **1**) and so forth and we would be restricted to at most eight digits for each telephone number. However, we would soon forget which telephone number was which.

If we could use letters as well as digits we could overcome this problem by halving the number of telephone numbers on the pad, using alternate lines for names and numbers as in Figure 1.3.

0			D	O	C	T	O	R
1	0	0	7	3	4	0	6	7
2					D	O	T	
3	0	0	3	5	4	2	0	1

Figure 1.3 *A telephone directory*

However we are not allowed to write letters on our pad – it allows for only digits. We are used to using digit sequences to represent numbers. There is no reason why we cannot use the digits to represent anything we like. Providing we know how to interpret what we see we could use pairs of digits to represent letters. Why pairs of digits? There are 26 letters and only 10 digits.

Let us agree the correspondence

     A 65
     B 66
     C 67

     .   .

     .   .
     Z 90

Thus DOCTOR becomes the sequence of **12** digits

   68 79 67 84 79 82

Our choice of coding may seem a little odd. There is a reason which we will give later but since it really does not matter how we choose to code the letters as long as we know the correspondence between the codes and the letters and the coding is convenient to use we can accept it without further justification.

By allocating three lines for each entry with the first two used to hold a name of up to eight letters and the third a number we might write out the above two entries as

0					6	8	7	9
1	6	7	8	4	7	9	8	2
2	0	0	7	3	4	0	6	7
3								
4			6	8	7	9	8	4
5	0	0	3	5	4	2	0	1

This does not quite work because we have not done anything about the unused digit positions on lines used for names. For example the entry for the name DOT makes use of only the last six digit positions on the two lines allocated to it. Recalling that our digit pad has digits in every digit position we must make sure that what precedes DOT is interpreted as a sequence of five spaces. We will give the space a code as well , namely **64,** which means our digit pad would finally look like

0	6	4	6	4	6	8	7	9
1	6	7	8	4	7	9	8	2
2	0	0	7	3	4	0	6	7
3	6	4	6	4	6	4	6	4
4	6	4	6	8	7	9	8	4
5	0	0	3	5	4	2	0	1

We need to code spaces in some way because the digit positions in the digit pad that correspond to spaces must contain some digit values and these must be different from those used for letters.

Names have been right justified in the sense that they are preceded with as many spaces as are needed to fill the 16 digit positions set aside for them.

Notice that in dealing with names we made use of two adjacent lines. Initially we thought of each line as holding a single number. We then saw that we were writing down a representation of a number using sequences of digits. In order to deal with names we viewed a line as four pairs of digits and used adjacent lines. We have made use of our digit pad to hold **values** of two essentially different **types** (names and telephone numbers). Both types of value are expressed using digits and if we did not know how to interpret what we found on the digit pad we could not make sense it. Digit sequences themselves convey no meaning. We need an interpretation rule to make sense of them.

We have already seen that telephone numbers are not really numbers in the normal sense. There is no point for example in adding together two telephone numbers nor do they in any sense measure quantity. They are simply sequences of digits that correspond to signals used within a telephone network to identify a network user.

Such sequences can however always be interpreted as numbers. The standard interpretation is that a sequence of digits corresponds to a particular sum of powers of **10**.

By **215** we mean

$$2 * 10^2 + 1 * 10^1 + 5 * 10^0$$

The position of a digit in the digit sequence determines which power of ten it applies to with the rightmost digit corresponding to the smallest power of **10**. We describe this system of number representation as base **10**. The invention of this positional form for numbers was one of the great advances in mathematics. Why **10** digits? There is no obvious answer. Any number of digits could have been adopted and positional systems using different bases are in use, in particular the **binary** system.

1.4 Binary numbers

We normally use the **10** digits **0,1,...,9** and (implicitly) successive powers of **10** to represent numbers. We could use any number of digits with an appropriate base. For example if we restricted ourselves to the two digits **0** and **1** then numbers can be expressed in exactly the same way except that we would be dealing with successive powers of **2**.

Using just **0, 1** and **2** as our base

$$11010111 = 1 * 2^7 + 1 * 2^6 + 0 * 2^5 + 1 * 2^4 + 0 * 2^3 + 1 * 2^2 + 1 * 2^1 + 1 * 2^0 = 215$$

That is the number normally written **215** (using the base **10** notation) could also be written **11010111** using base **2** notation. We are employing two different systems to write down the same number. The importance of the second system (called the binary system) is that it parallels the way computers store data.

1.5 The structure and organisation of main memory

Computer memory is made up of a large but finite number of storage cells called **memory locations** similar to the lines of a digit pad restricted to the digits **0** and **1**. The amount of memory will vary from machine to machine, but PCs often have associated with them memories with more than a million memory locations. Each memory location can be uniquely identified by its **memory address** (similar to the addresses of lines of a digit pad) but in all other respects memory locations are alike. A program will **access** a memory location by use of its address and such accesses will be to enable the program to obtain the value held in the memory locations (its **contents**) or place a new value there. A memory location will always have some value held in it.

Addresses are numbers starting at **0** and memory locations are assigned successive numbers. Thus a unique number is associated with each memory location and it is this number that is used for addressing purposes.

Figure 1.4 illustrates the way memory addressing is typically organised. A memory of over a millon locations is shown with the addressing running from **0** to **1048575**, the memory being made up of 2^{20} separate memory locations. (Memory sizes are always based on powers of two.) To reference the very first memory location an address of **0** is used. To address the very last memory location an address of **1048575** is used. The range of addresses is $0 .. 2^{20} - 1$.

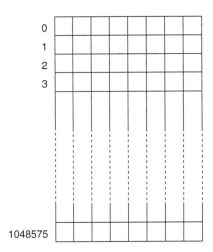

Figure 1.4 *The layout of main memory*

1.6 The contents of memory

Each memory location is constucted out of a small number (typically eight) of **two state** electronic devices called **bits**. Like our digit pad each device is always in one of its two possible states which can be thought of as the electronic equivalent of binary digits. That a bit can be in one of two states is to do with the physical properties of the material used to make the bits themselves. They can be switched between their two states electronically – this is analogous to making a mark on a piece of paper.

The **contents** of a memory location are determined by the combined states of the devices that make up a location. Where we need to discuss the contents of a memory location without making any assumptions about what the contents represent (a number, a letter or whatever) we will refer to the memory's state.

Memory locations can be set to any one of their possible states by the computer (memory is **written to**) and it is also able to determine the state of a given memory location (memory is **read from**).

The states of a memory location are used to **represent** data just as digits on a sheet of paper are. There is a correspondence between each physical state and a value. When a memory location is in a particular physical state this is **interpreted** as a particular value. Again, as with the digit pad, we can choose to interpret the same physical state in all sorts of different ways.

The most common location size, called a **byte,** gives **256** (2^8) possible states, being constructed out of eight bits but computer memories have been used with location sizes greater than this. If n bits are used for each memory location these locations can take 2^n possible states. Thus bytes are made up of **8** bits. The size of memory locations are measured in bits. A byte has a size of **8** bits.

The states taken by a memory location are in some respects similar to the states taken by a car mileometer. A milometer will have a fixed number of digit positions associated with it where each digit position can display a decimal digit **0 .. 9**. Each combination of digit values will correspond to a different state. Thus a mileometer with eight digit positions will have 10^8 possible states ranging from **0000000** to **99999999**. The mileage it can record is limited by the number of digit positions in its display. If we add **1** to a mileage of **99999999** the milometer cannot display **100000000**. The digit that would have been recorded if there was a ninth digit position on the milometer is lost and the display becomes **00000000**. In the same way the number of different states a memory location can take is limited by the number of bits used in its construction. These limitations are reflected in C. For example in using whole numbers (integers) in a C program the programmer should be careful not to generate numbers greater than the machine caters for.

Strictly the integers are all the numbers

... –3, –2, –1,0,1,2,3 ...

but there are an infinite number of these and only a finite number in some range

$-2^{n-1} .... 2^{n-1} - 1$

are normally available to the programmer. Again powers of **2** are being used to describe values associated with memory locations. Integers are normally held in either two byte or four byte fields. Thus either 2^8 or 2^{16} distinct states will be available to represent integers. Half the integers will be negative and half positive in the range $-2^7 ... 2^7 - 1$ or $-2^{15} ... 2^{15} - 1$.

If a calculation leads to a integer number larger than allowed for then the value generated in the program will be different from the true value. The most significant part of the number is lost much as it is with our mileometer. This unsatisfactory state of affairs (called **integer overflow**) exists with most programming languages. With integer overflow the C programmer is left to his own devices although most hardware recognises its occurance. Overflow checks could be incorporated into programs automatically. However this is not normally done because the resultant programs would be larger and run more slowly.

We think of memory locations as being in one of a number of states so that we can make a distinction between these states **and what they represent**. Given a **256** state memory location let us number the states **0,1,2, ... 255**. We can interpret these states as the non-negative integer numbers **0 ... 255**. But this is not the only interpretation. If we wanted to represent positive and negative numbers the numbers **0 .. 127** could be associated with the states **0 ... 127** with the numbers **–1 ... –128** being associated with states **255 ... 128**. This gives **256** integer values in the range **–128 ... 127**.

There is no reason why we cannot uses the states to represent any type of value we like provided we have enough states to work with. Characters such as the letters, digits, punctuation symbols and so forth can be coded in this way. Indeed a number of codings have been developed to represent letters, digits and other characters to allow text to be held in computer memory. The most widely used is the ASCII coding (American Standard Code for Information Interchange) given in Appendix 3.

The coding we chose for the upper case letters and for the space in our telephone example was taken from the ASCII coding.

The coding (ASCII or otherwise) used on a particular machine to represent characters is a feature of the hardware of that machine. IBM PCs make use of ASCII as do most micro-computers. Greater variety can be found in the larger mainframe computers.

Decimal numbers (numbers that include a decimal point), called **floating point** numbers in C, also have a representation on most machines which is normally quite different from the way integers are represented. In representing integers we found that we had to restrict ourselves to a finite set of integers in some range $- 2^{n-1} \dots 2^{n-1} - 1$ where **n** is the number of bits used to hold integer values. We did however get all the integers within that range. In general given two integers **n** and **m** with **m** greater than **n** there is a **finite** number of integers in the range **n … m** (namely **m − n + 1**). However given two decimal numbers **n** and **m** with **m** greater than **n** there is an **infinite** number of decimal numbers between them. This is easy to see by considering for example **1.1** and **1.2**. Certainly **1.11** and **1.12** are between them. Similarly **1.111** and **1.112** are between **1.11** and **1.12** and therefore between **1.1** and **1.2**. We can continue finding such pairs simply by extending the first number of a pair on the right with the digits **1** and **2**. It is therefore not possible to to represent all the decimal numbers between **n** and **m** using a fixed number of bits.

The standard way of representing decimals is based on the idea that any decimal **d** can be expressed using a value **m** between **0** and **1** along with a scaling multiplier **e** such that

$$d = m * 10^e$$

Thus for example given the decimal value **31.579** we have **m = 0.31579** and e = 2 with

$$31.579 = 0.31579 * 10^2$$

and given the decimal value **0.0005897** we have **m = 0.5897** and e = − 3 with

$$0.0005897 = 0.5897 * 10^{-3}$$

A decimal number is held as two values **m** and **e**. **m** is called the **mantissa** and **e** the **exponent**. The term **floating point** is used to describe this way of representing decimals because the decimal point has 'floated' from its normal position in the decimal number.

This way of representing decimal numbers allows a wide range of numbers but the numbers within that range that can be represented accurately are limited.

For example if the mantissa ranged from **− 99999 .. 99999** with the exponent ranging over **− 9 … 9** then the largest positive decimal number that could be represented is

$$999990000.0 \ (0.99999 * 10^9)$$

with the smallest being

0.000000001 (0.1 $*$ 10^{-9})

Decimal numbers that cannot be represented accurately will be **rounded**. For example with the above mantissa and exponent ranges the number **357.9724** will be rounded to **357.97** with mantissa **0.35797** and exponent **3**.

The number of digits that the mantissa can represent is called the precision of the floating point number. In our example the precision is **5**.

Why do we need to worry about how decimal numbers are represented? Decimal numbers are used widely and almost all programming languages support them. The programmer should be aware that arithmetic operations involving them may lose accuracy.

Again, with the above mantissa and exponent, adding **9999.56** and **0.0000001275** yields **9999.56**. The smaller decimal number makes no contribution to the summation.

A typical representation uses four bytes for floating point numbers with one byte used for the exponent and the remaining three used for the mantissa. Depending on the implementation, C provides at least two representations for floating point numbers. They differ only in the number of bytes used and therefore the sizes of the exponent and mantissa. These are usually four bytes and eight bytes.

Because numbers in memory are in binary both the mantissa and exponent will be in binary with the exponent representing a power of **2** rather than **10**.

Most machine instruction sets include addition and subtraction of integers which take into account the way integers are represented. With personal computers floating point arithmetic is not normally supported at the hardware level although what are called **floating point co-processors** can be added to provide such support. Without such a co-processor floating point arithmetic must be provided for in software.

Normally the programmer is not concerned about the fine detail of how numbers and characters are represented in memory but when programs are being moved from one machine to another difficulties can arise from both memory location size differences which might reduce the range of numbers that make sense ,and, in the case of characters from the possibility that a different character coding is used on the target machine.

We have seen that the most common memory location size is **8** bits. Although this is large enough to represent characters it is quite inadequate for numbers. To overcome this limitation locations are combined in twos or fours, where integer numbers and decimal numbers need to be represented. If a byte can take 2^8 states two bytes give $2^8 * 2^8$ (2^{16}) states, allowing non-negative integer numbers in the range **0 ... 65535** or numbers including negatives in the range **– 32768 ... 32767**. In using C there is some control over how many memory locations are used to represent numbers. Normally the choice is between one, two and four bytes but this can vary from machine to machine.

As we have seen, we can view the contents of memory in one of two ways. First we think of the contents as representing a value of some type. The contents of two bytes for example might be interpreted as an integer.

Our second view applies no interpretation to the contents. We are interested only in the bit settings without any interpretation. The term **bit pattern** will be used to refer to the contents of memory in such situations.

1.7 Memory addresses

Each memory location has an address associated with it. This means that every value held in memory also has an address. Where a value occupies more than one location adjacent locations are used with the lowest address normally treated as the address of the value.

Since the numbers **0, 1, ...** are used for memory addresses they can themselves be held as values in memory locations. Because machines invariably have more than **256** memory locations a single byte would not be large enough to hold memory addresses and two bytes or four bytes are normally used. In Figure 1.4 a memory with an address range of $0 \dots 2^{20} - 1$ is illustrated. Neither a single byte nor two bytes would be adequate to hold the highest addresses in such an address range. A single byte would cater for the addresses $0 \dots 2^{8} - 1$ with two bytes giving an address range of $0 \dots 2^{16} - 1$. The number of bytes actually used for addresses is a feature of the processor itself.

Because addresses can be placed in memory, addresses as well as characters and integers can be manipulated within programs.

In many programming languages the programmer is unaware of the way memory addresses are used. C is unusual in that the programmer has normally to be clear about when an address is used and when the value held in memory at a given address is used. This is in some respects a disadvantage of the language. Ideally a programming language should hide such hardware related features from the programmer, allowing him to concentrate on his programming in a totally machine independent way. However the design of almost all computers follows the same basic structure. This is often described as the von Neumann architecture after the man who, over 50 years ago, set out the principles underpinning the design of computers. Most of the programming languages in wide use today reflect this von Neumann architecture. Sooner or later programmers encounter situations where it is important to understand the nature of the machine their programs are executing on and this is very often to do with the distinction between the address of a memory location and its contents. C requires that the programmer is aware of such issues a little earlier than in most other programming languages.

Figure **1.5** shows a section of memory with values at addresses **1024** and **1025** and at **2058 ... 2061**. The bit patterns in these locations tell us nothing about what they are intended to represent. However if we interpret the first pair as an address and the second four bytes as an integer then

- the value held at address **2058** is the integer **657418**
- the value held at **1024** is an address, **2058**, that of the area of memory holding the integer **657418**.

We are assuming here that addresses require two bytes and integers four bytes. As has already been pointed out this is hardware dependent.

Although two bytes are set aside for addresses and four for integers, when we refer to the addresses of these values (as distinct from the addresses of the bytes used to hold the values) we use the lowest addresses (**1024** and **2058**) associated with them. Although both **1024** and **1025** are associated with the address **2058** as a value held in memory, we say that this address is held at **1024**.

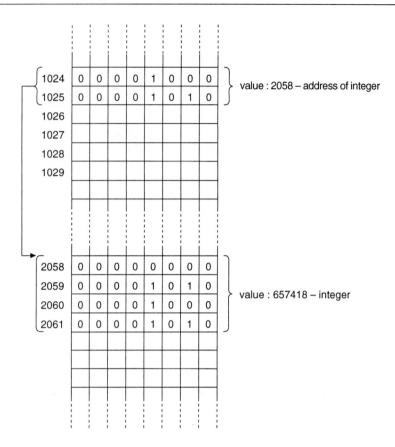

Figure 1.5 *Addresses and integers in memory*

How do we know that the first value should be treated as an address and the second as an integer? This is to do with type. The first value is an address of an integer with the second being an integer. Thus they are values of different type. In C, as in many other programming languages, whenever a value is created or used its type is known. This means that the way it is represented, how many bytes are required to store it and how it should be manipulated are also known.

There is no information about the type of a value held with the value itself. We could for example interpret the value at **2058** as an address. We are assuming that addresses use two bytes of memory so the contents of **2058** and **2059** get interpreted as the address **10**.

There is a danger that we use values in memory in the wrong way. We might unintentionally interpret an address as an integer or a character. In the early days of programming such errors were often the cause of program failure. We will see later that languages like C provide checks that help to reduce the likelihood of such errors.

We can store in memory the addresses of any type of allowable value, integers, characters and even addresses themselves. In Figure 1.6 the integer value is now at address **6154**. Its address is held as a value at **2058** and that address is itself held in memory at **1024**.

The type of value at **6154** is, as before, an integer, that at **2058** has type address of integer and that at **1024** is address of address of integer.

A value in memory has two attributes, the value itself and the address of the value. We use memory in two ways. Either we take the value at a given address and make use of it in some way or we change the value at a given address. In the first case both of the value's attributes are made use of. In the second only the address is used with the value discarded.

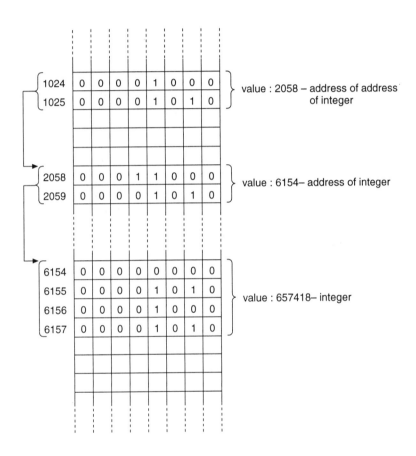

Figure 1.6 Addresses of addresses

In accessing a memory location we may reference it directly (as in 'the integer value at address **6154**') or our reference may be indirect (as in 'the integer value whose address is at **2058**'). As we will see later the use of indirection is common in programming with C).

1.8 Machine code programs and programming languages

We have said that the actions of the processor are directed by a program held in memory. The program is made up of a sequence of **instructions** and the processor is designed to step through these instructions **executing** them in turn. An instruction directs the processor to carry out an operation such as add together two numbers or copy a number from one part of memory to another. The processor treats the instructions held in memory as data, taking instructions one at a time from memory, determining the action indicated by each instruction and then carrying it out.

Instructions are held in memory as bit patterns just as addresses, integers characters and so forth are. Part of the bit pattern will indicate which operation should be carried out and part of it will indicate where in memory any values used by the operation are held. For example if the instruction is an integer add operation the processor will determine from the instruction not only that the operation is indeed the addition of two integers but also where the two integers are currently held and where the result should be stored. We saw that the various types of value that could be held in memory were held there as bit patterns. A bit pattern stands for an integer for example because we choose to interpret it in that way. Similarly a bit pattern becomes an instruction simply because it is interpreted as such by the processor. All programmers make errors in their programming. Those that program at the machine code level risk making errors of type. A value intended as an integer could be accidentally treated as an address or even an instruction. Such errors are often difficult to track down. We will see later that high level languages make this type of error much less likely.

The instructions held in memory are called **machine instructions** or **machine code.** It is very rare that programmers write programs in machine code. There are two reasons for this. First it is much more time consuming to write such programs compared with using a programming language such a C. This is because the programmer has to get very much more involved in the detail of how the processor works than is strictly necessary to describe the required action in general terms. For example if we want to describe the addition of two numbers this is very easy in principle. We simply place the operation + between the two numbers as in **3 + 4**. This is more or less how we would describe such an action in C. To express the same action in machine code we would normally have to explicitly direct the processor to

(a) move the number **3** from memory to a processor register R
(b) add the number **4** (again from somewhere in memory) to R
(c) move the value in R (**7**) back to memory.

Anyone who has struggled with an early model video recorder attempting to set it so that it will record automatically and who has given up in despair will know that it can be very difficult to direct programmable machines to do even very straightforward tasks. Modern video recorders often provide controls that are much easier to use, allowing the user to describe what he wants the machine to do in quite simple terms. What the video recorder does is the same. However the way of describing what happens has become much more related to how the user of the video understands things. This is what designers of programming languages have attempted to do. A language such as C allows us to make the computer do more or less anything that we can achieve through the use of machine code programs but in a much simpler way. For any C program there will be a corresponding machine code program but the C program will be much easier to understand.

A second reason why machine code programming is rarely used is that the program produced is restricted to computers with the same type of processor. There are a number of 'competitor' processors on the market, built by different manufacturers, from which computers can be built. These processors are often very different in detail although in general they have much in common. Certainly the instructions recognised by one type of processor cannot be executed on a different type of processor. Programming a task of any significance takes time and we would like to do this in a way that allows us to move our program from one machine to another without too much extra work. A number of programming languages have been developed that allow the programmer to write programs in a **machine independent** way. That is the programmer need not be aware of the detailed behaviour of the processor on which the program executes. Such languages are called **high level languages** . C is one of a fairly large number of high level languages.

Nevertheless if we write a program it has to end up as a machine code program before it can be executed. A C program for example needs to be translated into a machine code program. Turning such a program into its machine code equivalent is itself a programming problem. That is it is possible to write a program to do the job. A program which translates a program written in a high level language into machine code is called a **compiler**. The translation itself is called **compilation**.The compiler treats the program as data, constructing from it an equivalent machine code program. On any given machine each high level language that is used will have associated with it a compiler. Compilers tend to be large and complex programs. They are however freely available at a price for most languages on most machines from companies that specialise in their production.

The use of a high level language places some limitations on the programmer. He cannot, for example, access the processor data registers directly. They will be used in the compiled program but their use is entirely determined by the compiler. C is unusual in that it allows the programmer to influence in a very limited way how the compiler makes use of registers but this feature of the language is hardly ever used.

A further limitation, which most high level languages impose, is on the way data values are introduced and used. If we write in machine code we can do what we like with values in memory. Because no type information is associated with a value's representation in memory we can treat its corresponding bit pattern as an integer, a group of characters, an address or indeed a value of any type. At the machine code level the way a bit pattern in memory is **used** will determine its type. In allocating memory for values most high level languages require the programmer to state the value type and any use of the value must be consistent with its type. In C an integer for example cannot be used as an address and any attempt to do so will be picked up as **type error** on compilation.

Languages vary in the extent to which such checks are required of the compiler but few languages allow the total freedom found in machine code.

Many of the differences between languages arise from the way they support numbers. Almost all high level languages treat integers and decimal numbers as different in type even though in carrying out calculations using pencil and paper the distinction between the two types is largely ignored. This is because they are represented differently in memory and operations such as addition must be carried out differently. Integer addition is carried out directly by the processor whereas floating point addition is often dealt with by software.

This creates a problem when integers and decimals are mixed.

For **3 + 4** two integers are added giving the integer result **7**.

For **3 + 4.2** an integer and a decimal are involved. Since the addition operation will apply either to two integers or two decimals we must treat **3** as a decimal or **4.5** as an integer. A **type conversion** is carried out which finds a value of a second type in some way equivalent to the value of the first type. Here the obvious conversion is from the integer **3** to the decimal **3.0** since this does not lose accuracy and the result of the addition would be a decimal number. The alternative would be to convert the decimal **4.2** to the integer **4** losing accuracy.

Different languages deal with such mixed types in expressions in different ways. Most will automatically carry out the conversion with the least loss of accuracy. They also normally allow the programmer to control the conversion explicitly so that if for example in the above addition a conversion to integer was wanted where the automatic conversion was to decimal he could over-ride the automatic conversion.

Whatever the language, when the programmer makes use of a value he should be aware of its type and what operations are allowable on values of that type.

C is not as restrictive on the 'mis-use' of types as many other high level languages. For example most languages provide a character type where operations such as the addition of two characters do not make sense and are not allowed. C supports character type but allows character values to be treated as integers.

The type constraints discussed above are normally there to help the programmer. Many of the errors that arise when programming in machine code are to do with a mis-use of types inherent in the application for which the program has been written. Such errors are avoided by contraining the use of types.

1.9 The editor and text files

To develop a program using C we have seen that we must first write the program in C and then execute a C compiler which generates an equivalent machine code program from the C program. We are then in a position to execute our program. The C compiler will read the text of the C program, constructing from it the corresponding machine code program.

The C program is input **as data** to the C compiler which outputs **as data** the machine code program. Note the two views that can be taken of a C program. It is something that executes (at least once it has been compiled) and it is input data to or output data from another program (the C compiler). In fact, even when it is executing, what is actually happening is that the processor is moving through the machine code form of the program held in memory, executing instructions as it encounters them. It can be viewed as data even when executing.

Where does the C compiler obtain the text of the C program? We talked earlier about disk storage. On computer systems like the PC a program called an **operating system** is normally provided as part of the system. For example on PCs themselves the most common operating system used is a set of programs called MS-DOS. The operating system carries out a large number of different tasks. It effectively provides a high level language through which the computer user can direct the computer to carry out such tasks as executing programs. One of its tasks is to manage the disk storage in a way that makes life easier for the computer user. The behaviour of the disk drives and their controllers is complex and the operating system hides a lot of this complexity from the user. If a user had to deal directly with these hardware components he would have even more difficulty working out how to make them do what he wants than he would writing in machine code.

Almost every operating system organizes disk storage into **files**. Files are **named** sections of disk storage that hold data. The file name will be chosen by the creator of the file to distinguish it from other files and this name will be used by the operating system to identify the file. A file might be used to hold the text of a C program, its machine code equivalent, the names of employees in a company or indeed any data that needs to be treated as a unit in some sense or other. Of course files will vary both in size and in the nature of the data that they contain.

The contents of files are preserved even when the computer is switched off and change only when directly operated on by a program.

Files are normally grouped into **directories** and most operating systems allow directories to include further directories leading to a tree-like organisation of the files held on the disk storage of a system. This allows the user to organise his collection of files as he wishes, grouping together files and directories that are related in some way.

The operating system provides operations which allow the user to create, delete, copy and modify both files and directories.

Figure 1.7 illustrates how the files and directories might be organised on a floppy disk under MS-DOS. MS-DOS associates the names A:,B:,C: etc with the disk drives connected to the computer. If a disk is in on a drive then the files and directories on that disk are identified first by the name of the drive and then by a sequence of directory names leading to the file followed by the file name itself.

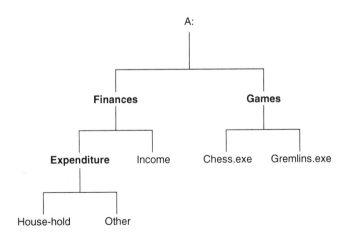

Figure 1.7 *An example of an MS-DOS file store structure*

The file Chess.exe is identified by the sequence

A:\Games\Chess.exe

Chess.exe is a file in the directory Games on a disk in drive A:

Figure 1.7 shows a disk organised into two directories. The directory Games holds two machine code games programs (MS-DOS associates the suffix .exe with files that contain executable code). The directory Finances hold a file called Income and a further directory Expenditure with two files within it.

We will sometimes use the term **file store** to mean the collection of files held on a computer system. The term covers both files held on any hard disk attached to the system and files held on floppy disks.

We needed to know about files to understand where the C compiler gets the text of the C program it is to compile. This will be held in a **text** file and the C compiler will be given the name of this file when the program is executed. As with main memory the file store can be used to hold files containing different types of values. We can create files of integers (where integers have a representation similar to or the same as their representation in main memory) or files of characters for example. Character files are called text files.

This still leaves the question of how such text files are created. Again almost every computer system will include a program called an **editor** which takes textual input from the keyboard storing it away in a file. MS-DOS provides two editors . The first, called Edlin, is a rather old fashioned editor that is probably little used now. The second, Edit, is relatively easy to use and is perfectly adequate for creating files containing C program text. Often a programmer makes use of an integrated package of programs which support file program file editing, compilation and so forth. The Borland C++ system is one such system.

1.10 Syntax errors

We have already seen that the primary job of a C compiler is to turn a program written in C into its machine code equivalent. All programming languages have rules of syntax which govern what a programmer can write down. Such language syntax rules are very like the rules of grammar associated with English with one major difference. We can normally get away with ungrammatical English because the reader or listener can often work out what is meant despite poor grammar. Compilers however will not accept program text that does not follow the syntax rules exactly. They will generate **syntax error messages** which indicate where the rules have not been followed. The human listener draws on a great deal of 'world knowledge' to make sense of badly expressed English. It is not possible to endow compilers with similar attributes and the safest course is to write the compiler in such a way that it reports any syntactically illegal program text. The quality of syntax error monitoring varies from compiler to compiler and almost all will from time to time give misleading messages. If a message does not appear to make sense the text of the program that precedes the point at which the error occurred must be carefully examined for syntax errors. In many ways the compiler writer has a more difficult task in dealing with errors than in generating machine code for programs that contain such mis-uses of syntax. We can get the syntax wrong in far more ways than we can get it right. Because of this even good compilers can occasionally mislead.

1.11 Linking separately compiled C programs

All programming languages have their strengths and weaknesses. One of C's strengths is that it allows the programmer to split his program up into separate **modules** for program development purposes. A module will be made up of C code held in a text file. By convention the file names of such files have suffixes '.c'. Each module can be developed in isolation from the other modules and when the programmer is satified with the individual modules these can combined to make a single program. There are several advantages in this approach. First, the work of a large program can be split up among a number of programmers in a relatively clean way. Second, a particular module of code can be incorporated into different programs.

Normally such modules would not make sense by themselves as executable programs since they almost certainly are referred to from other modules and themselves make references to other modules. They can however be compiled and, again by convention, most C compilers will use the file name of the input C code file as the name of the output file (which contains something very close to machine code) but with a suffix '.o' . Executable programs can then be constructed by linking together the '.o' files created by the compiler. It is at this stage that any references between modules are resolved. Associated with the C compiler is another program called a **linker** which carries out this job.

Given that we have designed and written our program the following steps are carried out to turn it into an executable program

(a) use the system editor to construct the C text files
(b) use the C compiler to compile these text files.
(c) use the linker to link together the output from the C compiler to form an executable program.

Figure 1.8 illustrates how the editor,compiler and linker get used in the contruction of a program. Here the task is to write a program that carries out a statistical analysis

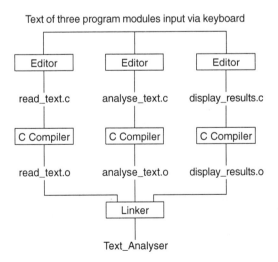

Figure 1.8 The construction of a 3 module program

of a piece of text. It might measure word lengths, sentence lengths and paragraph lengths, displaying statistical information based on these. The program has been split into three separate modules and the C code for these placed in files read_text.c, analyse_text.c and display_text.c. The editor is used to construct each of these files. These are then compiled and the compiler produces read_text.o, analyse_text.o and display_text.o. The linker is then used to bind these three files together to produce an executable program Text_analyser. Both the compiler and the linker may find errors. For the compiler these will normally be syntax errors which the programmer must correct before the corresponding '.o' file is generated. For the linker these will be because the linker has found inter-module references that do not make sense. Again the programmer must find out what is wrong and correct it before an executable program can be created.

Exercises

1. We have seen a number of examples of different types of values (names, tel-ephone numbers, etc.). List the different types given in Chapter 1 and add three further types to the list.

2. What forms of input/output devices other than those given here can you think of?

3. Main memory and storage media such as floppy and hard disks can be used to hold data. Give two ways in which they differ.

4. What are we doing when we interpret a bit pattern?

5. What does it mean to say that something is a representation of a value?

6. If two bytes are used to hold memory addresses what is the maximum size of addressable memory?

7. Section **1.4** describes how letters could be coded on a digit pad using the digits **0 ... 9**. (A code called the ASCII code which gave numeric codes for the letters is used.) The telephone numbers themselves were represented simply as digit sequences. Digits are characters and as such also have ASCII codes associated with them. ('**0**' ... '**9**' are coded **48 ... 57**.) Replace the digits used for telephone numbers by their ASCII equivalents in Figure 1.3. You will need to double the number of digit positions on the digit pad used to represent telephone numbers.

8. The ASCII codes range from **0** to **127**. How many bits are needed to represent an ASCII code?

9. How many bits would be needed to represent just the letters (both upper and lower case) and the digits?

10. In C a string is a sequence of ASCII codes with the last in the sequence being the code **0**. The tring 'DOCTOR' for example is represented as the sequence of codes **68**, **79**, **67**, **84**, **79**, **82** and **0**. Strings can include any ASCII code other than **0**. Suggest an alternative way of representing strings which allows all ASCII codes.

11. Most programming languages treat integers and decimals as different in type. Why is this?

12. Suppose that a floating point representation uses **8** bits for the exponent and **16** bits for the mantissa and that both the exponent and mantissa range from negative to positive values. Give the precision of this representation and give both the smallest and largest positive number that the representation allows.

13. Using the representation suggested in Question **12** how might the number **0.00005124** be held in memory.

14. In Figure 1.6 the integer value **657418** is held at address **6154** with this addess held at **2058** and the address **2058** itself held at address **1024**. The layout assumes that integers occupy **4** bytes and addresses occupy **2** bytes. Draw a diagram showing a similar layout but for the integer value **6574** and with integers occupying **2** bytes and addresses occupying **4** bytes.

2

Program design

Programs begin life as ideas. A need coupled with a belief that a computer can be used in some way to service that need leads to an idea for a program. Progress from that idea to a working program can be slow and painful if care is not taken. In this chapter we will look at some of the steps that should be followed to minimise the risk of failure. Much of what a programmer does is independent of both the machine his programs run on and the languages in which they are written. Given a **specification** of what the program should do he moves from an understanding of what is required through a process of program design to its implementation. Analysing a specification and developing a program design are largely language- and machine -independent activities. This chapter deals with some of the issues that arise in creating a program design.

Errors are made by the programmer throughout the development process and those that are made early are often the most expensive to correct if they are discovered only when the program is completed. In the worst case a misunderstanding about what is required could mean that the final program is useless and all the design and implementation that went into it has to be discarded.

Programmers have been around now for nearly four decades and the one certainty that has come from their efforts is that programs are very likely to have errors in them. It is often easy to produce programs that work some of the time. It can be extremely difficult to produce programs that work all the time. In fact we normally cannot say if a program we have written will always work and the right reaction to any such claim about a program is one of profound scepticism. We can of course produce programs that appear highly reliable. Compilers for example normally work. But they sometimes do not and the compilers of 30 years ago could make a programmer's life very exciting indeed.

It should be unneccessary to urge care at all stages of program development but people new to programming (and, sadly, sometimes very experienced programmers) tend to rush into writing code without a good understanding of what is required or an adequate design to work from. There is a feeling that the real work is in the production of the program, and that analysis and design should be dealt with as quickly as possible. Care from the outset pays dividends in that the overall development time is normally shorter and the final program better put together. In practice errors arise however careful we are and program development is iterative in the sense that at whatever stage we are at we may need to review earlier work. In attempting to design our program we may realise that our understanding of the specification is unsound, or in testing our program we may discover a design error.

2.1 Program specification

Program specifications are very often written in English. Because of this they can lack clarity or contain ambiguities. These difficiencies must be dealt with before any design can take place.

As a very simple example of how English is open to alternative interpretations consider

'Calculate the square root of x and print it out.'

What does 'it' refer to? The chances are that it refers to the square root but there is no certainty and the intended meaning could well be to print out x. In using English we employ such constructions freely and with one interpretation in mind we often do not see alternatives.

We also often leave things out of a specification in the belief that they are obvious.

For example a specification for a payroll program might include a description of how tax is to be dealt with.

'In calculating the annual tax liability if the annual income minus the employee's annual tax allowance is below the standard rate, threshold tax is applied at 25%. If it is above the threshold the residue is taxed at 40%.'

Although this conveys the essence of what needs to be done there are lots of problems with it.

- Is the standard rate tax applied to all income below the threshold or to the difference between that and the annual tax allowance?
- If the residue is taxed is the income below the threshold also taxed?
- What happens if the annual income is below the annual allowance?
- What happens at the threshold?

All these questions arise because the specification has been rather loosely written. Such specifications are not uncommon.

A further consideration in thinking about a specification is whether what is asked for is actually possible. Most people would be wary of attempting to write a program that was intended to correctly forecast the winner of the Grand National but there are some 'impossible' specifications that look very plausible.

Over 30 years ago workers in the area of artificial intelligence attempted to write a program that would translate between Russian and English. At the time it did not seem an unreasonable goal. Their attempts ended in failure and even today no such program exists although useful but limited language translators can now be built and it does look as if we will get there in the end.

A second example of a plausible sounding programming task is to do with what is called the **halting problem**. Programs are normally expected to finish execution at some stage. A common programming error arises because it is possible to write programs that do not. Such non-terminating programs are particularly irritating because it is often necessary to take quite drastic action to deal with them. For example we may have to switch the machine off. We can write programs that do things with other programs. Compilers take programs written in one language and turn them into equivalent programs expressed in a different language. A program that could infallibly tell whether a given program will terminate would be useful and does not look obviously impossible to write unlike our Grand National program. Alan Turing demonstrated in **1936** that such a program would indeed be impossible to write. Fortunately most programmers are never asked to write impossible programs.

Although the current practice is to write specifications in English, specification languages that allow precise descriptions of what is required have been developed and are gaining in popularity. The best known are VDM and Z. Both are based on set theory and the predicate calculus. This mathematical basis means that any specification written in either Z or VDM will be unambiguous. It is still possible however to leave thing out or specify impossible programs. But with the use of mathematical arguments we can analyse such specifications much more thoroughly than we can specifications written in English and as a result identify any problems with the specification at an early stage.

2.2 Program design

Given a good understanding of what is required in a specification, the next step is to develop a program design. Designing programs is in general a non-trivial activity and the programmer must avoid burdening himself with irrelevant considerations. At the design stage the programming language used is not important. Attempting to design and code a program in say C will almost certainly lead to difficulties unless the programming task is extremely simple.

Design is a creative activity and to some extent depends on the designer 'seeing' good ways of building programs but there are a number of techniques which help to give designers ideas and we will look at some of these in this chapter.

A program design needs to be written down. This is necessary in order to move from the design to the program itself. Translating a written design into a program is much easier than attempting to program from a design held in one's head.

Writing down a design helps in a number of other ways.

Often what appears to be a good approach proves very difficult to write down as a design. This is almost certainly because the design has not been thought through sufficiently and an attempt to write it down highlights difficulties with it and helps to clarify the design issues involved.

A written design can be analysed and discussed. A first attempt at a design could well be wrong. Analysing the design in its written form would hopefully reveal errors.

A general design principle that holds good for programming is that of 'divide and conquer'. A program can be thought of as being built from a number of sub-programs which, working together, achieve the effect required of it. The program design will reflect this and as part of the design process the programmer must try to identify these sub-programs. Since the sub-programs are individually likely to be simpler to deal with than the program itself the problem of program design has been simplified.

Often a program can be broken down into sub-programs in a number of different ways. Some will exhibit good structure and others not, although what we mean by 'good' in this context is difficult to define. Certainly the structuring of the program into sub-programs should be clear in the design. Each sub-program should have a well defined task and it should interact with other sub-programs in a simple and straightforward way.

A large number of notations for writing down designs have been invented. Which notation we choose will depend on the complexity of the programming problem in hand. In this chapter we will look at a notation called **pseudo code** which has much in common with languages such as C. This is normally used for programs (or sub-programs) which can be described in a page or less of pseudo code. Although a pseudo code description will leave out some of the detail that will appear in the final program there will be a close correspondence between the two.

A pseudo code description consists of a sequence of pseudo code **statements** where each statement can be interpreted as an action that the computer can carry out. Such statements may be very close to the final program in the sense that there is almost a direct correspondence between pseudo code statement and program statement. Quite often pseudo code statements are at a much higher level, corresponding to many program statements.

Although pseudo code cannot be compiled into machine code – it is too loose a description of program behaviour for that to be possible – we can nevertheless think of it as executing on some imaginary machine. This is what we mean when we say that a pseudo code statement is executed.

Pseudo code descriptions (or indeed any description of how to carry out a computing task) are called **algorithms,** provided each statement in the description makes sense as a computational action and combined collection of statements will not go on executing for ever. The term 'algorithm' is normally applied to those descriptions such as pseudo code where it is not possible to directly execute them on a machine. However, programs are themselves algorithms with the special property that they can be executed.

There is no universally agreed pseudo code language. Each text book on programming will offer an alternative. However they are all loosely based on one programming language or another. They all share two important properties.

- There is considerable freedom in the way actions are described.
- Almost no provision is made for describing the type of any data processed by the pseudo code.

The emphasis is on what is called **flow of control**. That is the order in which the actions described in the pseudo code are carried out by the computer. This flow oriented view of software contrasts with the currently fashionable **object** oriented view which emphasises data types. In practice the design and implementation of software has always recognised both views but flow of control has dominated programmers' thinking.

Here we will use a pseudo code based on C. The difference between the notation used here and that found in other text books is largely a difference of syntax. Flow of control is expressed using a C- like syntax. There is little or no difference in the nature of the flow. In fact we will freely plunder C in writing pseudo code where it is sensible to do so.

Pseudo code is a good way of describing the behaviour of programs at a level fairly close to the program itself. Earlier it was suggested that a program of any complexity should be viewed as being built from a collection of sub-programs. In later chapters we will make use of structure charts to describe program designs in terms of sub-programs where the links between sub-programs are shown but not the detailed behaviour of the sub-programs themselves.

2.3 Example 1 – Ordering three integer values

Suppose we want the computer to read in three integers and print them out in descending order of magnitude. Our first algorithm might be

> read three integer values into **a**, **b** and **c** from the keyboard;
> swap the contents of **a,b** and **c** so that **a** contains the largest integer and **c** contains the smallest;
> write out the values of **a,b** and **c** to the screen;
>
> ### swap 1

We have used the names **a,b** and **c** for the three memory locations that will be used to hold the input integers. **a**, **b** and **c** are examples of **identifiers**. In C, identifiers are used to name objects introduced by the programmer. We will discover later that identifiers are used to name a number of different classes of objects. Where they are used to name memory locations in the manner above they are called **variables**.

swap 1 is very close to English although there are some minor differences. Capitals are not used to start sentences and we end them with semi-colons rather than full stops. The semi-colon is intended to indicate the order in which actions should be carried out. The action described up to the first semi-colon should be carried out first with that up to the second next and so on. The semi-colon has been borrowed from C where it is used in much the same way.

Three actions are described here. The first and last are to do with the input and output of values. It turns out these map onto C in a very straightforward way. The second action needs to be developed further. Before carrying out the second action **a**, **b** and **c** contain the three values as they are read from the keyboard. We want to end up with **a,b** and **c** containing these same values but with the largest in **a** and the smallest in **c**. We do this by comparing them and if necessary swapping their contents. This leads to a second algorithm

> read three integer values into **a**, **b** and **c** from the keyboard;
> If (**b** < **c**) swap **b** and **c**;
> If (**a** < **b**)
> {
>   swap **a** and **b**;
>   if (**b** < **c**) swap **b** and **c**;
> }
> write out the values of **a,b** and **c** to the screen;
>
> ### swap 2

swap 2 is a development of **swap 1** in the sense that it is closer to the final program. It contains more detail about how the values in **a**, **b** and **c** are changed to get them in the required order. It illustrates an important point about program development. An initial algorithm is refined, producing a more detailed algorithm. This in turn may be further refined and the process repeated until an algorithm close enough to

Example 1 – ordering three integer values   29

the final program is obtained. Program code is then produced from this final algorithm. In doing this the programmer is able to control the detail of the final program.

The first line of **swap 2** is unchanged from its original form.

The second line swaps **b** and **c** if the value in **b** is less than that in **c**. (**b < c**) is called a **condition**. It is either **true** or **false**. If the value of **b** is less than the value of **c** then the condition is true. Otherwise it is false. The second line will only swap **b** and **c** if the condition (**b < c**) is false.

The second line is called a **conditional statement** and is an example of a **control** statement used to control the order in which statements are carried out. It is made up of a condition and a statement describing some action. The action described by the statement is only carried out if the condition is true. Executing a conditional statement of this form entails evaluating the condition. If it turns out to be true then the associated statement is executed. If it is false then the statement is not executed.

Note that conditons introduce a type we have not seen before. The values of this type are normally denoted by **true** and **false** which are called **Boolean** values. Although C allows the programmer to use conditions much as we have done here it does not support Booleans as such. Numeric values are used instead with **0** equivalent to **false** and any non-zero value equivalent to **true**.

We sometimes say a condition holds rather than it is true and condition does not hold rather than it is false.

Once the conditional statement on the second line is executed **b** will contain the larger of the two values in **b** and **c**. If at this stage the value in **a** is greater than or equal to that in **b** we have **a**, **b** and **c** as we want them. If it is not we certainly need to swap **a** and **b**. Because the original value in **a** could have been the smallest and because we have now swapped it with **b** we need to compare this new value in **b** with **c** to determine if a third swap is required.

The algorithm is made up of three **conditional** statements. Conditional statements occur frequently in both algorithms and programs and we adopt a standard way of writing them. Again our choice is influenced by C.

They take the form

> **if <condition> <statement>**

The key word 'if' always appears first. This is followed by a condition and then a statement. **<condition>** stands for **any** condition and **<statement>** any statement. In describing the form a statement may take anything that appears in angle brackets (< ... >) indicates what sort of thing can be written in that position in the statement. If we were describing a programming language such as C we should describe exactly what forms both conditions and statements can take. For algorithms we allow anything that can be sensibly interpreted. English language descriptions are allowed both for conditions and statements as long as they make sense.

Most programming languages provide for comparisons such as those used in **swap 2**. However they normally do not provide single statements equivalent for example to 'swap **a** and **b**'. This would need to be broken down further if we wished to express it in C. In writing an algorithm we are free to describe an action at whatever level we feel appropriate. Typically our algorithmic descriptions employ very specific high level actions with each action having associated with it a further algorithm that breaks the action down into lower level actions.

The second conditional statement has associated with it an action described by two statements. We need a way of grouping these together so that they are treated as a single statement as far as the conditional statement is concerned.

How should

> If (**a** < **b**)
>> swap **a** and **b**;
>> if (**b** < **c**) swap **b** and **c**;

be interpreted?

The indentation suggests that

>> swap **a** and **b**;
>> if (**b** < **c**) swap **b** and **c**;

should be viewed as a single statement associated with the conditional statement with both

>> swap **a** and **b**;

and

>> if (**b** < **c**) swap **b** and **c**;

being executed if **a** < **b** and neither executed if **a** >= **b**.

Most programming languages do not use indentation in this way and require some form of explicit bracketting to show how statements are grouped.

To make clear what is to be associated with a conditional and to be consistent with the way things work in C we will use curly brackets to group together statements that should be treated as a single statement under a condition. In C such a grouping is called a **compound** statement.

Thus we write

> If (**a** < **b**)
> {
>> swap **a** and **b**;
>> if (**b** < **c**) swap **b** and **c**;
>
> }

This now follows the general form of conditional statement described above. The statement part of the conditional statement is a compound statement. This is made up of two statements, one of which is also a conditional statement.

2.4 Dry running algorithms

Having devised an algorithm we need to be convinced that it does what we want it to. We cannot compile it and execute it on a computer so the only possibility left is to step through it trying it out using pencil and paper.

We can understand how a computer might behave if presented with an algorithm by conducting the following paper exercise. Using a blank sheet of paper which can be thought of as the computer's main memory

(**i**) Write out each statement of the algorithm on the piece of paper numbering them for identification purposes. This corresponds to the computer reading the program into memory.

(ii) Draw labelled boxes for each of the variables found in the algorithm. This corresponds to the allocation of memory to the variables.

(iii) Starting with the first statement use the labelled boxes to track the changes to the variables caused by the execution of each statement.

(iv) If a statement is a conditional statement only carry out the action associated with it if the condition holds.

As new forms of statement are introduced we will need to extend this procedure.

In carrying out **i** ... **iv** we will need to choose sample values for any inputs to the algorithm.

We can number the lines of our swapping algorithm as follows

```
1       read three integer values into a, b and c from the keyboard;
2       If (b < c) swap b and c;
3       If (a < b)
        {
4           swap a and b;
5           if (b < c) swap b and c;
        }
6       write out the values of a,b and c to the screen;
```

if we assume that the values **1, 2** and **3** have been read into **a, b** and **c** respectively the changes to the contents of **a, b** and **c** at each stage in the execution of the algorithm are as shown in the table below.

a	b	c	
1	2	3	after line 1
1	3	2	after line 2
3	1	2	after line 4
3	2	1	after line 5

This procedure is called **dry running** the algorithm. We would not normally include (i) above as a step in a dry run since we would almost certainly have the program written down in some form or other anyway. It is included here to highlight the fact that the computer needs to copy a program into main memory before it can execute it.

(iv) explains what to do with conditional statements. We will introduce more forms of control statement later which would need to be taken into account in dry running a program.

Dry running an algorithm or program is an extremely important aid in programming and should be used whenever possible. By following this practice the programmer develops a better understanding of what his program actually does and is often able to spot and correct program errors before the program is actually executed on a computer. Where a program is very large, dry running in the way described above may be impractical. We will see later however that a program of any size should be developed by identifying small sections of code and data that can form the 'building blocks' for the program which are then put together to form the program. The behaviour of these building blocks can often be analysed through dry runs.

Algorithms with conditional statements in them have alternative **execution paths**. If for the above algorithm the initial values of **a, b** and **c** are **3, 2** and **1** then no swaps take place whereas for the values **1, 2** and **3** we saw that three swaps take place. In analysing the behaviour of an algorithm all possible paths through the algorithm should be investigated. It is sometimes useful to show the various paths using a **flow diagram**. Such diagrams are made up of a collection of **nodes** represented by circles. Two nodes labelled **start** and **stop** represent the starting and finishing points of the algorithm. All other nodes represent places where a choice between alternative paths depends on a condition. In the diagram these nodes have been labelled with numbers corresponding to the line numbers of the algorithm where the condition appears with the condition itself appearing at the node. The nodes are joined by lines with arrows (called **directed arcs**) showing the direction of flow. An arc labelled **y** is followed if the condition holds. Otherwise the arc labelled **n** is followed. Actions carried out along a path are written alongside the corresponding arc. If no action appears against a directed arc no action takes places between the two nodes.

For example in Figure 2.1 given the values **3, 2** and **1** for **a, b** and **c** respectively the flow is from node **2** to node **5** via node **3** with no action taking place. Note that Figure 2.1 does not show input and output.

Six paths can be seen through the program. This does not however mean that it is necessary to invent six different sets of values for **a, b** and **c**. in order to test all the algorithm's paths.Starting with node **5** we want to devise two sets of data so that both paths from it are tested. Thus at node **3** we want **3** sets of data, the first set

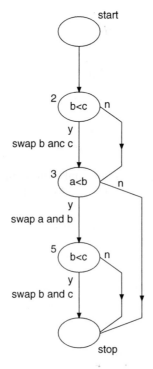

Figure 2.1 *A flow diagram for the second swap algorithm*

testing the path avoiding **5** and the remaining two testing the alternative paths from **5**. We can in fact choose these three sets of data in such a way that they also test the two paths from node **1**.

For our swapping algorithm we are interested in what happens to the contents of the variables **a,b** and **c**. The next section argues that it does what we want using assertions about the algorithm's behaviour.

2.5 Analysing an algorithm's behaviour

Dry running an algorithm helps to identify errors. A second approach is to find an argument based on general properties of the statements that make up the algorithm to justify our belief that the algorithm will do what we want. On executing **swap 2** we want **a** to be greater than or equal to **b** and **b** to be greater than or equal to **c**.

We will write this condition

$$(a >= b) \ \&\& \ (b >= c)$$

Here '**>=**' is used to stand for 'greater than or equal to' and '**&&**' is used to stand for 'and' following the notation used in C. The condition is true only if both comparisons in the condition are true.

We can be more precise about what our algorithm should do. It must ensure that when it terminates the above condition holds. By examining the effect of each statement we can demonstrate that this is indeed the case.

Before executing the first conditional statement on line **2** we have three values in the three variables **a,b** and **c** but we do not know which contains the largest and which the smallest. After executing this conditional statement it will certainly be the case that the value in **b** will be greater than or equal to the value in **c**. Thus the condition **b >= c** must be true at that stage. (**b** and **c** are swapped if **b < c** and otherwise left alone).

The second conditional statement compares **a** and **b**. If the value in **a** is at least as large as whatever value **b** now has then we have the values in **a**, **b** and **c** as we want them and the condition **(a >= b) && (b >= c)** must be true. Since in this case the algorithm takes no further action we end up with what we want.

If **a** is less than **b** lines **4** and **5** are executed. **a** and **b** are swapped, which ensures that the value in **a** is greater than or equal to that in **b**. At this stage **a** is greater than or equal to both **b** and **c**. We can write this down as the condition **a >= b && a >= c**.

Because **a** may have originally held the smallest value, **b** may now hold this smallest value. The final conditional statement checks for this and if necessary swaps the values in **b** and **c**, ensuring that **a,b** and **c** are in the required order.

We have examined the behaviour of our algorithm by identifying the condition that should hold when the algorithm terminates and then looking at how the condition is established. By considering the effect of individual statements we were able to make statements about what should be true at various stages in the execution of the algorithm and from these deduce that the required final condition would hold. It is sometimes helpful to write down such conditions as part of our algorithm .

They appear as **comments**. Comments are included with algorithms (and programs) to help anyone trying to understand how they work. Since they are not part of the algorithm they appear with we need a way of distinguishing them from it. Again we will follow C and bracket comments with '/*' and '*/'.

Adding the conditions that we know to be true after each statement as comments our **swap 2** algorithm takes the form

> read three integer values into **a, b** and **c** from the keyboard;
> If (**b** < **c**) swap **b** and **c**;
> /∗ **assertion 1: b >=c** ∗/
> If (**a<b**)
> {
>
>> swap **a** and **b**;
>> /∗ **assertion 2: (a >= b) && (a >= c)** ∗/
>> if (**b** < **c**) swap **b** and **c**;
>> /∗ **assertion 3: (a >= b) && (b >= c)** ∗/
>
> }
> /∗ **assertion 4: (a >= b) && (b >= c)** ∗/
> write out the values of **a,b** and **c** to the screen;

The conditions found in the comments here are sometimes called **assertions**. We are asserting that something should be true at these points in the execution of the algorithm. They should not be confused with conditions that appear in conditional statements which may be true or false.

We need to develop further the action of swapping the values of two variables before we are in a position to write a program to carry out our original task. We will leave this for the time being looking at a second example of algorithm development.

2.6 Example 2 – Finding the quotient and remainder of two numbers

In this example we will consider the problem of expressing a given division in terms of its quotient and remainder. For any pair of positive integers **a** and **b** we can find two positive integers **quotient** and **remainder** such that

> **a = quotient ∗ b + remainder**

We say **b** divides into **a quotient** times with remainder **remainder.**

One way of obtaining the quotient and remainder is to repeatedly subtract **b** from **a** until we get a result that is less than **b**. The quotient is then the number of times we subtracted **b** from **a** with the remainder the result of the last subtraction carried out.

Thus, given **10** and **3** we subtract 3 from **10** three times in succession giving **7** , **4** and **1**. The third subtraction gives a value less than **3** so we stop and we have a quotient of **3** and a remainder of **1.**

It is of course no surprise that we can substitute these values in our original relation between **a, b, quotient** and **remainder** giving

> **10 = 3 ∗ 3 + 1**

an equality that holds.

Note that the method described here is general. It will obtain the quotient and remainder for any pair of positive integers with one exception that we will come to later.. In constructing a program the programmer should aim for generality. A

Example 2 – finding the quotient and remainder of two numbers   35

program that works only for positive integers less than **100** is really not much use.

Most people would be happy with the description of how to obtain the quotient and remainder given above. However the description is given in English and computers are as yet a long way from being able to handle English. The phrase ' repeatedly subtract **b** from **a** until we get a result that is less than **a** ' asks that a number of things be done including a subtraction, a comparison and a repetition. These actions have to be given separately and explicitly in most programming languages.

We will recast the original description in a rather artificial way but one that is much closer to the way such descriptions are given in programming languages.

We will give an algorithm to find the quotient and remainder of two values and we will use the variables **a** and **b** to hold these values. Two further variables, **quotient** and **remainder,** will be used to build the quotient and remainder.

Thus for **10** and **3** at each subtraction the values for **a** , **b** , **quotient** and **remainder** will be as follows

a	b	quotient	remainder	
10	3	0	10	values before first subtraction
10	3	1	7	values after first subtraction
10	3	2	4	values after second subtraction
10	3	3	1	values after third subtraction

Note that before the first subtraction the count of the number of subtractions (the value for **quotient**) is **0** and the value of **remainder** is **10**. The justification for an initial value of **10** for **remainder** is that if **b** has been subtracted from **a** no times all of **a** will remain.

If we were trying to find the quotient and remainder using pencil and paper we would have to keep track of the values that **quotient** and **remainder** take at each repetition of the subtraction. We might do this by constructing a table of values like the one- above. Alternatively we might draw a box labelled **quotient** and one labelled **remainder** and write successive values for **quotient** and **remainder** in

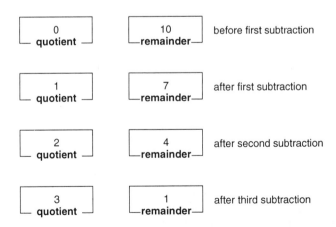

Figure 2.2 *The changing values of quotient and remainder*

each box rubbing out any earlier value. Figure 2.2 illustrates the different values that we write in the two boxes on successive subtractions.

We have seen that the main memory of a computer has some of the properties of our two boxes above. We can make a program put values into memory or make use of values held there. In the calculation of quotient and remainder four areas of memory will be employed corresponding to our four variables.

We need a way of describing the two ways of accessing memory (making use of a value in a memory location and changing the value in that location). We will use a notation found in most high level programming languages (although they will differ in detail).

2.7 Assignments and expressions

Whenever a variable name appears in an algorithm we may either be making use of or changing its value. The first conditional statement in **swap 2** has the form $(a < b)$. Here we make use of the values held by **a** and **b**. With 'swap **a** and **b**' the values held by **a** and **b** change.

Most programming languages provide a way of directly changing the value of a variable through what is called **assignment**.

We will use the general form

> **<variable> = <expression>**

to describe assignment. **<variable>** refers to the variable to be changed and **<expression>** gives the value that it should be changed to.
For example the assignment

> **a = 0;**

sets the value associated with **a** to **0**.

What do we mean by an expression? Expressions can take a wide variety of different forms in most programming languages. For now we will consider only very simple expressions. Expressions can be thought of as a way of writing down values. For example when we write **100** we know what value we mean. Using arithmetic operators we can write down the same value in lots of different ways. For example **100, 1 + 99, 2 + 98, 3 + 97,** ... all **express** the same value and are examples of expressions.

In the above assignment the expression is simply the number **0**. Among other things expressions can include arithmetic operators, numbers and variables. If they include operators they describe a calculation that the computer should carry out. Where a variable appears in an expression its value is made use of in the calculation.

For example the assignment

> **a = b + 1**

adds **1** to the value held in **b** and places the result in **a**. The value associated with **a** changes. The value associated with **b** is used in the calculation.

Although we use '=' for assignment this is not ideal because its use as an assignment operator is often confused with its normal algebraic meaning of equality. Indeed up to now we have used it in exactly this way as in

> **a = quotient ∗ b + remainder**

We use it for assignment here because it is the symbol used in the language C. Other languages use different symbols. For example Pascal uses ' **:=** ' which cannot easily be confused with equality and is thus considered a better choice of symbol. This may seem a rather unimportant issue but symbols often have meanings associated with them from for example the field of mathematics and to use them in a different way in a programming language can lead to confusion. A programming language which swapped the meanings of ' **+** ' and ' **−** ' would certainly be rather irritating to use. What is clear is that making assumptions about what a programming language operator actually does may lead to some nasty surprises. Most language designers make sensible choices in most cases but do not count on it, particularly with C. Always make sure you understand what a symbol is intended to mean.

Because '=' means assignment in C we need a symbol for equality. Since C uses '==' we will use that.

Again angle brackets are used to indicate that what appears in the general form stands for a range of possible actual variables and expressions.

We now know what a C programmer would understand by

remainder = 0

It describes the action of assigning the value **0** to the variable **remainder**.

Note that

remainder = 0

would mean something quite different to a mathematician who would interpret it as a statement about the value **remainder** namely that it was equal to **0**.

If we need to write down such comparisons again, following C we will write

remainder == 0

2.8 Operator precedence

In evaluating an expression we have to take into account the order in which operators are applied. Most programming languages would deal with the expression

3 + 4 + 5

by first adding **3** and **4** and adding **5** to the result, and this is very much what we would expect.

With the above expression it does not really matter which addition is carried out first; the result would be the same. If an expression involves subtraction then order is important.

With

3 + 4 − 5

we would expect the operators to be applied in a left-to-right order with the addition carried out first. This is indeed the case with C.

Where multiplication (or division) appears in an expression this is carried out before any addition or subtraction. For example with

3 + 4 ∗ 5

we would expect a value **23** and this would be obtained by carrying out the multiplication first. The order in which operators are applied to operand differs in the two cases. In the second case the multiplication is carried out before the addition. This is a matter of convention but one that we are so used to we apply the convention without thinking. In doing so we are giving the multiplication operation a **higher precedence** than the addition operator.

Programming languages also evaluate expressions following precedence rules and, for arithmetic expressions, these are normally what we would expect. C provides a wide variety of operations and where different types of operation are mixed in an expression we need to be sure about the order in which they are applied.

We saw earlier the condition

(a >= b) && (b >= c)

It is also an expression which makes use of a **comparison** operator (>=) and a **Boolean** operator (**&&**). The brackets make clear that the comparisons are carried out first. In C >= has a higher precedence than **&&** and so

a >= b && b >= c

would have the same meaning. Again it is probably what we would expect but it is certainly something that we need to be sure of and the only way to do this is consult the precedence rules associated with C.

Here is a further example of the order of operators. How are the following applied?

a * 3 + 1 <= b – 2 && b – 1 <= c * 4

C's precedence rules ensure that arithmetic operations are applied before comparison operators so again we get what we would expect. However different languages operate differently and where expressions involve a number of different types of operators it is always wise to check that the operators are applied in the order we want.

If the is any doubt brackets can always be used as in

((a * 3 + 1) <= (b – 2)) && ((b – 1) <= (c * 4))

We should also be clear about when the assignment operator is applied in C. The general form

<variable> = <expression>

given earlier is in fact a simplification of what is allowed. The assignment operator can appear anywhere in an expression provided its left operand can be interpreted as an address. It has a lower precedence than any of the arithmetic, comparison and Boolean operations.

Thus in C we view

quotient = quotient + 1

as an expression just as we would

quotient + 1

It describes a calculation and has a value associated with it. If differs from the second expression in that it **also** causes a change to the value associated with the variable **quotient**.

So an expression involving assignment does two things. It describes a value as all expressions do. It also describes a change to a variable. Evaluating such expressions both generates a value and carries out an assignment.
Since

> **quotient = quotient + 1**

is an expression what is its value? It is the value assigned to **quotient**.

We will see later that being able to use assignment in much the same way as other operators is useful in a number of ways. One of these is that it allows us to write down multiple assignments compactly. For example, if we wanted to initialise three variables **a**, **b** and **c** to zero we could do this using the single expression

> **a = b = c = 0;**

Assignments are carried out in a right-to-left order. **c** is assigned the value **0** first. As **c = 0** is an expression with value **0** this value is then assigned to **b**.However, **b = c = 0** is also an expression with value **0** which is assigned to **a**. What happens to the value of the expression **a = b = c = 0**? Written out in a C program in the form above its value is discarded.

We have digressed a little here to cover some aspects of expressions and in particular how they are treated in C. An important difference between C and other programming languages is the way it deals with assignments. In Pascal for example assignment is treated as a statement. In C, assignment can appear where ever expressions are allowed. This has some advantages but creates potential pitfalls for the programmer. The most common arises out of the choice of '=' for the assignment operator.

For example the condition

> **'a is equal to b'**

is often incorrectly written as the assignment

> **a = b**

This type of error arises so frequently that most compilers issue a warning that an assignment is being carried out where it might not be intended.

Note that in

> **quotient = quotient + 1**

the same variable name appears on the left and the right of the assignment operator and is used in two different ways. To the left of the assignment operator it indicates where in memory the value of the expression on the right of the assignment operator is to be placed. In the expression itself it indicates the value held in memory.

Again the mathematical interpretation of

> **quotient = quotient + 1**

is quite different and indeed would not make sense since its meaning would be that the value **quotient** is equal to the value **quotient + 1** which could never be the case.

2.9 Iteration and the while statement

With variables, expressions and the assignment operator we are almost in a position to write down a program-like description for the calculation of quotient and remainder. What is missing is a way of describing that an action be carried out repeatedly.

In our example we want to repeatedly carry out the subtraction of **b** from **a** until we have **remainder** less than **b**. The way we will do this is to assign the value in **a** to **remainder** and repeatedly carry out the assignment

remainder = remainder – b

until **remainder** is less than **b**.

Note that we could have chosen to change **a**. This would have meant that we would not have needed the variable **remainder** and the final algorithm would involve fewer steps. The use of **remainder** is to make clearer what is going on in calculating **quotient** and **remainder**.

We can think of the repetition in two ways. First as a repetition **until remainder** is less than **b** as we have done above. Second as a repetition that continues **while remainder** is greater than or equal to **b**. We will treat repetition in this second way because in doing so we follow more closely the way it would get done if we were writing a C program.

We will use the general form of while statement

while <condition>
 <statement>

to describe repetitions.

We interpret this as repeatedly executing **<statement>** until **<condition>** becomes false.

The repeated execution of a statement is sometimes referred to as **iteration** and the statement repeatedly executed is sometimes referred to as the **body** of the **while** statement.

If **<condition>** is false initially the **while** statement has no effect. **<condition>** will normally be an expression that involves variables that are changed by **<statement>**. If this were not the case and the condition was initially true it would remain true and the **while** would execute endlessly. There are applications for such non-terminating loops but these are rare. Whenever a while loop is used care should be taken to ensure that the condition will eventually go false. Neglecting to ensure this is a very common and particularly irritating form of error because its effect is that the program never stops. Most computer systems provide ways of 'killing' such programs but certainly the chances are that the programmer does not know how to do this the first time it happens.

We may want several actions to be carried out repeatedly while a condition is true. As with conditional statements the brackets '{' and '}' are used to group statements together so they are treated as a single statement.

We can now use the **while** statement and the assignment statement to describe the calculation of quotient and remainder. The algorithm makes the assumption that the variables **a** and **b** have already been assigned the values involved in the calculation. We will see later how **a** and **b** can be set up as required.

Our algorithm consists of the following statements

```
quotient = 0;
remainder = a;
while (remainder >= b)
{
    quotient = quotient + 1;
    remainder = remainder - b;
}
```

The first two statements are assignment statements which **initialise quotient** and **remainder** to appropriate initial values ready for the iteration of the **while** statement. Most programs contain variables that need to be given initial values. A common error is to leave out such initialisations.

The body of the **while** statement will repeatedly execute until the condition **remainder >= b** becomes false. The number of repetitions will depend on the values of **a** and **b**. The effect of executing the **while** statement would be that the two assignment statements following the condition would be executed. If **a** is less than **b** initially these two assignments would not be carried out at all.

Does the body of the **while** statement ensure that the condition will eventually go false? The second assignment ensures that **remainder** decreases in value **provided b is greater than zero**.

If **b** is zero then then the assignment

remainder = remainder - b

will not change the value of **remainder** and the condition

remainder >= b

will remain true. Since **b** is not changed within the body of the **while** statement if it is initially zero it remains zero. Thus if the body of the **while** statement executes once it will continue to execute because the controlling condition will never become false.

Can we be certain that **b** will always be greater than zero? What we have to be clear about is what range of values our algorithm is intended to deal with. We have decided to deal only with natural numbers ignoring the possibilty that **a** and **b** might be negative. Should we also ignore the possibility that **b** might be zero as well? The algorithm deals with natural numbers and zero is a natural number so it is appropriate to deal with the zero possibility within the algorithm.

We want to say something like

' If **b** is greater than zero then compute the quotient and remainder for **a** and **b**.'

in our algorithm and we will use a conditional statement to do this as in

```
quotient = 0;
remainder = a;
if b > 0
    while remainder >= b;
    {
```

```
        quotient = quotient + 1;
        remainder = remainder – b;
}
```
quotient remainder algorithm

Now if **a** and **b** are natural numbers our **while** loop is certain to terminate, since the value of **remainder** decreases on each cycle of the while loop and will certainly be less than **b** eventually.

In the example used earlier with **a** taking the value **10** and **b** taking the value **3** the while statement would execute the two assignments three times with **quotient** and **remainder** taking the values listed in Figure 2.2.

2.10 Assignments, pre-conditions and post-conditions

We have seen that although dry running an algorithm or program is an important step in checking that it behaves as we want it to, this process provides no guarantees. We also attempt to find arguments based on the algorithm's underlying logic to provide a justification that it does what it is intended to do. We did this with our 'swapping' algorithm.

Let us return to this briefly to illustrate another way of analysing the behaviour of an algorithm.

We need to work out a way of swapping the values of two variables in order to develop, for example,

swap **b** and **c**

We can make use of a third variable **temp** and carry out the following sequence of assignments

```
temp = b;
b = c;
c = temp;
```

We can now replace in the 'swapping' algorithm both occurrences of 'swap **b** and **c**' with this sequence and 'swap **a** and **b**' with an equivalent sequence. To check that **b** and **c** are indeed swapped a dry run with a pair of values for **b** and **c** would be adequate. We could however argue more generally as follows.

Suppose that **b** and **c** initially have values b_0 and c_0 respectively. Prior to executing the sequence of assignments the condition

$$b == b_0 \ \&\& \ c == c_0$$

holds. Notice our C like use of '==' for equality.

After the last assignment we want the following to hold:

$$b == c_0 \ \&\& \ c == b_0$$

We call the first condition a **pre-condition** and the second a **post condition** of the assignment sequence. In this example the pre-condition says no more than **a** and **b** have some arbitrary values. The post condition makes use of these values to indicate the effect of the assignments.

Pre- and post conditions can be thought of as specifying the behaviour of a program. The pre-condition specifies the conditions under which it makes sense to execute a program. The post condition specifies the program's effect.

In our example, if we examine how the pre-condition is transformed by each assignment we can determine whether the post condition holds on completion of the sequence of assignments.

If we consider the first of the assignments we can write down the pre-condition and what we know to be true following this assignment in the style of assertions given earlier.

> * **assertion 1: b == b_0 && c == c_0 ***
> **temp = b;**
> * **assertion 2: b == b_0 && c == c_0 && temp == b_0 ***

assertion 1 is our pre-condition. **assertion 2** follows from **assertion 1** because if it is true then the assignment will ensure that **assertion 2** is also true.

Using **assertion 2** in conjunction with the second assignment we can write

> \ **assertion 2: *b == b_0 && c == c_0 && temp == b_0 ***
> **b = c;**
> * **assertion 3: b == c_0 && c == c_0 && temp == b_0 ***

with **assertion 3** following from **assertion 2** and the meaning of assignment.

We can argue

> * **assertion 3: b == c_0 && c == c_0 && temp == b_0 ***
> **c = temp;**
> * **assertion 4: b == c_0 && c == b_0 && temp == b_0 ***

in a similar way.

We can therefore conclude that if the pre-condition (**assertion 1**) holds then the condition

> ***b == c_0 && c == b_0 && temp == b_0**

holds on completion of the sequence of assignments and so the post-condition

> **b == c_0 && c == b_0**

holds.

What have we done here? First we have written down a condition that should be true in order to execute the algorithm. We have then identified conditions that we assert to be true at each stage in the algorithm. The truth of each assertion is justified by the truth of an earlier assertion and the effect of the algorithm from that earlier assertion. We have then found a final assertion that can be justified in this way **and** that establishes the post condition. Since the post condition describes the desired effect of the algorithm we conclude that the algorithm behaves as we want it to.

The pre-condition used here is always true. It was chosen to make demonstrating that the post condition would hold easy to do. The sequence of assignments always works whatever the initial values of **b** and **c**. Not all algorithms work under all circumstances. The **quotient remainder** algorithm only works for positive numbers. If we supply it with negative numbers then it will generate meaningless values for **quotient** and **remainder**. In designing an algorithm we need to be clear about the range of data values it is intended to deal with. Any program developed from the algorithm may have to carry out **data validation** to ensure that only data values that the algorithm is designed to handle (**valid data**) are used, with other data values treated as errors.

2.11 Analysing iteration

The **quotient remainder** algorithm processes a pair of natural numbers **a** and **b**. Recall that the natural numbers are the positive integers so in thinking about our algorithm we shall ignore negative values. When we come to write the corresponding C program we will have to take negative values into account because we will have to use integers for **a** and **b**. We could of course have designed our algorithm to cope with integers rather than natural numbers. The reason we have not done so here is to keep the algorithm as simple as possible. In moving from an algorithm to a program we make choices about what language features best model the values that our algorithm deals with.

When the algorithm finishes we want **quotient** and **remainder** to have values such that

$$(a == quotient * b + remainder) \ \&\& \ (remainder < b)$$

With **a = 10** and **b = 3** we find that **quotient = 3** and **remainder = 1**. If we use these values in the above post condition we find that it is true.

The condition

remainder < b

is needed because we want **quotient** and **remainder** to be what we normally understand by quotient and remainder. Without it **quotient** and **remainder** could take a number of different values with

a = quotient * b + remainder

holding. For example it holds with **quotient = a** and **remainder = b**.

Let us re-write the algorithm with some assertions added.

```
quotient = 0;
remainder = a;

/* assertion 1: a == quotient * b + remainder */

if b > 0
    while remainder >= b;
{
        quotient = quotient + 1;
        remainder = remainder – b;
}

/* assertion 2: (a == quotient * b + remainder) && (remainder < b) */
```

assertion 1 holds because of the two assignments that precede it. If we can show that **assertion 2** holds then we have shown that the algorithm's post condition holds on termination of the algorithm and we can be confident that the algorithm behaves as we want it to.

The key is to show that

$$a == quotient * b + remainder$$

holds after each execution of the body of the while statement and that when it terminates

$$remainder < b$$

Given that **assertion 1** holds before the **while** statement is executed can we show that it still holds on a single execution of the body of the **while** statement? If we can then we can conclude that it holds at the end of each execution of the body of the **while** statement and in particular after the last.

Calling each execution of the body of the **while** statement $cycle_1$, $cycle_2$, ... $cycle_n$ with $cycle_n$ its last execution we show that an arbitrary cycle, $cycle_i$, leaves the truth of **assertion 1** unchanged. Since **assertion 1** is true at the start of $cycle_1$ it is therefore true at the start of $cycle_2$ Since it is true at the start of $cycle_2$ it is true at the start of $cycle_3$. This argument runs through to the last cycle.

Call the **values** taken by **quotient, remainder, a** and **b** at the start of $cycle_i$ $quotient_0$, $remainder_0$, a_0 and b_0.

We are trying to show that if the condition

$$a == quotient * b + remainder$$

holds at the start of $cycle_i$ it holds at the end. Thus we are assuming

$$a_0 == quotient_0 * b_0 + remainder_0 \qquad \textbf{1.}$$

at the start. Here we have simply replaced the variable names by their values in the condition.

At the end of $cycle_i$ **quotient** has been incremented by **1** and **remainder** has been decremented by b_0. That is they have the values $quotient_0 + 1$ and $remainder_0 - b_0$ respectively. Both **a** and **b** are unchanged.

For the condition

$$a == quotient * b + remainder$$

to hold at the end of $cycle_i$, again by replacing the variables by their new values in the condition, we want

$$a_0 == (quotient_0 + 1) * b_0 + remainder_0 - b_0 \qquad \textbf{2.}$$

to hold. Now

$$(quotient_0 + 1) * b_0 + remainder_0 - b_0$$
$$== quotient_0 * b_0 + b_0 + remainder_0 - b_0$$
$$== quotient_0 * b_0 + remainder$$
$$== a_0$$

We have simplified $(quotient_0 + 1) * b_0 + remainder_0 - b_0$ to

$$quotient_0 * b_0 + remainder_0$$

which by **1.** equals a_0. Thus if **1.** holds **2.** must also hold.

Thus the truth of **assertion 1** is unaffected by the **while** statement. Assertions that are unchanged by the execution of a **while** statement are called **loop invariants**. The style of argument used here depends on identifying a loop invariant from which the desired post condition can be derived. For any **while** statement there are many invariant conditions. Most will be of little use in establishing a given post condition. For example the condition **remainder >= 0** is also an invariant for the **while** statement in our algorithm. It does not however help in establishing **assertion 2**. Although the post condition itself is a good starting point in looking for a suitable invariant it is often necessary to experiment a bit before one is found.

We need to be sure that the **while** statement terminates. We have assumed that both **a** and **b** positive. **remainder** is initialised to **a** and **b** is non-zero. Thus the assignment

remainder = remainder – b;

reduces the value of **remainder** on each iteration of the **while** statement. **remainder** must therefore reduce to a value less than **b** at some stage so condition **remainder >= b** must eventually be false. Therefore the **while** statement terminates and we can add **remainder < b** to **assertion 1** giving **assertion 2**.

From this we see that if **assertion 1** holds then **assertion 2** must also hold and since **assertion 1** does indeed hold we have established the algorithm post-condition.

In this chapter we have looked at two ways of treating algorithms in order that we can be confident that they do the job they are intended to do. We can dry run them and we can construct arguments based on their general properties from which we can deduce that they do what we want. Neither approach is foolproof. Our tests may not be exhaustive and our arguments may be unsound. Nevertheless we should attempt to carry out both activities as thoroughly as possible. Programmers make errors and we need as much help as we can get to minimise their number.

In summary the programmer should bear in mind the following.

1. Before developing a program make sure you understand exactly what the program should do.
2. Programs need to be designed before they can be written. How one approaches the design of a program varies from program to program but designs need to be written down so that they can be analysed and so that they can be used in developing the
3. Provided the programming task is small enough the design of a program can be expressed as an algorithm using a notation similar to but simpler than typical programming languages.
4. Ideas for program designs come in many ways and there is no one certain way of obtaining the best design. Experimenting by trying to do by hand what the program is intended to do can often generate ideas.
5. Having written an algorithm it should be dry run using different test cases to get a feel for how it really works and to identify any errors.
6. General arguments should be found to try and establish that the program does what is wanted.
7. Care and patience in programming pays enormous dividends.

The reader may form the impression that the development process runs smoothly from one stage to the next. It never does. In developing an algorithm a problem in the original specification may become apparent. In trying to justify an algorithm a fundamental flaw may emerge. We can add

8. Be prepared to start again.

If a problem is discovered in a program which has taken a considerable time to develop there is a great temptation to try to botch the program in some way in the hope that this will save time. If the problem is to do with the program's design it rarely does and it certainly leads to a poorer quality program than would otherwise have been the case. Re-thinking the design and if necessary re-writing part or all of the program is almost certainly the wisest approach.

Exercises

1. Section 2.4 introduces the idea of dry running algorithms. Given that values **1**, **3** and **2** read into **a, b** and **c,** dry run **swap 2** showing how the values associated with **a, b** and **c** change.

2. Figure 2.1 gives a flow diagram for **swap 2**. Find three sets of values for **a, b** and **c** that ensure that all the paths in 2.1 are traversed.

3. Write down the steps you need to take to sort a deck of playing cards into rank order. The highest ranking suite is spades followed by hearts, diamonds and clubs. The highest ranking spade (the ace of spades) should be first in the deck with the lowest ranking club (the two of clubs) last.

4. If a golf ball dropped onto a concrete floor bounces up **90%** of the height it fell from give an algorithm that will count the number of times the ball bounces before it bounces up less than **10%** of the height it was originally dropped from.

5. A vending machine allows a customer to feed in more money than required for his selected item. It will give change of up to one pound using **1p, 2p, 5p, 10p, 20p** and **50p** coins. Give an algorithm that calculates the change in the minimum number of coins.

6. Given that **a == 1, b == 5** and **c == 10** write down the values of the following expressions and the values of **a, b** and **c** after each expression has been evaluated using the operator precedence and order of evaluation given in Section **2.8**.

    (i) a = b = c + 4
    (ii) a + (b = c) * 10

    If all operators have the same precedence and are applied left to right what values would the above expressions have and what values would **a, b** and **c** end up having?

7. The following sequence of assignments

    a = a – b;
    b = a + b;
    a = b – a;

    swaps the contents of **a** and **b** without the use of a third variable. Using the style of argument presented in Section 2.10 demonstrate that it works.

    In what way would this sequence and that given in Section 2.10 behave differently if executed as programs? You will need to consider the limitations placed on the size of integers in order to answer this.

8. The following algorithm

    y = 1; z = x; k = n;
    * assertion 1: y * z^k == x^n *\
    while (k <> 0)
    {
        k = k–1;
        y = y * z
    }
    * assertion 2: y * z^k == x^n && k == 0*\

    computes x^n given that **n >= 0** initially. Assuming the pre-condition **k >= 0** show that the post condition **y == x^n** holds by showing that **assertion 1** and **assertion 2** hold.

9. The greatest common devisor of two non-zero positive numbers is the largest number which divides exactly into each of the two numbers. We write **gcd(a,b)** to stand for the greatest common devisor of **a** and **b**. One way of obtaining **gcd(a,b)** is to successively subtract the larger from the smaller until the two are equal in value. This value is then the greatest common devisor.Express this as an algorithm by initialising two variables **x** and **y** to **a** and **b** and then repeatedly subtraction one from the other until they become equal.

    You will need to construct a **while** statement with a body that deals with the two cases **x > y** and **x < y.** This can be done using two instances of the form of conditional statement described in Section 2.3. The alternative is to use a conditional statement of the form

    if <condition> <statement_1>
    else <statement_2>

    where **<statement_1>** is executed if **<condition>** holds and **<statement_2>** if it does not.

    Given the post condition **gcd(a,b) == x** and using the loop invariant **gcd(a,b) == gcd(x,y)** identify two assertions equivalent to **assertion 1** and **assertion 2** of the previous question and add them to your algorithm.

    Show that both assertions hold and hence that the post condition holds.

    In showing that your second assertion holds you will need to use the two properties of greatest common devisors **gcd(x – y,y) == gcd(x,y)** where **x > y** and **gcd(x,y – x) == gcd(x,y)** where **y > x**.

3

Turning algorithms into C programs

In Chapter 2 we developed an algorithm for the calculation of the quotient and remainder of two numbers. In the first part of this chapter we will look at how to turn this description into a C program. C language features will be introduced as they are required. In particular we will see how functions may be declared and used.

3.1 Algorithms

We have called the following description an **algorithm**:

```
quotient = 0;
remainder = a;
if (b > 0)
    while (remainder >= b)
    {
        quotient = quotient + 1;
        remainder = remainder - b;
    }
```

An algorithm gives the steps that have to be carried out in order to achieve some result. In its original meaning the result was normally the calculation of some numeric value and algorithms were concerned with numeric calculations. Because computers can be used for non-numeric tasks such as sorting a list of names into alphabetical order its meaning has widened to include the description of these non-numeric tasks.

However our algorithm is not a C program. It will need to be changed in a number of ways before it can be compiled and executed.

Why did we bother to develop the algorithm if we have to re-draft it? There are several things we have to do in writing a program. Certainly we have to sort out what actions the program should carry out and in what order. We must also use our programming language correctly. By developing an algorithm first we can ignore (to a large extend) detailed language considerations and concentrate on what the program should do. Experienced programmers writing small and very straightforward programs often develop programs without developing an algorithm first. In some circumstances this is all right. It is however a good practice to develop algorithms for all but the simplest programming tasks. No painter starts a major picture by applying paint to canvas. He first tries to imagine the picture and then makes preliminary sketches of how it should look before taking brush to canvas. He works out much of the picture's general structure through thought and experimenting with sketches beforehand. The programmer must do a similar thing. In particular he must experiment by constructing algorithms and thinking through how they might execute. In this way he develops an understanding of how to organise his program before he has written a single C statement.

There is a second way in which algorithms help. They **document** a program. It is often easier to understand the behaviour of a program by first looking at its underlying algorithms. It is almost certainly the case that far more code is produced through the modification of existing programs than through the creation of entirely new ones. Such modifications are often made by programmers who were not involved in the original development of the program. Without supporting documentation, including algorithms or their equivalent, the task of program modification is considerably (and unnecessarilly) more difficult. Programmers have a responsibility to those who come after them.

Once we have an algorithm it is often fairly straightforward to produce the C program from it. Much of the art of programming is in the development of the algorithm itself which is in many ways language independent. The notation used in describing the above algorithm was drawn from C. C was chosen as a basis simply because we want to develop C programs from any algorithms that we write. There is no standard way of writing down an algorithm although there are various alternatives used in the literature on programming that we could choose from. The choice does not matter too much provided it is reasonably easy to read.

3.2 The role of the semi-colon in C

All statements other than compound statements written in C must be followed by a semi-colon. We adopted this convention in our algorithmic notation. This rule of syntax is a bit like the rule that requires a full stop after English sentences. Given a piece of English without full stops we could probably work out from the meaning of the English where the full stops should go. In a similar way we could also make sense of a C program that did not include semi-colons. This is possibly why it is quite common for people learning to program to leave out semi-colons. They do not seem very important. Unfortunately however they are required and if they are left out the C compiler will generate error messages.

3.3 The do statement

If initially the condition associated with a **while** statement does not hold then the body of the statement is not executed. There are some situations where an iteration should execute at least once and it is more convenient to place the controlling condition after the body of the iteration. Since the case study in Chapter 8 makes use of it and it relates closely to the **while** statement we describe the C statement that allows us to write down iterations in this way here. The statement, called the **do** statement, takes the general form

do <statement> while <condition>

Its effect is to execute **<statement>** and then evaluate **<condition>**. If **<condition>** holds this is repeated. If it does not the iteration terminates.

3.4 Declaring variables

In Chapter 1 we saw that an area of memory could be used to hold different types of values (integers, decimals, addresses and so forth). Most high level languages ensure that once an area of memory has been set aside for a particular type of value then it is used in a way consistent with that type. If an area of memory is being used to hold a character then it should not be treated as if it held an integer. Languages vary quite considerably in how strict they are in requiring consistency of use. In Pascal inconsistent use is almost always prohibited. C is much less restrictive in this respect. Pascal is said to be **strongly typed** whereas C would at best be described as **weakly typed**. There are situations in which it is useful to be able to treat a variable as of one type in one context and as a different type in another. Such situations are however quite rare and it would be fair to say that the rather lax approach adopted in C is one of its weaknesses. The C programmer does not have the same level of consistency checks carried out by the compiler that the Pascal programmer has. Nevertheless C needs information on what types of values are to be associated with any variables used in a program in order to determine how much memory to set aside for each variable. In common with most programming languages C requires that any variables that are to be used in a program are **declared** before their use and part of that declaration will include the variable type.

We will see later that C provides a very rich set of declaration features. For now we will describe how the positive numbers that our algorithm manipulates are declared. In constructing algorithms we invent data types best suited to the problem in hand. In converting an algorithm to a program we have to make use of what is available in the language. We may not find an exact match and as we will see later the choice we make can lead to difficulties. Our algorithm deals with positive integers. Although C allows us to declare variables as either signed or unsigned integers it does not provide sufficient control over the use of unsigned integers to make their use worthwhile here. **quotient, remainder, a**, and **b** are thus declared as signed integers. This declaration should appear before any use is made of these variables. A variable is introduced by giving first its type followed by its name. Integer declarations can be made in a number of ways in C. One way is to use the key word **int** followed by the names of one or more variables. The four variables needed here would be declared by

      int quotient,remainder,a,b;

quotient, remainder, a, and **b** are thus introduced into the C program as being of type **int**, a form of integer. We will place this declaration immediately before the first assignment statement giving :

      int quotient,remainder,a,b;
      quotient = 0;
      remainder = a;

```
if (b > 0)
while (remainder >= b)
{
    quotient = quotient + 1;
    remainder = remainder – b;
}
```

3.5 C functions

We used statements like the assignment statement and the while statement as building blocks in developing our original algorithm. The typical C program is not however simply a collection of statements. Normally it is build from a collection of **functions,** each of which is itself build from a collection of statements. Thus C provides a way of grouping together statements, giving the group of statements a name and then treating the group as if it were a single entity. Each such grouping is called a function.

We should think of C programs as being built from one or more functions, with the functions themselves being built from statements. This form of structuring is not to be confused with that introduced in Chapter 1. There we saw that a C program could be organised as a number of **.c** files. Each **.c** file can contain one or more functions. Thus a C program is structured in two ways. First the program is split across several source files. Second the C in each source file is organised into functions. The experienced C programmer uses both types of structuring to organise the code of his program. The larger and more complex the program the more important it is to use the two forms of structuring wisely.

The proper study of C functions must be left until much later in the text. However C functions have some properties in common with conventional mathematical functions. For example the square root function (written '$\sqrt{}$') found in mathematics takes a number as an **argument** and gives the square root of that number as a **result**.

Thus $\sqrt{9}$ has argument **9** and result **3**. It is a **use** of '$\sqrt{}$' to find the square root of **9**.

Like mathematical functions C functions take arguments and return results. The arguments take the form of expressions which are evaluated before the function is called with the values given to the function to work on. Again like mathematical functions if we quote the name of a function, giving it appropriate arguments, we should get back a result. In mathematics we think of the function and its argument as being replaced by the associated result. Where we see $\sqrt{9}$ we can read **3**. In C, in common with most programming languages, for a function to be usable, it has to be described somewhere. Code associated with the function should exist which when executed achieves the desired effect. Using a C function is described as **calling** the function. The function **returns** its result as a value to be used at the point at which the function is called. Functions can appear as operands anywhere within an expression and the function result is used in evaluating the expression.

The C system provides a number of functions which the C programmer can call. For example the function **sqrt** takes as an argument a number and returns as a result the square root of that number. (In C special characters such as $\sqrt{}$ cannot be used as the names of functions.)

In the assignment statement

r = sqrt(9) + 1;

sqrt(9) is a function call appearing in an expression. In C, arguments to a function should follow the function and be enclosed by round brackets. The function will return **3.0** which is used as the first operand of the addition. The result of the addition it then assigned to **r**. The code associated with **sqrt** is given the value **9**. It computes the square root of **9** and this value is returned as the result of the function call. The function is designed to work with decimal numbers. Both the argument and the result will be decimal. The integer value **9** will be converted to its floating point equivalent before the square route is computed.

The following examples using **sqrt** demonstrate the flexibility of functions.

Example 1

r = sqrt(a + b + 2);

Here, the argument is the expression **a + b + 2**. This expression must be evaluated before **sqrt** is called. If **a == 5** and **b == 81** then its value would be **88** and **sqrt** returns a value close to **9.38**.

Example 2

r = sqrt(a + sqrt(b) + 2)

Here, the argument is the expression **a + sqrt(b) + 2**. Again this expression must be evaluated before **sqrt** is called. Since the expression itself involves a call to **sqrt** this must be done first. Using the same value for **a** and **b sqrt(b)** returns **9.0** with the expression evaluating to **16.0**. This is now the argument to the 'outer' call to **sqrt** which returns **4.0**.

Example 3

r = sqrt(a) + sqrt(b);

Here, **sqrt** is used to find the square root of both **a** and **b**. These are then added together with the sum assigned to **r**.

C functions differ from mathematical functions in a number of ways.

A C function need not return a value. We can call a function that executes code but which does not return any value. Another of the functions to be found in most ANSI C systems is the function **memmove** which the programmer can use to move sections of memory. Although its use is not to be recommended it does illustrate a function that does some work but does not return any result.

If

memmove(addr1,addr2,len);

appears as a statement in a program where **addr1** and **addr2** are **memory addresses** and **len** gives the number of bytes to be moved then **len** bytes starting at **addr1** will be copied to the area of memory starting at **addr2**. No result is returned by the function.

Further, a C function which would normally return a value can be used in such a way that its value is ignored.

We could write

sqrt(9);

as a statement in a program. Using **sqrt** in this way would serve no useful purpose but it is allowed.

What we have seen are examples of how existing functions may be used within a program. Programs consist of collections of functions which must be written by the programmer. These functions call one another to carry out the job that the program is designed to perform. They may also make use of functions provided by the C system.

If a programmer writes a function he is free to choose a name for that function more or less as he pleases. There is always one function however that must be included in a C program whose name is fixed. The function name is '**main**' and C statements that are to be executed first appear in this function. '**main**' is always the starting point of the execution. In our example **main** will take no arguments and return no result.

The algorithm we developed now becomes the function **main** and its further modified to

```
main()
{
    int quotient,remainder,a,b;
    quotient = 0;
    remainder = a;
    if (b > 0)
    while (remainder >= b)
    {
        quotient = quotient + 1;
        remainder = remainder – b;
    }
}
```

Notice that '**main**' is followed by the a pair of round brackets ('()'). If there are no arguments the brackets are still required. Again a detailed explanation of C function arguments must be left until later.

The statements that go to make up the function **main** are always enclosed in curly brackets. In our example a '{' immediately follows **main()** and a matching '}' terminates the **main** function.

This is an example of a C **block**. A **block** is a compound statement with declarations added at its start.

Normally space is allocated for the variables declared at the start of a block, on entry to the block, and freed on exit. However, we will see later that it is possible to ensure that the space is allocated when the program starts executing.

The use of variables declared within a block is restricted to the block in which they are declared. No other part of the program can refer to them directly, although we will see later that both the value associated with a variable **and** its address can be made available indirectly by using function arguments.

If we used a text editor to create a file containing this latest modification and presented it to a C compiler it would compile and we could obtain an executable program from it. As a program however it is not much use. At no stage have we considered how values for **a** and **b** can be given to the program nor how it makes its final values of **quotient** and **remainder** available. We remedy this in the next section.

3.6 Streams and standard input and output in C

The designers of C wanted to keep the language as simple as possible. The philosophy was that the language itself should be simple but designed in such a way that it was very easy to include in any program functions that in some way or another extended the language. Most C systems give you not only the compiler but a collection, useful functions (called **library** functions), including functions to handle input and output. C programs can input data from a variety of sources, ranging from files held on disk to characters typed in at the keyboard, with a similar variety for output. This input and output is based on the concept of a **stream**. For example an input file held on disk is accessed as a stream of bytes starting at the beginning of the file. A number of streams are created automatically when the program begins execution, including the streams called **stdin** and **stdout**. Input from the keyboard is made available to the program via **stdin** and output to the screen is generated via **stdout**.

There are several library functions that are specific to **stdin** and **stdout**. Two of these, **scanf** and **printf** we make use of here.

Recall what we mean by input and output. When a program is executing it is often necessary to supply data to the program by typing it in at the keyboard and if we want to observe the results of a calculation the program has to display these at the screen. Both the keyboard and the screen are devices that an executing program can communicate with (as are the hard disk drive and the floppy disk drive). This is quite different from the movement of data in main memory through, say, assignment. Such movement in not observable by someone sat at the computer nor can he directly write in to memory other than through input functions provided by the C system.

Both **scanf** and **printf** allow the programmer to carry out a wide range of different types of input and output. For example, **scanf** allows the programmer to read integers, characters, decimal numbers and other types of values into variables in the executing program. Normally the programmer types the value at the keyboard and **scanf** will take the typed value and place it in the specified variable.

There are two things **scanf** needs to be told. What type of value is being typed in and which variable the value is to be placed in. For our example we want to type in 2 integer values which we want placed in **a** and **b.**

Clearly **scanf** needs to know which variables are to receive input. Does it need to know the type of the input? Could it not work this out for itself? If **10** is input at the keyboard why is it not always to be treated as the integer **10**? The keyboard is a character device. Input via the keyboard is always as a sequence of characters corresponding to the key strokes that generate the input. **10** as input at the keyboard is given to **scanf** as the two characters **'1'** and **'0'**. It is quite possible to input the sequence '**10**' to a program which does not treat it as an integer. The word processor that has been used for this book treats all digit sequences simply as sequences of characters. **scanf** can be used to process keyboard input in a variety of different ways. However, we need to indicate which. This is done using a **format string**. Format strings are used in input and output functions to direct how the input or output will work.

To read into **a** and **b** two integer values from the keyboard we call **scanf** as follows:

   scanf ("%d%d",&a,&b);

The first argument, **"%d%d"** , is the format string. It is in fact an example of a C string constant. A string is simply a sequence of characters. String constants are always written between quotes (" ... ").

The first **%d** is a format directive which directs **scanf** to take digits from the keyboard and convert them into an integer, placing this integer in the variable **a**. Directives within a format string always begin with the character '**%**'. When **scanf** executes under this directive the next keyboard input should be a sequence of digits. This may be preceded by spaces and end of lines (generated by the 'enter' key or 'return' key on most keyboards) and should be followed by some non-digit character (for example a space or an end of line). If **scanf** finds no digits this is treated as an error. Such errors can be handled within the executing program but to keep things simple we will assume that they do not arise. (**scanf** returns a result code which can be used to see if an error has occurred but we will use **scanf** in such a way that this result code is lost.)

The second **%d** acts in a similar way to the first, except that the variable **b** is used. As many format directives as required can appear in a format string. There should be variable references following the format string for each directive, and each such reference is expressed as a separate argument to **scanf**. The arguments supplied to a C function are always separated by commas. In the above use of **scanf** , three arguments are supplied," **%d%d**", **&a** and **&b**, the first being the format string, with the remaining two being the variable references.

All the other variable references we have seen have consisted simply of the name of the variable. Here the name is prefixed by an '**&**' character. Recall the two ways in which a variable might get used. We may want the value held in the area of memory associated with the variable or we may want to place a new value in memory in which case the variable reference is interpreted as an address. Up to now the context in which the variable reference occurred determined how it was to be treated. Because **scanf** is changing the contents of the two areas of memory associated with **a** and **b** it needs the addresses of these two areas. But context here does not help. In fact if a variable reference appears as an argument to a function C will always interpret this as meaning the value of the variable. If an '**&**' appears before a variable in an expression the address of the variable not its value to be used in the expression. By giving **scanf** the arguments **&a** and **&b** rather than **a** and **b** it is given the addresses of the two areas of memory rather than their contents. **scanf** asumes that arguments corresponding to inputs such as **&a** and **&b** above are addresses and treats them as such.

What happens if we write

   scanf("%d%d",a,b);

scanf would be given the values associated with **a** and **b**, not their addresses. Since it expects these arguments to be addresses it will treat them as such. If for example **a** held the value **0** at the call to **scanf** this would be given to **scanf** as an address. **scanf** would attempt to write the input value into this address. What happens next is system dependent but what is certain is that it would not be what the programmer expects.

The use of addresses in C will be developed in later chapters. For now, whenever making use of a function provided, for example, as part of the C system be very careful to supply arguments correctly. It is very easy in C to fail to do this. In particular, where an address is required by a function, it is very likely that any variable reference given as an argument needs to be prefixed by an '**&**'. If the '**&**' is omitted the function will be given the value associated with the variable which it will treat as an address, leading to unpredictable results. In the worst case this could be a total failure of the C system itself.

Having worked out what arguments we need to give **scanf** we add it to our program as a function call. We place this function call somewhere before the input values are made use of by the rest of the program. Here we place it after the declarations and before the first assignment.

The program will now read in two integer values, storing them in **a** and **b**. It will then calculate quotient and remainder, leaving these values in **quotient** and **remainder.** To display these values on the screen we use a second function **printf**. As with **scanf**, **printf** has as one of its arguments a format string. **printf** is general, allowing the output of integers, characters and other types of values. The format string is followed by expressions for the values to be output, successive format directives in the format string indicating how the values of each expression are to be treated (as integers, characters or whatever). The format string can include text to be output.

The two expressions will be references to the variables **quotient** and **remainder**. The call to **printf** with its arguments will look like

> **printf("quotient = %d remainder = %d",quotient,remainder);**

If the values **10** and **3** are supplied as input to our program this call to **printf** would generate as output

> **quotient = 3 remainder = 1**

Using the format string

> **"quotient = %d remainder = %d"**

'**quotient=**' will be output to the screen, followed by the value of the first expression after the format string (**quotient**). ' **remainder=**' will then be output with the value of the second expression following this. In this example of a format string the format directives are embedded in text to be output.

Expressions in calls to **printf** take the same form as expressions appearing on the right hand side of assignments. For example

> **printf("%d",0);**

would generate **0** as output, and

> **printf("quotient plus remainder = %d",quotient + remainder);**

would generate as output

quotient plus remainder = 4

Since we want to output **quotient** and **remainder** only if we have calculated them we need to be careful where we place **printf** in our program. These are calculated only if **b** is greater than zero and so we need to associate **printf** with the if statement. We need to group together the while statement and **printf** under the if statement. Again we use curly brackets to do this, giving

```
main()
{
    int quotient,remainder,a,b;
    scanf("%d %d", &a,&b);
    quotient = 0;
    remainder = a;
    if (b >0)
    {
        while (remainder >= b)
        {
            quotient = quotient + 1;
            remainder = remainder – b;
        }
        printf("quotient = %d remainder = %d",quotient,remainder);
    }
}
```

as our more or less complete program. What remains is to ensure that **scanf** and **printf** are found by the C system.

3.7 Include files

scanf and **printf** are functions that are provided as part of the C system. They will almost certainly be held in a form very close to machine code. (It would be possible to provide them as C code but this would require their recompilation every time they were needed in a program. It is therefore more sensible to have them pre-compiled.) The linker has access to a **library** of pre-compiled functions. If a program references one of these functions then the linker will ensure that it is made part of the executable program.

Recall the two stage process that is applied to C programs coded in several **.c** files. Each **.c** file is compiled, with the compiler producing a **.o** file which contains something very close to machine code. The various **.o** files are then linked together by the linker to produce the final executable program.

In compiling a **.c** file the compiler will restrict itself to what is described in that file. Effectively it treats all **.c** files as independent and unrelated.

But the **.c** files that have been used to hold the text of the C program cannot really be all entirely independent. Although a single program can be spread over several files there must be references in some of the files to functions that are described in other files. If there were not then there would be no way that bits of the program in separate files could communicate. References in one **.c** file to functions in another **.c** file are called **external** references. If the compiler encounters an external reference how can it check that the reference is consistent with the thing referenced? For example, how can it check that the right number and type of arguments are supplied to a function in a function call? The answer is that without help it cannot. In the original implementations of C this was accepted as one of the areas where programmers had to be particularly careful. The ANSI standard for C requires that in such situations a function **prototype** is provided in the **.c** file making the reference. A function prototype describes in C as much of the function as is necessary for the compiler to carry out its consistency checks on the use of the function. We will look at how to write function prototypes when we look at how to write functions. Because the program we have written makes use of functions (**scanf** and **printf**) to conform to the ANSI standard we should provide prototypes. To make the C programmer's life a little easier than it would otherwise be C systems provide files that contain prototypes for the functions provided by the C system. These files have a special suffix, **.h**, which distinguishes them from **.c** files. They nevertheless contain C and as such are recognisable by the C compiler. A programmer can put whatever he likes into a **.h** file. If it is valid C then the C compiler will accept it. By convention these files contain prototypes and a small number of other types of C construct. Functions themselves would not normally appear in **.h** files.

The prototypes for the input and output functions are always held in a file called **stdio.h**. The names of prototype files for library functions have been standardised.

If either

       #include <f>   or   **#include "f"**

appears in a **.c** (or **.h**) file it is replaced by the contents of the file **f**.

Files are usually organised into directories. Although the names of the files containing prototypes for the library functions have been standardised, where these files are held in the directory hierarchy has not. They will of course be somewhere. This will vary from C system to C system. The angle brackets tell the compiler to look in the directory where the C system **include** files are normally kept.

If the second form of **include** is used **f** should name a file and if necessary the directory hierarchy that the file is embedded in depending on the file naming conventions of the operating system being used.

We add

       #include <stdio.h>

at the start of our program to ensure that the prototypes for **scanf** and **printf** are made available.

Adding **#include <stdio.h>** gives

```
#include <stdio.h>
main()
{
    int quotient,remainder,a,b;
    scanf(" %d %d", &a,&b);
    quotient = 0;
    remainder = a;
```

```
if (b > 0)
{
    while (remainder >= b
    {
        quotient = quotient + 1;
        remainder = remainder – b;
    }
    printf("quotient = %d remainder = d",quotient,remainder);
}
}
```

which should compile and execute.

We took care in our algorithm to compute quotient and remainder only if **b** is positive and non-zero. Do we need to do anything if this is not the case? As the program stands it will terminate without output if a **b** is input that is not positive and non-zero. This is hardly helpful to any user of the program who would at least like to know why he is not given the quotient and remainder for the values he has input. Since this easy to do it would be rather churlish not to oblige.

Our algorithmic language allowed us to write if statements that execute one way if the condition held and another if it did not. C provides a similar extended form of the if statement. By following the statement after the condition with an **else** we can include in our program actions to be carried out if **b** turns out to be less than or equal to zero. The obvious action is to output an appropriate message. Our program becomes

```
#include <stdio.h>
main()
{
    int quotient,remainder,a,b;
    scanf("%d %d", &a,&b);
    quotient = 0;
    remainder = a;
    if (b > 0)
    {
        while (remainder >= b)
        {
            quotient = quotient + 1;
            remainder = remainder – b;
        }
        printf("quotient = %d remainder = d",quotient,remainder);
    }
    else printf("The second input value must be positive and non-zero");
}
```

3.8 Program testing

Although the program given above should compile and execute, in practice what happens is that we create a **.c** file which contains some syntactic errors. However careful we are to avoid these they arise with irritating regularity. The C symbols that punctuate our programs are common sources of such errors. Semi-colons or brackets **seem** less important than assignments and arithmetic operations and we can we less careful in their use. The compiler will identify and report on such errors although compiler error messages can sometimes be rather obscure. If the compiler generates an error message there is certainly a syntax error in the program and it is probably somewhere near where the compiler has indicated its occurrence. Very often the error message accurately pinpoints the cause of the error. When it does not it may be necessary to look back through the program text from the point where the error is indicated for **any** misuse of the syntax of the language. Once all syntactic errors have been corrected we have what is called a clean compilation.

In the earlier sections of this chapter we created a program which we can compile and execute. This was based on an algorithm developed in Chapter 2 which we were very careful to check by dry running on sample input. Does the program behave as we want?. Errors may exist in a program for a number of reasons.

- We may not have been thorough enough in checking out our original algorithm. There may still be errors in the algorithm.
- We may have introduced errors in converting our algorithm to a program. Such new errors arise either because we have not understood the way in which a particular language feature works and our use of it is incorrect or because we have not been able to match the algorithm exactly to code. The language we are using forces us to make adjustments to the algorithm. Errors arise when we make these adjustments

Because we cannot be certain that our program will behave as it should we must subject it to the same sort of analysis as our original algorithm. We used a technique called dry running on the algorithm. We can do the same thing to our program. We select sample input values and manually step through the program examining the effect of each program statement, checking that it does what we want it to. This is a paper and pencil exercise that needs to be carried out very carefully. It can also be very time consuming and for large or complex programs it is not practical. It makes sense only for small sections of code which may of course be parts of larger programs.

Since we can execute our program we can subject it to a far wider range of tests than is practical with dry running either algorithms or programs. This stage in the development process, called program testing, often reveals errors in programs and as a result the associated **.c** file needs to be modified and re-compiled.

Such errors are called **bugs**. A test may show that a program is not behaving as it should. It will not however help in finding out **why** this is the case. Some detective work needs to be carried out to find the cause. This activity, called program **debugging**, can be the most time consuming of the whole development process. A bug can sometimes take days of investigation to uncover and is the price paid for careless design and implementation.

Tests should be chosen with care. We need to construct tests which test different aspects of a program and avoid those which simply repeat earlier tests.

For our program tests, using the inputs

10   3 and **100   30**

would be so similar that either one of these would do.

However the test

−10 3

would reveal something that we overlooked in developing the program. At the algorithm stage we dealt with positive integers. We used variables of type **int** in our program. But such variables can take negative values and when we run our program it will accept negative input, producing rather odd results. We should really check the input and if it is negative output a message rather than calculating quotient and remainder.

In devising tests we must try and cover all possible classes of input, with a representative from each class testing the program in a different way. How we split possible inputs up into different classes is partly to do with the nature of the application and partly to do with the way in which the program is implemented.

If for some reason it was found convenient to treat single digit numbers as a special case in computing quotient and remainder, treating all other numbers in a general way, then the two tests

7   2   and   **70   20**

would test different aspects of the program.

When you are constructing tests, determine the expected output from the program manually or at least in a way unrelated to the program under test. On applying a test **carefully** compare the expected output with the actual output. It is not uncommon for programmers to devise and apply tests concluding that the program works because the output looks roughly as expected. The test reveals a program error but too casual an approach on the part of the programmer causes it to be overlooked. We often see what we expect to see not what is there.

However careful we are in designing our algorithm, however well we know the programming language we are using to implement the program and however thorough we are with our program testing we can never guarantee that our program works. If we are very careful at **each** stage in the development of a program we reduce the risk of errors. In particular errors in a program that are introduced in the early stages of the development process can be more difficult to correct than those that are introduced later. Errors that arise because the language is used in the wrong way can normally be corrected more easily than those that arise from flaws in the underlying algorithm.

In both dry running a program and executing it the behaviour of a program can be determined for a given input. By executing a program we can test it over a much wider range of possible inputs than we could by simply dry running it. What then is the advantage of dry running? Before we can really benefit from testing a program the program must hold together to some extent. If it is a very long way from working executing it would probably give little or no useful information about its behaviour other than it does not work. We normally cannot see what it is doing as it does it. Because of this we cannot see where it starts to go wrong. In dry running a program we are able to check that at each stage it does what we want it to do. Many of the errors in the program will be revealed as a result and we can move onto the program test stage with more confidence in the program than would otherwise be the case.

Modern C systems often provide what are called **symbolic debuggers**. A symbolic debugger allows the programmer to control the execution of his program stopping and starting it at will. He can examine and change the values assigned to variables as the program executes. This provides a very powerful way of checking the behaviour of a program and can be used instead of dry running. It also takes a lot of the pain out of locating the causes of program errors. Although it is difficult to obtain realistic figures on how much time is spent on design, implementation and testing, it is very likely that often over half the total time involved will be dedicated to testing and debugging. A symbolic debugger can reduce that time significantly. An error that might otherwise take hours to identify can often be tracked down in minutes. The value of such a tool cannot be over-estimated and if one is available the time invested in learning how to use it is well worth it!

3.9 Converting digit sequences to numbers

A number of lessons came out of the development of the above program. In particular functions were used and we saw that input from the keyboard required conversion from character form to integers. We will consider a second example which develops these last two points in particular.

In using **scanf** we assumed that whenever it was called within the program it would be presented with a sequence of digits for conversion to integer. In many applications numbers are embedded in input in such a way that such an assumption cannot be made. We may find that we have to read the digits as characters within the program and carry out the conversion ourselves.

3.10 Character constants

Let us suppose that for the above program this is indeed the case. We will need to read the digits in as characters and use them to produce the corresponding integer. We have used **int** to introduce variables that take integer values. If we precede a variable name with **char** rather than **int,** a **char** variable is created. Enough space in memory for the representation (ASCII or whatever) of a character will be set aside and labelled with the variable name. Normally a byte is used. In fact type **char** is based on integers. A variable of that type has many of the characteristics of **int** variables and we could even use **int** instead of **char** below.

In the above program we used the integer value **0** in the assignment

quotient = 0;

The use of **0** here is as an integer **constant**. Digit sequences in C are used to represent integer constants within a program.

We can make use of character constants as well. We must however place the character between a pair of quote characters. Note that two types of quote characters, ''' and '''', appear on the keyboard. We have already seen that '''' is used with strings. Strings start and end with this character. For character constants the character '"' is used.

Thus if we write **9** this is treated an integer constant, if we write **'9'** this treated as a character constant and if we write **"9"** this is treated as a string constant. Only single characters can appear in character constants and they translate into the corresponding character code, whereas string constants can have any number of characters from **0** upwards and translate into a sequence of corresponding character codes terminated by the ASCII code **0**.

Given a variable **ch** of type **char**

> **ch = 'a';**

assigns the representation of the character **a** to **ch**.

Because type **char** is integer based, values of that type can appear in arithmetic expressions. For example

> **'9' – '0'**

causes the code for **0** to be subtracted from that for **9**.

In all the codings that have been developed for the characters the digits **'0'**, **'1'** , ... **'9'** have always been allocated successive values. For example the ASCII codes for **'0'** ... **'9'** are **48** ... **57**.

If the characters are coded in ASCII the expression

> **'9' – '0'**

is equivalent to the expression

> **57 – 48**

which of course gives the integer value **9**.

This gives us a very easy way of converting a digit character into its integer equivalent. We simply subtract the code for the character **'0'**.

3.11 Generating a number from its digit characters

We need to deal with more than one digit however. If the characters **'7'** and **'8'** are read in from the keyboard we must convert these to the integer **78**. If the characters **'3'**, **'5'** and **'4'** are read in then these become the integer **354**. We must read digits from the keyboard until the sequence of digits ends and convert the complete digit sequence into its corresponding integer value.

If it is not obvious how to tackle a given programming problem it is always a good idea to look at an example. By trying to do with the example what you want the program to do you often gain insights into how the program might work.

Here suppose the digit sequence **'4'**, **'5'** and **'3'** is input to the program. The program receives the digits from most significant (**'4'**) digit to least significant digit (**'3'**) because this is the order that we type them at the keyboard.

If digits are read one at a time then we cannot tell on reading a digit if it is the last digit in the sequence of digits being read. We only know it is the last if we discover that the character following it in the input is **not** a digit.

In our example when **'4'** is read it may be that this is the only digit in the digit sequence, in which case the number would be **4**. The second digit **'5'** would mean that the number will certainly not be **4**. The digit '**4**' might however occupy the 'tens' position in the number in which case the number could be **4 * 10 + 5 = 45**. On reading the third digit '**3**' again we have to modify what we thought was the number. Now the digit '**4**' might occupy the 'hundreds' position with '**5**' occupying the 'tens' position. Our number then might be **45 * 10 + 3 = 453**. If no digit immediately follows the '**3**' in the input then the digit sequence did indeed stand for the number **453** with '**4**' giving the number of hundreds, '**5**' giving the number of tens and '**3**' giving the number of units.

Two things are happening here.

First the number associated with a digit sequence is being treated as a sum of powers of **10**.

$$453 = 4*(10*10) + 5 * 10 + 3 = 4*10^2 + 5*10^1 + 3*10^0$$

Second, the required powers are obtained by successive multiplications by **10** as successive digits are encountered.

Thus the strategy we shall adopt in converting the digit sequence into its associated integer is

- intialise an **int** variable **number** to zero
- read and discard any space characters in the input
- read successive digits updating **number** as described for each digit input until a space character is encountered.

Once again we have made some simplifying assumptions the most important of which is that only spaces and digit sequences appear in the input.

3.12 The conversion algorithm

C provides a function **getchar** which **returns** the next character typed at the keyboard. Using this the conversion can be expressed as an algorithm as follows

```
number = 0;
ch = getchar();
while (ch is a space) ch = getchar();
while (ch is not a space)
{
    number = number * 10 + ( ch - '0');
    ch = getchar();
}
```

The first line of the algorithm initialises **number** to zero.

The second line reads a character from the keyboard, placing it in the variable **ch**. It takes the form of an assignment. When **getchar** is called it will cause a character typed at the keyboard to be read and converted into its internal code, which is returned as the result of the function call. This result is then assigned to the variable **ch**.

The third line of our algorithm reads successive characters until a character other than a space is input. Our assumption means that this must be a digit. A while statement is used with the condition **ch is a space** and an assignment **ch = getchar()**.

Each time **getchar** is called the next character typed at the keyboard is assigned to **ch**. Thus each time the condition **ch is a space** is encountered it will be for a different input character. Assuming that at some stage a digit is typed this condition will eventually become false and execution will move on.

The fourth line begins the loop that reads in successive digits carrying out the conversion. Again, because we are catering only for spaces and digits in the input, if a character is not a space then it must be a digit.

The body of the loop consists of two assignment statements.

The first assignment statement does quite a lot of work. It

- ensures that the current value of **number** is multiplied by **10** to reflect the fact that because a new digit has been encountered the current value must be a factor of **10** out (**number * 10**)
- converts the internal code for the input digit into a number in the range **0 ..9** (**ch – '0'**)
- adds the number associated with the input digit to the updated value of **number**. (**number * 10 + (ch – '0'**))

The second assignment uses **getchar** to read the next character from the keyboard and assign it to **ch**. At each cycle of the loop **ch** will change. Since we are assuming that digit sequences will always be followed by spaces eventually a space will be read in and assigned to **ch,** causing the loop to terminate because the condition controlling the execution of the loop is **ch is not a space** .

3.13 C code for the conversion

Once again we need to turn the algorithm into C code. The condition '**ch is a space**' is expressed in C as the comparison

    ch == ' '

A space character is written ' '. (The space bar on the keyboard generates a space character. It, like all other characters, has an associated internal code. For example the ASCII code for a space is **32**. We have seen that character constants appear in C programs between a pair of '''' characters. Here the space character appears there.)

The condition '**ch is not a space**' is expressed in C by the comparison

    ch != ' '

where the symbol **!=** is used for inequality.

We move our algorithm a little closer to its C equivalent by replacing the loop conditionals appropriately, giving

```
number = 0;
ch = getchar();
while (ch = ' ') ch = getchar();
while (ch != ' ')
{
    number = number * 10 + ( ch – '0');
    ch = getchar();
}
```

We at last have the C code that will convert digits input at the keyboard to the number that they correspond to. We need now to decide how to 'package' this code in such a way that it can be used conveniently. In our original program we read numbers in in two places in the text of the program using **scanf**. We could use the conversion code developed here rather than **scanf** in one of two ways. We could place the code directly in our program (with some minor changes to variable names) at the two places where conversion of input is required. Alternatively we could use the conversion code as the basis of a function that we use much as we used **scanf**.

3.14 The conversion code in the form of a function

The second approach above is by far superior to the first and should almost always be adopted. If the same action (more or less) crops up in several places in a program then making a function for it offers the following advantages:

- The code associated with the action appears only in one place, namely in the function.
- The function can be tested as an independent program before being made use of in the program for which it was originally designed.
- The function may prove to be useful in more than one program. The conversion described above could well be needed in many different programs.
- A program built out of well chosen functions is normally better structured than would otherwise be the case and as a result is easier to follow and test.

In the last point the phrase 'well chosen' is used. How a program is structured as a collection of functions is often a difficult design problem and we will need to look at program design in much more detail later. Although it is sometimes possible to find several different structures involving different functions each of which is acceptable, dividing a program into functions needs to done with care. Ideally each function should have associated with it a single clearly defined action and it should relate to the rest of the program in a straightforward way. Part of the skill of programming is to do with identifying structure within a program and expressing that structure through language features such as functions.

Since the conversion code is best packaged as a function we need to decide on a function name, whether the function needs any arguments and whether the function returns a result. We will call the function **getint** and since, like **scanf**, it works only on input from the keyboard it needs no arguments. We will however design it so that it returns a result. We want it to be used in a similar way to **getchar**. **getchar** reads a character from the keyboard, returning its internal code as a result. We will ensure that **getint** reads a sequence of digit characters from the keyboard returning the corresponding integer as a result. It can then be used in a similar way to **getchar**.
   Thus the assignment

   a = getint();

causes the function **getint** to be called. **getint** reads the next sequence of digit characters from the keyboard calculating the corresponding integer which it returns as its result. This result is then assigned to **a**. Note that the assignment has the same effect as **scanf("%d",&a)**.

3.15 The general structure of a function declaration

User defined functions need to be declared before they can be used. In ANSI C the general form of a function declaration is

> **<result_type>**_{opt} **<function_name>** (**<parameter_list>**_{opt})
> {
>
> .
> .   body of function
> .
>
> }

where **<result_type>** (which is optional and may be omitted) indicates the type of the result returned by the function; **<function_name>** is a name chosen by the programmer for the function; and **<parameter_list>** (which is again optional) is a list of argument descriptions. If **<result_type>** is not given then result type **int** is assumed.

Since we have decided that **getint** will take no arguments we need not worry about the complexities of argument descriptions at this stage. Our result type is **int,** giving

> **int getint()**

as the first line of our function declaration.

The function makes use of two variables **number** and **ch**. These need to be declared within the function and this is done in much the same way that we made variable declarations in **main** earlier. **number** is declared as a variable of type **int** and **ch** is declared as a variable of type **char**.

3.16 Returning results from functions

Finally we need to indicate in the function where to exit from the function and what value should be returned as the function result. C provides the **return statement** to achieve this, which takes the general form

> **return <expression>**

where **<expression>** is an expression whose result is of the type given with the function name. If no **return** appears in a function then the function will exit at the last statement of the function. If a function without a **return** is used in an expression, then the program containing that expression will behave unpredictably.

Using **return,** our function declaration becomes

```
int getint()
{
    int number; char ch;
    number = 0;
    ch = getchar();
    while (ch == ' ') ch = getchar();
```

```
    while (ch != ' ')
    {
        number = number * 10 + ch – '0';
        ch = getchar();
    }
    return number;
}
```

3.17 Using getint

We can demonstrate the use of **getint** by using it instead of **scanf** in the program given in Section 3.7 We simply replace

```
scanf("%d %d", &a,&b);
```

by the two assignment statements

```
a = getint();
b = getint();
```

giving

```
#include <stdio.h>
main()
{
    int quotient,remainder,a,b;
    a = getint();
    b = getint();
    quotient = 0;
    remainder = a;
    while (remainder >= b)
    {
        quotient = quotient + 1;
        remainder = remainder – b;
    }
    printf("quotient = %d remainder = %d",quotient,remainder);
}
```

As we have seen, C provides a library of functions any of which we can call from within our C programs. A number of **.h** files are associated with this library and we indicate our use of particular functions by including the corresponding **.h** files. The function **getint** is our own creation and we must make it available to any program that we want to make use of it. This can be done in several ways.

We could place the text of the function in the same **.c** file as the text of the program that calls it. In our example our **.c** file would then contain two function declarations, one for **getint** and the other for **main**. This is quite a common approach: **.c** files often consist of a number of function declarations.

If the function is general enough for it to be useful to a number of different programs then it can be placed in a file of its own. For example we might choose to place **getint** in a file which we call **getint.c**. (Two very similar names are used here,

getint and **getint.c**. The first names a C function that has significance only within a C program. The second names a text file containing the C code for that function which has significance within the filestore of whatever operating system the editor and C compiler used operates under.)

If a program used input/output functions from the C library we made sure that

```
#include <stdio.h>
```

appeared in the program in order that the compiler could check that the functions were being used in an appropriate way. the file **stdio.h** contained enough information about each of the functions for the compiler to do this, although the code for the functions was held in a compiled form in the C library.

If we want to make our function generally available we need to create a file, **getint.h,** say, in which we place a description of **getint** that the compiler can use for such checks. This description contains the name of the function, the type of its result and the type of its arguments. For **getint** there will be just one line in **getint.h**

```
int getint();
```

which provides this information. Finally we add **#include "getint.h"** to our program giving

```
#include "getint.h"
#include <stdio.h>
main()
{
    int quotient,remainder,a,b;
    a = getint();
    b = getint();
    quotient = 0;
    remainder = a;
    while (remainder >= b)
    {
        quotient = quotient + 1;
        remainder = remainder - b;
    }
    printf("quotient = %d remainder = %d",quotient,remainder);
}
```

Let us call the file that contains this program **main.c**.

Why did we use **"getint.h"** rather than **<getint.h>**? This we covered in Section 3.7. When compiling a program the C compiler will need to know which directory holds the **.c** file to be compiled. Most C systems are implemented on operating systems that use the idea of a **current working directory**. The system user is working somewhere within the file store. The directory he is using is termed the current working directory. A programmer building an application will normally create the various **.c** and **.h** files used in the same directory. In using the C system the programmer will 'position' himself in this directory, which as a result will be designated the current working directory and any file references are to files in that directory. When the C system encounters a **#include "fname.h"** it looks for **name.h** in this directory. In our example we assume the file **getint.c**, the file

getint.h and the file containing the program that makes use of **getint** are all held in the same directory – the current working directory.

C library files apart, if **.c** files in different directories make use of the same **.h** file then a name must be used that gives the exact location of the **.h** file and since it may be nested within several directories this name will be made up of the directory names involved as well as the file name.

We have three text files: **main.c, getint.c** and **getint.h**. Executable code can be obtained for our program by compiling **getint.c** and then **main.c**. Compiling **getint.c** causes the creation of a **getint.o** file. Although this .o file cannot itself be executed since it does not include a **main()** function, it will be used by the linker to make an executable program from **main.o** (obtained by compiling **main.c**).

3.18 Processing text

As a further example of program design involving the processing of characters we will examine the problem of recognising word boundaries in a sequence of words. To keep things simple we will restrict the program to a single line of input consisting of words made up from upper and lower case letters with the text terminated by a full stop. No other punctuation characters are catered for. The program will output each word of the line of text on separate lines.

3.19 Buffering keyboard input

A line of text is input at the keyboard by typing the text of the line followed by an 'enter'. We have seen that these characters can be read using **getchar**. There are two ways in which this might work

- characters can be read by **getchar** as they are typed
- the complete line of text needs to be typed before characters can be read.

Where input is from the keyboard and output to the screen the approach adopted can make a difference to the way input and output appear on the screen.

For example

```
ch = getchar();
while (ch != '.')
{
    printf("%c",ch);
    ch = getchar();
}
printf("%c",ch);
```

reads and outputs characters until the character '.' is encountered. Note that we have made use of a new directive, '%c', to indicate that a character is to be output using **printf**. This ensures that a character is displayed. If we had used '%d' the character code (ASCII or whatever) would be output as an integer value.

If characters are readable as soon as they are typed then a typed line would be interleaved with the program's output, since each time a character is typed it is read by the program and displayed on the screen.

When, for example, **hello** was typed what would appear on the screen would be

hheelllloo

If a complete line of text needs to be input before its characters are made available the output generated from that line of text would follow it on a new line.

When **hello** was typed, what would appear on the screen would be

hello
hello

The C input system ensures that the complete line of text is read in and stored before the program can access it. The text is said to be **buffered** by the input system.

3.20 The program algorithm

Since the program is intended to process just one line of text and since the text is buffered our program can read characters with the certainty that any output follows the line of input.

The action of the program can be described by the while statement

> **while (not at end of input line)**
> **{**
> > **read and output a word;**
> > **read and discard spaces;**
> > **move to the next line of output;**
> **}**

We will assume that only spaces separate words with the only punctuation being a full stop which appears at the end of the line. Further we allow words to be made up of any characters other than spaces and full stops. Our program will treat

the cat sat on the mat.

and

th%$$$ and $£'''''' +eq.

in exactly the same way. That is the program does not check that only letters are input.

If a character is read initially then, since the last character on the line is a full stop, the while statement becomes

> **ch = getchar();**
> **while (ch != '.')**
> **{**
> > **read and output a word;**
> > **read and discard spaces;**
> > **move to the next line of output;**
> **}**

We are going to read each word letter by letter. This gives

```
ch = getchar();
while (ch != '.')
{
     while (ch != ' ')
     {
          printf("%c",ch);
          ch = getchar();
     }
     read and discard spaces;
     move to the next line of output;
}
```

Reading and discarding spaces is dealt with by

while (ch == ' ') ch = getchar();

which simply reads characters until a non-space character is encountered.

3.21 Control characters

The character set used with most programming languages is made up of two types of characters, **printable** and **non-printable**. The printable characters are those that can be seen when displayed on a screen or printed. These include the letters, digits, punctuation characters, and arithmetic operators among other printable characters. The non printable characters include what are called **control** characters which allow for example the programmer to direct output to the next line on the screen. The ASCII character set includes a number of control characters and these characters will thus have ASCII codes associated with them. For example the code for the new line control character is **10**.

If we are certain that our system is making use of ASCII coding we could force a new line by

printf("%c",10)

which outputs the value **10** as a character. The use of the format directive **%c** will ensure that the value **10** will be treated as the ASCII character code for new line and if it is sent to the screen further output will be on a new line.

Because some C systems operate on machines that use different character codings, C provides a machine independent way of specifying a new line. This entails the use of an **escape sequence** in a format string. The character '\' is a normal printable character available on almost all keyboards. However it is used in a special way in C where it is always followed by a second character that is interpreted differently from normal.

In C the character sequence, \n stands for the new line character where it appears in a format string or between character quotes. '\' is called an **escape character** and the above character sequence is an example of an escape sequence. If you actually want the character '\' you have to write it '\\'.

Character constants have to be single characters. Note that although '\n' looks like two characters it is still a single character.

The machine independent way of forcing a new line is by

> printf("\n")

and should always be used in preference to

> printf("%c",10)

If we add a loop to discard spaces and this use of **printf** the algorithm develops into the program

```
main()
{
    char ch = getchar();
    while (ch != '.')
    {
        while(ch != ' ' )
        {
            printf("%c",ch);
            ch = getchar();
        }
        while(ch == ' ') ch = getchar();
        printf("\n");
    }
}
```

This last example illustrates two points, the first to do with program development and the second to do with programming languages.

First in moving from algorithm to program the algorithm went through a number of transformations or **refinements**. The inital algorithm dealt with words and lines. Words were treated as single atomic objects found in a line of text. The first refinement of the algorithm recognised that words were separated by space characters and that the full stop character ended the line. The second refinement took into account the nature of words as sequences of characters. The program was developed from an initial algorithm through a succession of refinements that took into account more and more detail.

Second we have an example of a nested loop. The while loop that deals with characters (the inner loop) operates within the loop that deals with words (the outer loop). For each cycle of the outer loop there are a number of cycles of the inner loop. In general statements defined in terms of other statements can be nested to an arbitrary depth.

Exercises

1. Write C programs for the algorithm given in Question 8 of Chapter 2 and for the algorithm developed for Question 9.

2. Write a C program which reads a binary number and outputs it in its decimal form.

3. Write a C program which reads an integer and displays it as a binary number.

4. The program given in Section 3.7 does not check for negative input. Modify it

so that it does.

5. Floating point numbers can be declared using the key word **float** to indicate the variable type. Constuct a function that reads in a sequence of digits with a possible embedded decimal point converting the sequence to its corresponding floating point number.

    You will need to use **printf** and the format directive **'f'** associated with floating point numbers to test your function. So for example if **fl** is a variable of type **float**

    printf("%f",fl)

    displays the value in **fl** as a decimal value. The number of digits following the decimal point can be controlled by placing a point followed by an integer constant before the directive.

    printf("%.3f",fl);

    displays the value in **fl** with three digits following the decimal point.

6. The calculation of quotient and remainder given here makes use of successive subtraction. It was done in this way as an example of program development. However C provides arithmetic operators that generate quotient and remainder. For two **integer** numbers **a** and **b a/b** gives the quotient and **a%b** gives the remainder. Modify the program to make use of these operators.

7. Construct a program which generates a table of integer powers. The program should take as input an integer **n** and create an n line table. Numbering the lines from **1** the **i**th line should consist of the **i** powers of **i** (**i, i * i, i * i * i, ...**). For example a table with **n > 3** will take the form

1			
2	4		
3	9	27	
4	16	64	256

    .

    .

    .

    To ensure a satisfactory layout you will need to specify a field width within your output format string. This can be done in one of two ways. An integer constant immediately preceding the format code **d** can be used. For example **printf("%6d",i)** outputs the value in **i** as an integer in a six character field width. If '*' is used then the field width is given by an expression following the format string. For example **printf("%*d %*d",s,i,s + 1,j)** outputs the value **i** in a field of size **s** followed by **j** in a field of size **s + 1**.

4

Modular program structure

The programming problems examined in Chapters 2 and 3 resulted in a fairly small programs. Such programs are in fact quite uncommon in the world of professional programming, although the programs that do occur are very often made up of small sub-components that carry out simple tasks and the overall effect of the program is achieved through combining the effect of these sub-components. Indeed a goal in the design of any program should be the identification of simple sub-components that the program can be built from. In this chapter we will illustrate this aspect of programming using as our example the development of a program that evaluates arithmetic expressions. Before doing so we will look at some aspects of the development process of such programs in general terms and also some of the skills required of a professional programmer.

The size and complexity of a program depends on the nature of the task that it carries out. Some programming tasks may require large teams of programmers working together over a period of months or years before a program is produced. Teams of 20 or more programmers working on the same overall task for two or more years are not uncommon. Often the overall task may lead to several large programs (program suites) working together to achieve the desired effect.

A very large percentage of professional programming involves the modification of existing programs. Indeed many companies employ programmers for no other purpose than to maintain software. The need to maintain software arises either because errors are found in the software or because the task carried out by the software has changed.

Even though a program has been in use for several years it could still contain errors. Most programs are designed to deal with situations with very large possible combinations of input. Even the very simple program given in Chapter 3 deals with a very wide range of possible input values – all allowable pairs of integers. A particular combination of inputs that causes a program error may arise so rarely that it is several years before the program is presented with it. The program may have been tested fairly thoroughly before being accepted as working but because it is very rarely possible to test exhaustively it has never met the combination of values that causes the error before.

Software in use today can often be more than ten years old and much of the work done on it over that period has been to correct errors and update it in response to changes in the context in which it gets used. Thus many programmers spend their time dealing with code that they did not write often in organisations where the author of the program has long since left. Even though a program may do the job it was designed for it may be so poorly written that understanding how it works is almost impossible. A good program not only works but is written in as clear a way as possible. This should always be borne in mind when writing programs.

The image of the programmer as a solitary being working at his PC until the early hours is therefore quite wrong . He normally works in a team, is very dependent on the work of others and, if he is any good, attempts to produce programs that are easy to maintain by other programmers.

Of course programmers also get involved in the development of entirely new software and this needs to be done in a methodical way. We have already noted that the programmer must have a very clear idea about what the program is to do. This may be obvious but it is an unfortunate fact of programming life that programmers often rush into coding ill prepared. It is very easy to underestimate the complexity of a programming task. Difficulties then emerge during coding which are to do with a poor or incomplete program design.The remedies found for these difficulties often need to take into account the coding that has already been carried out and as a result are clumsy and unsatisfactory.

The problems of poorly developed software have been with us for over 30 years and in that time many **methodologies** have been proposed as ways of reducing the risk. A typical software development methodology is a rather loose collection of guide-lines, techniques and notations that have come to be accepted as helpful in the development of software. Most methodologies are based on the notion of a **software life cycle** and break software development down into a number of steps moving in time from the initial concept behind the software through to the working system.

The development steps taken may vary depending on the nature of the software but will almost always include

- **requirements analysis** – given the possibility that some task may be carried out by a computer program this stage of the development attempts to clarify exactly what the that task involves. It leads to a **program specification** which describes the task as precisely as possible.
- **program design** – a strategy is devised by which a computer can be made to perform the task identified in the program specification. This strategy is developed into a design often captured in some form of **design document**.
- **detailed design** – using the design document as a basis a program structure in terms of program modules is identified and each module is expressed in an algorithmic form.
- **program implementation** – the algorithms developed at the detailed design stage are coded in a programming language.

Each step calls on special skills, with those of the programmer normally being associated with the last two steps. However we take the view here that the programmer's job begins with the specification and continues through the maintenance of the resultant software.

4.1 The program specification

The purpose of a program specification is to describe the task that the program is to perform. It is very often given in terms of input and output. A specification was given in Chapter 2 for the program which calculated quotient and remainder which was expressed in terms of inputs **a** and **b** and outputs **quotient** and **remainder**.

A specification should not normally force the programmer to make choices about input or output. For example it should not be up to the programmer to decide in what order the input from the keyboard is read. This should be clear from the specification.

Normally any unusual situations that the program might encounter should also be dealt with. For example if a program processes positive integers the specification should describe what action the program should take if it is given negative integers.

Sometimes a specification is deliberately incomplete. The customer for the program does not care for example what the program does if it encounters illegal input (for example negative integers if it processes positive integers) as long as something sensible is done. Where a specification is incomplete some limitation should be placed on the options available to the programmer. A program which fails on illegal input would not be acceptable but if a specification does not cover illegal input then the programmer may simply ignore the possibility.

The specification is the programmer's starting point. He must therefore be very clear about what the specification is asking for. This is often not as simple as it sounds because specifications are normally written in English and can be quite vague. Authors of specifications are often not computer specialists. They may produce specifications that in principle identify a useful task but contain inconsistencies and irrelevant material. The specification may be incomplete in ways that the programmer cannot resolve. For example unusual sets of circumstances that could arise may not have been adequately dealt with in the specification.

Most programmers at some stage in their programming career will be given specifications that appear to make sense but on completion of the program they find that what the author of the specification wrote and what he meant were two different things. As a result a lot of programming activity is wasted. This arises out of the potential for ambiguity in English. Again the programmer must be on his guard. Ambiguity is particularly tricky because if we see a meaning in a piece of English we often assume that this is the only possible meaning. Specifications can be written using special languages designed purely for program specification. The problems of vagueness, woollyness and ambiguity do not arise in such specifications and these languages are gradually becoming established in the computing community.

4.2 Finding a suitable design

Given a specification, the first difficulty the programmer encounters is knowing where to start his design. He has to create, apparently from nothing, a program that will satify the specification. Where creativity is required it is never possible to give a recipe that will ensure success. There are however a number of things a programmer can do that may help him.

Different programs often have similar designs because there are similarities in the tasks they carry out. For example programs often have to sort things into order. Suppose the names and company telephone numbers of employees within a company are held on a computer. A company telephone directory could be produced by sorting the pairs of names and telephone numbers so that they were ordered alphabetically by name. Or we may have the examination results of students on a degree course held on a computer and the requirement may be for a ranked list of students. Here the ordering is based on marks rather than names but the same basic method of sorting could be used as that used to produce the telephone directory.

When faced with a programming task a useful first step is to study the design of programs that carry out similar tasks. It may be necessary to make use of ideas from several different programs but certainly take advantage of what has already been done, particularly if the programming problem is a complex one. New programming languages are invented fairly regularly. No one would attempt to write a compiler for a new language without first studying how compilers for existing languages are written.

A second way of trying to get some feel for the design of a program is to take an example of what the program is to do and see how it might be done using pencil and paper. The form that the algorithm for the quotient remainder program should take emerged by taking a pair of numbers and working out their quotient and remainder by hand. Looking at a manual approach to achieving the task required of the final program may not suggest the best way of doing things at first but it gives a starting point for an algorithmic description and as this description is written out improvements often present themselves. Writing down ideas is important even if they cannot be expressed as an algorithm. This forces a clearer vision of the idea and the very act of writing can cause new ideas to spring to mind.

It is worth repeating here a comment made in Chapter 2. The way forward is very rarely to start writing code. This tactic, however tempting, normally leads to disaster. The feeling that time spent on analysis and design is unproductive time is common and understandable. There is no code to show for it. However this is wrong. The better thought through the design the easier the programming task and the shorter the overall development time. No one would start laying out a new garden without a very good idea of how it is to be organised. There would be a plan. This must be so for programs as well.

This does not preclude experimentation however. There is nothing wrong in trying out programming ideas on the computer. A programmer may have developed a design that he is reasonably confident he can implement. However there is perhaps an aspect of that design that is a little unusual and he wants to assure himself that it is not going to create major problems. A bit of programming in this situation is not unreasonable.

Good design is of paramount importance. However 'good' and 'complex' are not synonymous. Keep designs simple and avoid over-designing. It is much better to review a simple design that proves to have some inadequacies at the implementation stage than to create an over-complex program from an over-complex design.

Sometimes a design is unavoidably complex because of the nature of the programming task. Often such designs have evolved as ways have been discovered of extending a simpler design to cater for a more sophisiticated application . The very first operating systems were extremely simple. This was not because the machines they ran on could not support more complex operating systems. They almost certainly could. It was because not enough was known about how to build more complex systems.

The construction of complex systems with many components has always proceeded slowly through a process of evolution. The modern airliner is extremely complex compared with the airliners of 60 or 70 years ago but its design developed out of those earlier designs. In general, simple systems that work are extended or modified to provide more sophisticated systems. Software often follows this same evolutionary path.

An evolutionary approach in developing a program can pay dividends. If the design of a program is proving difficult to identify, simplifying the task can help. Its design can then be extended to cater for the original problem. For example the task of developing a word processor with features similar to those found in commercial word processors could be simplified by initially including only a small number of the required features in the design.

We saw in Chapter 2 how the design of algorithms could be expressed in a program-like notation. This notation is called **pseudo-code**. A design will normally be described at several levels. The highest level will give an outline design with each lower level providing more design detail than the level above. A design will not always develop in this way – we sometimes want to examine some aspect of a design in a little more detail before developing further the overall design – but once a design is complete it should be possible to describe it in this hierarchical way.

At the lowest level a design may consist of a number of algorithms expressed in pseudo-code. At higher levels different notations for describing the design may be used. There are many notations available for describing designs at these higher levels. Normally they allow the program to be described as a collection of **modules,** each module having associated with a clearly identified task. The way these components interact will also be shown. This interaction takes one of two forms:

- One module calls on another module to do carry out its associated task.
- One module passes data to another module.

Of course the two types of interaction are related. In calling on a module to carry out a task it may be necessary to pass data to that module or to receive data from it. For example, if a program design included a module to compute quotient and remainder for two numbers any other module making use of it would need to pass it the two numbers and obtain from it the quotient and remainder.

We will make use of a graphical notation in the example below which works well for describing designs at a level above pseudo-code. It will be used to describe programs in terms of what are called **module structure charts**. Unlike an algorithm what it will not show is **flow of control**. The order in which statements are executed is given in an algorithm. A module structure chart shows what modules go to make up the program, and how they interact. The order in which modules execute is **not** given. Again some detail is being left to a later stage in the design description, following the philosophy that a separation of issues in design (here program structure and flow of control) helps in the production of good designs.

4.3 Detailed design and program implementation

Detailed design turns a higher level of design into a collection of algorithms and data descriptions. We have so far said very little about data but the modules that appear in structure charts may well be implemented as functions operating on a collection of data values. Data values can sometimes take quite complex forms and program design must take into account the structure of data along with the code that processes the data. For example, software to do with currency transactions is likely to include a module which manages the exchange rates. An essential part of this module would be a table of exchange rates between the various currencies. This table might well have a structure similar to the mileage tables giving distances between towns found in road atlases. The exchange rate module would be made up of the table and code to carry out currency conversions.

How such data structures are described will be dealt with in later chapters.

4.4 An example – Arithmetic expression evaluation

To illustrate the organisation of a design into modules we will develop a program that evaluates arithmetic expressions involving integers, addition, subtraction, multiplication and division. The completed program will behave a little like a pocket calculator. It will read arithmetic expressions, evaluate them and display the result of evaluation.

An arithmetic expression takes the form of a sequence of integers separated by arithmetic **operators** and the input to the program will follow this form with its output being the result. The integers that appear in our expressions are examples of **operands** in expressions.

The input to the program will range from the very simple, a single integer, to expressions involving a mix of integers and arithmetic operators.

As discussed in Chapter 2, when we write down an expression such as

$$3 + 4 * 5$$

there is a convention that the multiplication will be carried out before the addition. That is the expression is evaluated in the order

$$3 + 4 * 5$$
$$= 3 + 20$$
$$= 23$$

Note that we could have treated it as

$$3 + 4 * 5$$
$$= 7 * 5$$
$$= 35$$

There is nothing special about multiplication that requires that we calculate in the way that we do. However everybody agrees to treat multiplication and division as taking precedence over addition and subtraction but otherwise to carry out the calculation by applying the operators from left to right. Therefore we will ensure that our program works in the same way.

If we applied **all** operators in the order that they appeared designing the program would be relatively easy. Having to take precedence into account means that we may have to apply an operator appearing later in the input first as in the calculation above.

We will allow brackets in expressions and treat them in the conventional way. Thus for example

$$4 * (5 + 6)$$

takes the value **44**.

This adds a further difficulty to our programming task. We must evaluate expressions in brackets first.

We will also allow spaces between the integers and the operators that make up the input expression. This follows the style of expressions in C and some other languages. For the last expression we could input it to the program in many different ways including

$$4*(5+6)$$
$$4 \ * (5 + 6)$$
$$4 * (5 + 6)$$

The program will need to identify the end of an expression. We will use the character '.' for this.

Here then are some examples of input to the program and the corresponding output.

Input	Output
3.	3
4 + 5 .	9
4 * (5 – 2) .	12
5 * 5 * (2 * 2 + 50/ (4 + 1)).	350

Although the program developed here is primarily intended to illustrate a number of design issues it should also help the reader understand better the nature of expressions in general and how more general expressions might be dealt with. The expressions found in C programs may involve operands other than integers. Variables as well as constants usually appear in them. They may also involve a wider range of operators. However they are structurally similar to those that our program will process and could be dealt with a similar way.

There is a principle in tackling program design that works very well in many cases.

> **If the program design for a programming task is difficult to determine simplify the task.**

By removing some of the complexity in a given task a design may be easier to identify and this design can then be developed to cater for the original task. We noted earlier that complex designs often evolve from simpler designs. The approach suggested here echoes that.

Following this principle we will develop the required program in three stages.

- A program that handles expressions involving integers and the operators '+' and ' – ' is developed.
- The program is extended to include the operators '*' and '/'.
- The program is extended again to include bracketted expressions.

In each case we will assume that expressions submitted are in their correct form. In practice this would be a dangerous assumption. A robust expression evaluator would generate error messages if the input did not make sense. Once we have a program that handles correctly formed expressions it can be extended in a straight-forward way to deal with ill formed expressions and we make this an exercise at the end of this chapter.

4.5 Dealing with addition and subtraction

Because the operators '+' and ' – ' have the same precedence we can apply them in a left to right order. As a consequence the general strategy is fairly straight forward. We know when we have reached the end of an expression that a '.' character is encountered. We also know there will be at least one operand since at this stage we are assuming that the input to our program does not contain errors.

The program will read the very first operand as the result so far. It will then read what follows. If this is the ' .' character the program will output the result so far and terminate. If not an operator and operand should follow. Both the operator and operand will be read and a new result is calculated from the result so far and the operand just read using the operator. Again if what follows is the '.' character the result so far will be output and the program will terminate, otherwise the cycle will repeat.

Note that we do not have to read in the whole expression before evaluating it. Indeed to do so would lead to a much more complicated and less satisfactory program. Let us call the proposed program **evaluate** and our first version **evaluate_1**.

Our first goal is to create a general structure for our program and express this in the form of a module structure chart. This will provide a framework to support the detailed development of the program. We need to identify the major building blocks that will be used in constructing the program and how these blocks relate to each other. Each building block will appear as a module in the chart. Each module should have a clearly defined task associated with it. Where it is sensible to break such tasks down into sub-tasks in some way then subordinate modules will be associated with these sub-tasks.

The structure chart will show two things

- which modules are subordinate to which
- what communication takes place between modules.

There is a widely accepted notation for structure charts and we shall follow this, introducing notation where necessary.

evaluate_1 reads in and evaluates an arithmetic expression and then outputs the result. We have decided that our program will apply operators as soon as their operands are available. This suggests two sub-tasks

- read and evaluate expression
- output result

which can be treated as building blocks for **evaluate_1.**

The module '**evaluate_1**' therefore has the two subordinate modules '**evaluate_expression**' and '**output_result**'.

Although these two subordinate modules carry out separate tasks, they do need to communicate. Once '**evaluate_expression**' has calculated the value of the expression it needs to make this value available to '**output_result**'. Subordinate modules communicate via their parent module. '**evaluate_expression**' communicates with '**output_result**' via '**evaluate_1**'

Figure 4.1 expresses the design of our program as a module chart. An arrow from '**evaluate_expression**' to '**evaluate_1**' is used in the diagram to show a data flow from the subordinate module to '**evaluate_1**'. Such arrows in structure charts are called **data couples**. A data name (in our case '**result**') is associated with the data couple.

A data flow from '**evaluate_1**' to '**output_result**' also appears again with the associated data name '**result**'. The association of the same name with different data flows in a structure chart allows the flow of a given data value throughout the chart to be shown.

The arrow used has an arrow tip and a small circle at its tail as in

'**evaluate_expression**' needs to read both operators and operands. Two modules are associated with these tasks, '**get_operator**' and '**get_operand**' which are both subordinate to '**evaluate_expression**'. The relationship between '**evaluate_expression**' and these two modules and the flow of data between them is shown in the struture chart.

We now give brief descriptions of the role of each module in the chart.

- '**evaluate_1**' obtains the value of the input expression from '**evaluate_expression**'. This value is repesented by '**result**' in the structure chart and the direction of the data couple linking the two modules indicates the direction of the data flow. It then makes use of '**output_result**' to output the value of the expression.
- '**evaluate_expression**' obtains successive operands and operators from '**get_operand**' and '**get_operator**' building up the value of the expression by applying operators until the expression is exhausted.
- '**output_result**' outputs the value of the expression.
- '**get_operand**' reads the next integer in the expression.
- '**get_operator**' reads the next operator.

A module structure chart gives the sub-tasks that need to be carried out in order that a program performs its task. It is drawn in such way as to show the hierarchical nature of a piece of software. It reflects an approach to design that seeks to identify building blocks for a program at a fairly high level and then apply the same approach to the design of these building blocks, repeating this until the building

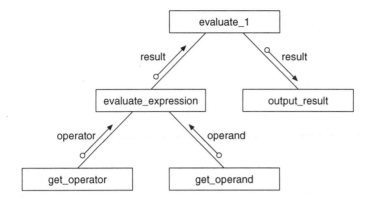

Figure 4.1 *The module structure chart for evaluate_1*

blocks identified are at such a level that they can be turned into code fairly easily.

What it does not show is flow of control. That is in what order things get done. There is no significance in the order on which sub-modules are written down under a given module in this type of structure chart.

Although it leaves out a lot of detail it helps the programmer to understand better how the program should be put together and it also helps the programmer to organise the actual programming.

A major objective in program design is the subdivision of the task required of a program into sub-tasks. There is always a degree of flexibilty in such subdivisions and often several equally good alternatives may present themselves.

Figure 4.2 gives an alternative structure for **'evaluate_1'** . In this design the expression is read in completely before it is evaluated. As far as the user is concerned there would be no difference in the way the program behaves whichever of these two designs is chosen. However the second design would be considerably more difficult to implement. The data value **'expression'** passed between **'evaluate_1'**,**'read_expression'** and **'evaluate_expression'** is considerably more complex than the data value **'result'**. **'expression'** must take as its value the

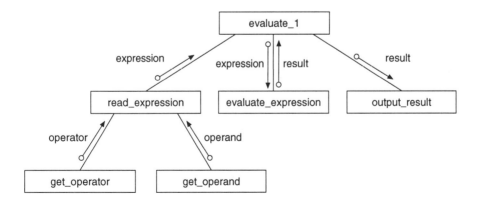

Figure 4.2 *evaluate_1 , reading the input expression first*

unevaluated expression in some form. This will mean its value must represent the operators and operands that appear in the input expression. This type of value can be dealt with in most programming languages but the language constructs needed to deal with them are considerably more complex than those we have met so far.

The program structure expressed by Figure 4.1 can be realised in a number of different ways. Structure charts are language independent, but the translation of a chart into a program will be largely influenced by the chosen language.

In general a module will translate into one or more functions and variables (among other things). Access to these from other modules should be controlled. If for example a module includes variables that are local to its operation these should not be accessible from outside the module. In C, as we have seen, this type of control is provided through the use of **.c** and **.h** files. The module's functions, variables and so forth are held in a **.c** file with a **.h** file controlling access to the **.c** file. Any module making use of that module must include the **.h** file.

We will again make use of **.c** and **.h** files here. All but one of the modules in Figure **4.1** will map onto a **.c** file with a corresponding **.h** file defining the allowable access to that module. Each module will consist of a single function. The module '**output_result**' will translate into the C library function **printf** directly. We have seen that library functions can be used anywhere in our C programs provided we include the appropriate **.h** file – in this case **stdio.h**.

It is not necessary to place each module in a structure chart in a separate **.c** file. We could have placed all the functions and variables needed for **evaluate_1** in just one file. Compiling the program would then have been more straightforward. However it is important to understand the role of **.c** and **.h** files in the organisation of C programs and we are taking advantage of this example to illustrate their use.

Why would we distribute a program over several files? Certainly with large programs implemented by teams of programmers it makes organisational sense. A second reason it to do with re-usability. If a program module is general purpose then it may form part of many different programs. Placing it in a **.c** file and providing an interfacing **.h** file makes its use in this way easy.

We have used names for three types of object

- structure chart modules
- files
- C functions and variables.

A structure chart module will have associated with it at least a **.c** file and possibly also a **.h** file. Each **.c** and **.h** file will contain C functions, variables etc. Table 1 gives the module names, the corresponding file names and the function names in the **.c** and **.h** files.

The following sections describe the contents of the **.c** and **.h** files associated with the four modules that appear in the table. The module **output_result** maps directly onto the library function **printf**.

Table 1

Module Name	File Names	Function names
evaluate_1	evaluate.c	main
evaluate_expression	eval_exp.c	evaluate_expression
	eval_exp.h	evaluate_expression
get_operator	get_op.c	get_operator
	get_op.h	get_operator
get_operand	get_opnd.c	get_int
		get_operand
	get_opnd.h	get_operand

4.6 get_operator

The files **get_op.c** and **get_op.h** hold the C code that implements the module **get_operator**. The file **get_op.c** contains one function, **get_operator**, which reads and discards spaces returning as its result the first character that it reads that is not a space. The assumption is that it will be either the character '+' or the character ' – ' and therefore represent the operation of addition or subtraction. In practice such an assumption would be unacceptable since the possibility that keyboard input is incorrectly typed always exists. Where a program may encounter incorrect input the programmer must make sure that in such cases the program recognises and deals with it. Adding code to **get_operator** to deal with this possibility is a good place to start in dealing with Question 6 at the end of this chapter.

The function **get_operator** is extremely simple. It is essentially a while loop that reads characters until a character other than a space is encountered. We saw exactly this loop in the code for **getint** developed in the last chapter. Since it makes use of the library function **getchar** it is preceded in the .c file by **#include <stdio.h>**.

get_operator makes use of the character variable **ch**. The declaration that introduces **ch** introduces a new feature of C. Variables can be given initial values as part of their declaration.

The declaration

```
char ch = getchar();
```

not only introduces **ch** as a variable of type **char** it also reads a character and initialises **ch** to that character value. Such initialisations look like assignments. The expression to the right of the assignment operator is evaluated with its value used to initialise the variable. There are no constraints on the form that such expressions can take.

The reader has been encouraged to construct algorithms that leave out a lot of program detail before developing C code. Sometimes the programming task in hand is so straightforward that this stage can be omitted. That is the view taken here for the module **get_operator**.

The file **get_op.c** will contain

```
#include <stdio.h>
char get_operator()
{
    char ch = getchar();
    while (ch == ' ') ch = getchar();
    return ch;
}
```

with the corresponding **.h** file **get_op.h** containing

```
char get_operator();
```

We can now make use of the function **get_operator** in any C program provided **get_op.c** is compiled and we include **get_op.h** in our program. In compiling the program the compiler will need to know where to find **get_op.h** in the file store and the linker will need to know where to find the compiled form of **get_op.c**.

4.7 get_operand

The operands that the module **get_operand** deals with are integers. We saw in the last chapter two ways of reading integers from the keyboard. The simplest way of doing this was to read into an integer variable using **scanf**. The required conversion from a string of digit characters into an integer was carried out by **scanf**. As a programming example we also developed a function, **getint**, which read digit characters until a character other than a digit was encountered, carrying out the conversion to integer value explicitly. We will use **getint** here changing it a little to illustrate one or two further features ot the C language.

It is often the case that functions written for one application can be made use of in an entirely different one. A well thought out design which separates out the functions needed in an implementation in a clean way creates a greater chance of such re-usability of software. It would be foolish not to take advantage of such opportunities when they arise. Even where there is not an exact match savings in effort can often be made through modifying an existing function.

We will make three changes to **get int**.

The first simply encorporates the the initialisation of the variables **number** and **ch** into the declaration of these variables.

The second change is to the condition associated with the while statement in **get int**.

As it stands **get int** requires that a space follows a number. Having read and discarded any spaces that precede the number it reads characters until a space is encountered, treating these characters as digits. We have made it a requirement of the program that expressions may be input with or without spaces between operators and operands. Therefore a number may be followed by a space, an operator or a '.' character which is used to signal the end of an expression.

The third change ensures that any character following a digit sequence is not lost.

There are two ways in which the end of a sequence of characters drawn from a given sub-set of characters might be determined. The first way, used in **getint**, is to read characters until a particular character known not to be in the sub-set is encountered. Here the sub-set in question is the set of characters '**0**' ... ' **9**' and the terminating character is the space character. What would happen if for example the sequence included letters? As it stands **getint** would treat them as digits using them in the computation of the corresponding integer value.

A second, safer, approach is to read characters, checking that they are in the the required sub-set, until a character not in the sub-set is encountered. Each character read is tested to ensure it is in the sub-set and input stops when this test fails. This is the more convenient way of dealing with the new situation required of **getint** and so becomes our second change. In order to make this change we will need to use a condition that employs two comparison operators.

4.8 Conditions involving more than one operator

The loop in **getint** that reads in the digits was expressed in the algorithm for **getint** as

> **while (ch is not a space)**
> **{**
> > **number = number * 10 + (ch – '0');**
> > **ch = getchar();**
> **}**

This becomes

> **while (ch is a digit)**
> **{**
> > **number = number * 10 + (ch – '0');**
> > **ch = getchar();**
> **}**

The **while** loop now terminates when it encounters a character that is not a digit rather than terminating when it encounters a space.

When expressed in C the condition **ch is not a space** uses a single comparison operator '**!=**'.

We have so far only used conditions with a single comparison operator although in Chapter 2 we used more complex conditions in assertions. C places no limit on the number of operators that can appear in an expression and we will express the condition **ch is a digit** as a condition using two comparisons.

The condition **ch is a digit** in C terms is the condition that **ch** is one of the characters '**0**' ... '**9**'. We once again make use of the ordering associated with the internal codings for these characters. They are consecutive, with '**1**' higher than '**0**' in the ordering, '**2**' higher than '**1**' and so forth.

The condition **ch is a digit** becomes **ch >= '0' && ch <='9'**. Recall that in C **ch**, '**0**' and '**9**' can be used as if they were integers, their integer values being the internal character codes.

ch >= '0' && ch <= '9' is interpreted in the obvious way. The condition holds if both the conditions **ch >= '0'** and **ch <= '9'** hold.

ch >= '0' && ch <= '9' is built from two simpler conditions and it holds only if both the simpler conditions hold. **&&** is called a **logical** operator. C supports a number of such operators. Since it will be used shortly we will introduce a second C logical operator ‖ which again combines conditions.

For example the condition

ch is not a digit

would be expressed in C as

ch <= '0' ‖ ch >= '9'

with ‖ corresponding to **or.**

Again **ch <= '0' ‖ ch >= '9'** is built from two simpler conditions. It holds if one or both of the simpler conditions holds. In this example at most one of the conditions can in fact hold but ‖ can be used in situations where the two conditions it applies to are not exclusive.

We have already noted that C does not support boolean values and that conditional expressions are really arithmetic expressions with a zero result interpreted as false and a non-zero result interpreted as true if the expression appears as a condition in, for example, a conditional statement.

How do we interpret an expression such as **ch <= '0'**? It takes the integer value **1** if the value in **ch** is less than or equal to the ASCII code for **'0'** and **0** otherwise.

Again how do we interpret an expression such as **ch >= '0' && ch <= '9'**?

We must be clear about the precedence of the various operators that appear in it. The operators '>=' and '<=' have a higher precedence than '**&&**' or '‖'and are therefore applied first.

What type of value does '**&&**' generate? The way it is evaluated is quite complicated. The left hand operand (**ch >= '0'** here) is evaluated first. If it is **0** then the result from '**&&**' is **0**. The right hand operand is not evaluated. If the left hand operand has a value other than **0** the right hand operand is evaluated. If the right hand operand has a value **0** then the result from '**&&**' is **0**. Otherwise it is **1**.

Since **0** corresponds to false with all non-zero values corresponding to true '**&&**' behaves in exactly the same way that conventional boolean conjunction behaves where if both operands are true the conjunction is true otherwise it is false.

With '‖' again the left operand is evaluated first. If it has a value other than **0** the result from '‖' is **1**. In this case the right operand is not evaluated. If the left operand is **0** then the right operand is evaluated. If the right operand has a value other than **0** the result from '‖' is **1**. Otherwise it is **0**.

Again this is what we would expect. Disjunction is invariably interpreted as inclusive disjunction where the disjunction is false only if both operands are false.

This raises a second issue. For '**&&**' and '‖' the left operand is evaluated first. This is not the case for all operators. For example with addition C leaves up to the compiler writer which order the operands are evaluated in. Thus for example in

sqrt(x) + sqrt(y)

we cannot assume that **sqrt(x)** is evaluated first. Normally this makes no difference. There are times when it might.

The expression

getchar() > getchar()

appears to take two characters from the keyboard, examining whether the first character typed in is greater than the second. This is however implementation dependent. The compiler writer is free to organise the compiled code in such a way that the right hand call to **getchar** is made first in which case the result could be quite different from that expected.

The while statement can now be written

```
while (ch >= 0 && ch <= 9)
    {
        number = number * 10 + ( ch – '0');
        ch = getchar();
    }
```

This reads the digits and any character that might follow. If this character is not a space then it should be one of the characters '+',' – ' or '.'. The function **get_operator** is also expected to read this character returning it as its result. If it has been read by **getint** how is this possible? C provides a built-in function **ungetc** which establishes a character as the next input character. Any request for input will start with this. It is normally used to return a character to an input stream. **getint** reads one more character than it needs. It uses **ungetc** to return that character to the input stream so that it becomes available to **get_operator**. We saw in Section 3 that input from the keyboard is associated with a stream called **stdin**. **ungetc** takes two arguments, the character and the name of the source of the input. Thus **getint** includes the call **ungetc(ch,stdm)**. This is our third change to the original version of **getint,** giving the final version

```
int getint()
    {
        int i = 0; char ch = getchar();
        while (ch == ' ') ch = getchar();
        while (ch >= '0' && ch <= '9')
        {
            i = i * 10 + ch – '0';
            ch = getchar();
        }
        ungetc(ch,stdin);
        return i;
    }
```

Since the only type of operands invisaged are integers it would be perfectly acceptable to implement the module **get_operand** using just **getint**. We have chosen here to include a function **get_operand** which simply calls **getint**. The justification for this is that we might want to add further forms of operand. For example we might want to allow identifiers as operands. **get_operand** would then call different functions depending on the type of operand it was given.

Placing **get_operand** after **getint** in the **.c** file and including **stdio.h** the **.c** file looks like

```
#include <stdio.h>
int getint()
```

```
        {
            int i = 0; char ch = getchar();
            while (ch == ' ') ch = getchar();
            while (ch >= '0' && ch <= '9')
            {
                i = i * 10 + ch - '0';
                ch = getchar();
            }
            ungetc(ch,stdin);
            return i;
        }

        int get_operand()
        {
            return getint();
        }
```

The **.h** file **get_opnd.h** will contain

```
        int get_operand();
```

4.9 evaluate_expression

The module **evaluate_expression**, the code of which is held in the **.c** file **eval_exp.c**, makes use of both **get_operand** and **get_operator**. Its behaviour is outlined in the program fragment

```
        result = get_operand();
        op = get_operator();
        while (op != '.')
        {
            opand = get_operand();
            if (op = '+')
                result = result + opand;
            else
                result = result - opand;
            op = get_operator();
        }
```

The variable **result** is used to hold the accumulated result as the expression is evaluated. The variable **op** is used to hold the next operator to be applied. It is assumed that there will be at least one operand in the input expression and that the expression will always be terminated by the '.' character.

The first two lines of the algorithm initalise **result** to the first operand of the expression and **op** to either the first operator or the terminating character '.'.

If **op** is not '.' it is assumed to be either '+' or ' – '. Recall that no error handling is included in the program being developed although in practice a program user could easily inadvertently input a character other than '+', '–' or '.' as an operator.

Where the input is either '+' or ' – ' a further operand is expected. Again the assumption is that the operand will be input and **get_operand** is employed to do this.

The operator in **op** is used to determine whether an addition or subtraction is required and the appropriate operation is then carried out.

The C code above can be turned into the function **evaluate_expression** without difficulty. Before doing this we will take the opportunity of extending the concept of an expression and introducing more of the C language.

4.10 Conditional expressions

Expressions describe how to calculate values. The program being developed here allows expressions involving integers and the operators '+' and '−' although we will be extending it further. C provides considerable variety in the form expressions can take.

We could view

if (x >= 0) then x else − x

as an expression which gives the absolute value of **x**. (If **x** is greater than or equal to **x** then the value of the expression is **x** and otherwise it is − **x**.

Such expressions are called conditional expressions and are supported in many programming languages, including C, although the way they are written will vary from language to language.

C has a rather cryptic syntax for conditional expressions but one that is not difficult to get used to. The above conditional expression for the absolute value of **x** would be written

x >= 0 ? x : − x

The condition appears first followed by the character '?'. This is then followed by two expressions separated by the character ':'. If the condition holds then the value of the first expression is the value of the conditional expression. Otherwise it is the value of the second expression.

Conditional expressions can appear as operands within expressions. Using this idea we want something like

result = result + (op == '+' ? opand : − opand)

to update **result**. The value of **opand** is added to **result** if the operator is a '+' and otherwise it is subtracted from **result** to give the new value of result.

The file **eval_exp.c** will contain the function **evaluate_expression** and will include **get_op.h** and **get_opnd.h** as in

```
#include "get_op.h"
#include "get_opnd.h"
int evaluate_expression()
{
    int result = get_operand(), opand;
    char op = get_operator();
    while(op != '.')
    {
```

```
        opand = get_operand();
        result = result + (op == '+' ? opand : - opand);
        op = get_operator();
    }
    return result;
}
```

It will have associated with it the **.h** file **eval_exp.h** which contains

int evaluate_expression();

providing the interface with the module **evaluate_expression**.

4.11 evaluate_1

The final module to be dealt with is **evaluate_1**. It is coded as the function **main** in the **.c** file **evaluate.c**. We have seen that all C programs require a **main** function, which is where execution of a C program begins. Here **main** consists of just two statements, both calls to the library function **printf**.
    The call

printf("input expression\n");

displays a message to input an expression. Embedded within the output string is a directive (**\n**) to move to a new line after the output. On the screen the cursor will be positioned at the start of a new line.
    The call

printf(" %d",evaluate_expression());

makes use of the function **evaluate_expression** to read and evaluate the expression typed in at the keyboard. We have seen that the values given to **printf** for output can be variables. In fact they can be any expression that evaluates to an appropriate value. As an argument to **printf evaluate_expression** is an expression that evaluates to an integer value which is then output.
    The code for the module **evaluate_1**, placed in the file **evaluate.c** looks like

```
#include "eval_exp.h"
#include <stdio.h>
main()
{
    printf("input expression\n");
    printf(" %d",evaluate_expression());
}
```

The above functions have been presented starting with **get_operator**. The order of presentation is also the most likely order of implementation because it allows testing to be carried out earlier rather than later. We cannot test **evaluate_expression** until we have written **get_operator** and **get_operand** so it makes sense to implement them first.

4.12 Adding multiplication and division

In extending **evaluate_1** to cater for multiplication and division operator precedence needs to be taken into account. The operators '*' and '/' must be applied to their operands before the operators '+' and ' − '.

For example in the expression

2 ∗ 2 + 4 ∗ 4

2 ∗ 2 and **4 ∗ 4** must both be evaluated before the **'+'** operator can be applied.

Again in

3 ∗ 4/2 + 9/3 ∗ 9

3 ∗ 4/2 and **9/3 ∗ 9** must be evaluated first.

In each of these examples the operands associated with the operator **'+'** involve operators which must be applied before **'+'** can be applied. The operands turn out to be sub-expressions that need to be evaluated.

In C the operators **'+'** and **' - '** are called **additive** operators and the operators '∗' and '/' **multiplicative** and we will use the same terminology here. In our examples the additive operators have operands that may be described in terms of multiplicative operators.

In the program developed for **evaluate_1** the function **evaluate_expression** uses **get_operand** to obtain the integer operands for the additive operators. This uses **getint** to read integers from the keyboard.

Here **evaluate_expression** must do something more. It must ensure that the operands for an additive operator are fully evaluated before the additive operator is applied. We will introduce a function, **evaluate_mult**, to do just that.

evaluate_mult behaves in a way similar to **evaluate_expression** above. It reads an integer and an operator from the keyboard. If the operator is multiplicative it reads the next operand applying the operator. It repeats this until no further multiplicative operators are encountered. This is expressed in the program fragment

```
result = get_operand();
op = get_operator;
while (op == '*' || op == '/')
{
    opand = get_operand();
    if (op = '*')
        result = result * opand;
    else
        result = result / opand;
    op = get_operator();
}
```

By adding

- a function header **int evaluate_mult()**
- declarations for **result, opand** and **op**
- a call to **ungetc** to restore the operator last read
- a **return**

we obtain

```
int evaluate_mult()
{
    int result = get_operand(),opand;
    char op = get_operator();
    while(op == '*' || op == '/')
    {
        opand = get_operand();
        result = result*(op == '*'?opand:1.0/opand);
        op = get_operator();
    }
    ungetc(op,stdin);
    return result;
}
```

Once again we have turned a conditional statement into a conditional expression. This is done by treating

result/opand

as

result*(1/opand).

However in the C program we have used **1.0/opand** rather than **1/opand**. To understand why we need to examine the behaviour of the operator '/' and the way decimal numbers are treated in C.

4.13 The behaviour of the division operator / and decimals.

When the operator '/' is given integer operands it generates an integer result. Where the second operand divides exactly into the first there is no loss of accuracy. Where there is a non-zero remainder this is lost.

The expression

1/opand

would always yield **0** if **opand** is an integer greater than 1. So if, for example, **result** initially has the value **4** and **opand** has the value **2** then in **result*(1/opand)** the calculation carried out is

4 * (1/2)

which gives the incorrect integer value **0**.

Using **result * (1.0/opand)** it is

4 * (1.0/2).

Because the dividend is **1.0** the expression evaluates to **2.0**.

he symbol '/' has two meanings in C (and in most other programming languages). For integer operands it means integer divide giving the integer quotient. For decimal operands it means floating point divide.

If one of the operands is decimal then the other is converted into a decimal value and floating point division takes place. This conversion is automatic. In general where an operator is applied the C system will carry out whatever type conversions are necessary for the application of the operator to make sense. When the C compiler encounters a constant such as **1** in an arithmetic expression it interprets it as an integer constant. If a decimal point appears as in **1.0** a floating point constant is assumed. In **1.0/opand** because **1.0** is a floating point number the division is interpreted as floating point division and in carrying out the division **opand** is converted to floating point.

This has an influence on the assignment as a whole. For example in

> **result = result ∗ (1.0/opand)**

because the second operand of '∗' is a floating point the first operand **result** is converted to floating point; floating point multiplication is then carried out giving a floating point result.

Because the resultant floating point value is then assigned to the integer **result** a further conversion back to integer takes place.

Our first version of **evaluate_expression()** obtained operands to apply either '+' or '−' to using **get_operand**. Since these operands may now involve multiplicative operators we replace calls to **get_operand** by calls to **evaluate_mult** giving

```
int evaluate_expression()
{
    int result = evaluate_mult(),opand;
    char op = get_operator();
    while(op != '.')
    {
        opand = evaluate_mult();
        result = result + (op == ' + '?opand: – opand);
        op=get_operator();
    }
    return result;
}
```

We have extended the class of expressions that our program can handle by adding a new function and modifying an existing one slightly.

We need to decide how the new function fits in to our overall design. We can either treat it as part of the module **evaluate_expression** or introduce a new module into our module structure chart sub-ordinate to **evaluate_expression**. The first approach is the easiest to implement so we follow it.

The function **evaluate_mult** and the modified function **evaluate_expression** are held in the .c file **eval_exp.c**. No other files need altering and by compiling and linking the four **.c** files we obtain a program that can evaluate expressions that include both additive and multiplicative operators.

In particular we do not alter **eval_exp.h** the interface file for **eval_exp.c**. Although there are two functions in **eval_exp.c** only **evaluate_expression** is made visible through **eval_exp.h**. **evaluate_mult** is required only by **evaluate_expression** and is not made available through **eval_exp.h**.

4.14 Adding brackets

It is sometimes desirable to override the default order of operator application . This is done using brackets.

The expression

$$3 + 4 * 5$$

evaluates to **23**. If however we want the addition operator to apply before the multiplication operator we would write

$$(3 + 4) * 5$$

which evaluates to **35**.

How can we extend what we have so far in order to deal with brackets?

It should be apparent by now that expressions have a structure that we are taking advantage of in processing them. An expression is viewed as a sequence of operands separated by additive operators where each operand is either a number or a sequence of numbers separated by multiplicative operators.

For example the structure of the expression

$$3 * 4 + 12/6$$

can be expressed as the inverted tree (see Figure 4.3).

The additive expression consists of two multiplicative sub-expressions separated by an addition operator. Each multiplicative sub-expression is made up of two numbers with each pair of numbers separated by a multiplicative operator.

The way the expression is evaluated can also be expressed using a tree (see Figure 4.4).

evaluate_expression calls **evaluate_mult** to deal with the first operand in the addition. **evaluate_mult** uses **get_operand** to read the numbers **3** and **4** before

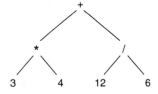

Figure 4.3 *The expression tree for 3 ∗ 4 + 12/6*

multiplying them together. **evaluate_mult** is called a second time for the second operand of the addition. Again **evaluate_mult** uses **get_operand** to read the numbers **12** and **6** to apply the division to.

The two trees in Figures 4.3 and 4.4 have essentially the same shape. This is not of course surprising. The first tree shows what operators should be applied to what operands. The second tree shows how the functions that make up **evaluate_1** are called to carry out the evaluation.

Expressions involving brackets also exhibit structure. For example the expression

$$(3 + 4) * 5 + 6$$

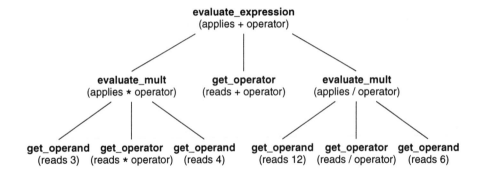

Figure 4.4 *The evaluation tree for 3 * 4 + 12/6*

has the structure shown in Figure 4.5.

The **second** addition operator takes as its operands the value of **(3 + 4) ∗ 5** and **6.**

The value of **(3 + 4) ∗ 5** is obtained by applying the multiplication operator to the value of **3 + 4** and **6.**

Whatever the arithmetic expression found in the brackets to the left of the multiplication operator it must be evaluated fully before the multiplication operator can be applied. In our example the expression in the brackets is an additive expression – it makes use of the addition operator. This suggests that we use the

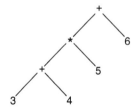

Figure 4.5 *The expression tree for (3 + 4) * 5 + 6*

function **evaluate_expression** to evaluate it since this was designed to deal with additive expressions.

Note that because **evaluate_expression** handles multiplication operators via **evaluate_mult** if we can use it to deal with bracketted expressions, such expressions can use multiplicative operators and, as it turns out, further bracketted expressions.

The evaluation of our expression would then be described by the tree shown in Figure 4.6.

evaluate_expression is called to evaluate the whole expression. Since it uses **evaluate_mult** to obtain the operands for the additive operators it calls this function twice for the two operands that the second addition operator in the expression applies to.

The second operand associated with the addition does not involve multiplication. **evaluate_mult** simply returns whatever value it gets from **get_operand.**

The first operand does however involve multiplication. The second operand to this multiplication is straightforward. The first operand is where a bracketted

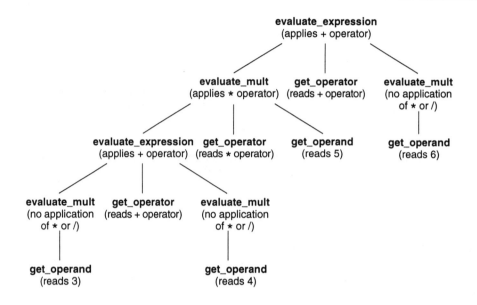

Figure 4.6 *The evaluation tree for (3 + 4) * 5 + 6*

expression is encountered. Here the evaluation tree indicates that **evaluate_expression** is used to deal with the bracketted expression.

Something rather unusual appears to be happening. In the example, **evaluate_expression** calls **evaluate_mult** to deal with the first operand. This in turn calls **evaluate_expression** to deal with the first operand of the multiplication. In C and in many other programming languages a function may call itself either directly or indirectly. Such calls are called **recursive** calls and functions that make calls to themselves either directly or indirectly are called **recursive** functions. Here **evaluate_expression** calls itself indirectly through **evaluate_mult**.

Recursion presents a number of difficulties when first encountered. These include:

- understanding the effect of recursive calls
- recognising when recursion can be used
- understanding how recursion works.

For the first of these, simply accept that recursive calls can be made and analyse the behaviour of such calls as you would any function call.

Recognising when recursion can be used is a matter of practice. In analysing a programming task its recursive nature may become apparent but this can only happen if there is an awareness of the potential for recursion in such a task.

An understanding of how recursion works requires a good knowledge of the way the machine code equivalents of programs written in languages like C work and this study is beyond the scope of this book.

At this stage it is enough just to understand the effect of recursive calls.

Figure 4.6 has **evaluate_mult** calling **evaluate_expression** directly. We could extend the program we have developed so far by extending **evaluate_mult** to deal with bracketted expressions but this would be rather clumsy.

Our program must also handle expressions like

$$3 - (8 - 4)$$

where again we have a bracketted expression that must be evaluated before the subtraction can be carried out. Since subtraction is dealt with in **evaluate_expression** we would also have to extend this function to deal with bracketted expressions. This type of duplication is unsatisfactory and should be avoided if possible. Doing things in the wrong place in a program is one of the most common causes of unnecessary complexity.

In both

$$(3 + 4) * 5$$

and

$$3 - (8 - 4)$$

the bracketted expression has the same status as the second operand which is a number. Numbers are dealt with in **get_operand**. This suggests that bracketted expressions should be dealt with within **get_operand**.

The **get_operand** developed so far is extremely simple. All it does is call **getint**. In extending it to deal with bracketted expressions it has to be able to distinguish between numbers and bracketted expressions. Since a number starts with a digit and a bracketted expression with an opening bracket there is no difficulty here. **get_operand** reads characters until it encounters a non-space character. This should be either a digit or a bracket. If it is a bracket, **evaluate_expression** will be called to deal with the bracketted expression. If it is a digit then **getint** is called. In this second case **ungetc** is used to make the digit available to **getint**.

get_operand now becomes

```
int get_operand()
{
    char ch = getchar();
    while (ch == ' ') ch = getchar();
    if (ch == '(') return evaluate_expression();
    else
    {
        ungetc(ch,stdin);
        return getint();
    }
}
```

get_operand now removes spaces before calling **getint**. Since **getint** also has code to do this we can simplify **getint** by removing this code.

We have not quite finished. The current version of **evaluate_expression** will read additive operators and operands until a full stop is encountered. Since it is now also dealing with bracketted expressions an expression may be complete either if it is followed by a full stop or by a closing bracket. This requires a very minor change to the condition associated with the while loop in **evaluate_expression,** leading to

```
int evaluate_expression()
{
    int result = evaluate_mult(),opand;
    char op = get_operator();
    while(op != '.' && op != ')')
    {
        opand = evaluate_mult();
        result = result+(op == '+'?opand: - opand);
        op = get_operator();
    }
    return result;
}
```

Figure 4.6 shows how the expression **(3 + 4)** * **5 + 6** might be evaluated. With the above changes Figure 4.6 becomes as shown in Figure 4.7.

Note that, in the evaluation of both expressions for which trees are given calls to **getint** are not shown. **get_operand** will always eventually call **getint** to read numbers even if this is through a call to **evaluate_expression**.

We have made alterations to the files **get_opand.c** and **exp_eval.c**. No other files have been changed. Once again compiling **get_opand.c** and **exp_eval.c** and linking together all the **.o** files gives us a program that will evaluate arithmetic expressions including bracketted sub-expressions.

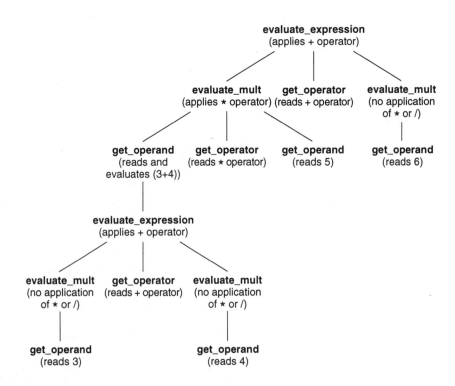

Figure 4.7 *A modified evaluation tree for (3 + 4)* * *5 + 6*

Our final program was developed from an initial design for a simpler programming task through a process of evolution. This evolutionary process seemed without difficulties. In reality problems would emerge at each evolutionary stage that might necessitate a re-think of the design of an earlier stage. Given the creative nature of design there is no way of ensuring that this does not happen.

At first sight the program seems little more than an exercise in programming. However the design arrived can be used as the basis of seemingly quite different programming problems as the exercises at the end of this chapter should illustrate.

Exercises

1. In implementing the expression evaluator described in this chapter your C system may have generated a number of warning messages. You may encounter two types of warning. First your system may warn you that your **main** function does not return a value. All C systems assume **main** has a result type of **int**. Returning **0** (which indicates that the program has executed successfully) eliminates this warning. Second your system may warn you of problems with function calls. Strictly,where a function is parameter-less the key word **void** should appear in its declaration where parameters would normally appear as in

   int evaluate_expression(void)

   .
   .
   .

   Adding this key word to each of the function declarations other than **main** eliminates this second type of warning. Modify the function declarations given in chapter 4 to take these points into account.

2. Draw trees similar to that of Figure 4.6 to show the evaluation of

   (i) **3 + 4 * 5**
   (ii) **3 + (4 * 5)**

3. Modifying the value in a variable in some way to give it its new value is a very common.For example incrementing a variable by **1** through assignments like

   x = x + 1

   probably occurs more than any other assignment. Because of this C provides a shorthand called **compound assignment** which allows the above assignment to be expressed as

   x + = 1

   The shorthand takes the general form

   <variable> <operator> = <expression>

   where **<variable>** is a variable, **<operator>** a C binary operator and **<expression>** an expression and is equivalent to

<variable> = <variable><operator><expression>

Although not a particularly significant shorthand it is useful and is normally made use of by experienced C programmers. Modify the functions developed in this chapter to take advantage of the shorthand.
Early versions of C provided the shorthand but in the form

<variable> = <operator> <expression>

Why do you think this could create problems?

4. Modify the expression evaluator so that the end of an expression is indicated by an end of line rather than '.'. Recall that the end of line character as a character constant is written '\n'.

5. Division by zero is normally treated as an error because the result of such a division is infinitely large. Modify the expression evaluator so that it generates an error message whenever a division by zero is attempted.

6. Exercise 5 in Chapter 3 required the modification of **getint** so that it takes as input decimal numbers such as **1.0**, **3.1416** and **33.34**. Modifying the types of variables and functions to floating point where appropriate, develop a program to handle expressions involving decimal numbers. Just as **int** is used to indicate integer type **float** is used to indicate floating point type.

7. The functions developed above take no account of incorrectly formed exressions. For example the expression

   3 * (4 + \5)

   makes no sense because the '+' operator is immediately followed by the '\' operator.
   What types of errors in the input can you identify?
   Change the functions so that error messages are output where such errors are encountered. The call **exit(φ)** to the library function **exit** (in stdlib.h) causes normal program termination. Use this to terminate execution on encountering an error in the input.

8. In FORTRAN the operator '**' raises a value to a power. For example 3 ** 3 raises 3 to the power 3 giving 27. Implement this operator ensuring both that it is treated as having a higher precedence than '*' and '\' and that it is evaluated right to left. That is expressions like 3 ** 4 ** 5 are interpreted as 3 ** (4 ** 5). You will need to write a new function **evaluate_power** and in doing so a recursive approach to dealing with successive '**' operators is recommended.

5

Functions, parameters and pointers

5.1 Function arguments

In Chapter 4 we saw how C functions could be used as building blocks for programs. The functions we have developed so far return results but take no arguments, although we have made use of C library functions such as **scanf** that do. In this chapter we look at how functions can be given arguments.

5.2 Declaring functions that take arguments

The first example of a C program given involved the calculation of the quotient and remainder of a pair of positive numbers by successive subtraction. To illustrate the use of arguments we will program this problem in a different way making use of two functions, one of which returns the quotient of the two numbers, with the other returning the remainder. The point of the example is to show how functions taking arguments can be declared and used. We have already seen that the arithmetic operators '/' and '%' can be used to find the quotient and remainder of two integers. We will however still use successive subtraction, since the use of '/' and '%' would make the use of functions to calculate quotient and remainder look less convincing.

We will call the function that calculates the quotient **quotient,** with the second function called **remainder.** The body of the function **quotient** follows very much the pattern of our original program. A variable in which the quotient is generated is initialised to **0** with a second variable, used for the remainder, initialised to the divisor. We will use the variable names **q** and **r** for the quotient and the remainder.

The calculation of quotient and remainder is very much as in our earlier program. Using compound assignment to shorten the assignments we have

```
while (r >= b)
{
    q + = 1;
    r – = b;
}
```

We have already seen the general form that a function takes, namely

result_type function_name (param_1,param_2, ...)
{
.
. **body of function**
.
}

where

result_type function_name(param_1, param_2, ...)

(called the function **header**) provides information essential to the function's use, with the body describing the behaviour of the function.
The header provides

- the function name
- the type of the result
- the names and types for each of the arguments that the function may take.

The last section of the header gives the argument descriptions in the form of a sequence of declarations, **param_1,param_2, ...** , separated by commas. These look very much like variable declarations being made up of a name which stands for an argument preceded by a type specification.

One difference between parameter declarations and variable declarations is that **each** parameter must be preceded by a type specifier, whereas a group of variables can be introduced using a single type specifier.

The variable declaration

int a,b;

introduces the variables **a** and **b** as being of type **int**.
If we want a function to take two **int** arguments the parameter declaration must take the form

int a,int b

The style of parameter declaration given here follows the C ANSI standard discussed in the preface. In earlier forms of C the parameters appeared in the header without preceding type specifiers, with the type for each parameter given later.

A parameter name has meaning only within the body of the corresponding function. It is very much like a variable declared within the function body, with the property that it is initialised to a value when the function is called. It can be used within the body just like a normal variable. This includes changing through assignment the value it gets initialised to at function call.

We have already found that one of the benefits of using functions is that we can use them to structure the text of a program, making it easier both to understand and modify. For a given programming task we attempt to identify sub-tasks that taken together help to carry out the overall task.

We sometimes find that a sub-task is sufficiently general for it to be used in several different places in our program. A second benefit of the use of functions is that the same function can be used in different parts of a program. We saw this with the function **getint()** which indeed proved general enough to be used in different programs.

Where a function that takes arguments is used a number of times the arguments that it is given may well be different each time it is used.

Again we saw a number of examples of this in our uses of **printf**. Because of this the names that appear in the header of a function declaration cannot have anything to do with any actual argument. They must stand for any potential argument that the function may be given.

To emphasise this distinction the declarations that relate to arguments that appear in a function header are called **parameter** declarations with the names themselves being called **formal parameters**. An argument is a value given to a function when it is called.

In the body of a function formal parameters can be treated as if they were variables declared within the function. The main difference between the two will be that formal parameters are assumed to have values associated with them that are obtained from the arguments supplied to the function when it is called. Thus formal parameters may take different values from call to call.

The function header for **quotient** looks like

> **int quotient(int a,int b)**

where the result type is **int**, the function name is **quotient**, the parameter declarations are **int a** and **int b** and the formal parameters themselves (both of type **int**) are **a** and **b**. **a** stands for the dividend and **b** the divisor in the calculation of the quotient.

To complete the function we need to add only declarations for **q** and **r** and a **return** which returns **q** as the result of the function. We then have

```
int quotient(int a,int b)
{
    int q = 0,r = a;
    while (r >= b)
    {
        q + = 1;
        r - = b;
    }
    return q;
}
```

as our final form for the function **quotient**. Note that although **quotient** calculates both quotient and remainder only the quotient is returned from the function.

5.3 Calling functions with arguments

Function calls take the general form

> **function_name(expression_1,expression_2, ...)**

where the expressions in the function call and the formal parameters in the function declaration correspond positionally. The first formal parameter is associated with the first expression, the second with the second and so forth.

Implicit assignments take place when a function is called. Formal parameters and arguments are paired up by position, with the formal parameter acting as the left hand value of the assignment and the argument acting as the right hand value. The arguments are evaluated and the resultant values assigned to their corresponding formal parameters.

The order in which the arguments are evaluated is up to the compiler writer and it should not be assumed that this is left to right. For example

printf("%c%c",getchar(),getchar());

reads two characters from the keyboard, displaying them on the screen. For the input **ab** either **ab** or **ba** is possible as output. If the second argument is evaluated before the third then we get **ab**. Otherwise we get **ba**. In fact many C systems evaluate function arguments right to left because it is convenient to do so.

Expressions can include assignments. Arguments are expressions and therefore can include assignments.

Given that **i** is an integer with value **0** then

printf("%d %d",i + = 1,i + = 1);

is allowable and causes the values **1** and **2** to be output. The second and third arguments involve assignment and again the order in which they are evaluated will determine the order that the values **1** and **2** are output.

quotient can be called wherever we need to calculate the quotient of a pair of positive numbers. For example the statement

printf("%d",quotient(10,3));

will display the value **3**.

Here **printf** will display as an integer whatever value it gets back from the call **quotient(10,3)**. The call causes the function **quotient** to be activated with the parameter **a** taking the value **10** and the parameter **b** taking the value **3**. The code in the body of **quotient** is then executed with the value **3** generated in **q** within **quotient** being returned as its result.

Since the arguments to functions are expressions they can be arbitrarily complex, involving variables, constants, operators and even function calls themselves.

For example in

printf("%d",quotient(x + y − 1,x − y + 1));

The expressions **x + y − 1** and **x − y + 1** are evaluated with their values assigned to the formal parameters **a** and **b** before **quotient** is called.

Indeed calls to **quotient** can make use of quotient in the argument expressions.

Although not very useful the call

quotient(quotient(15,3) + 1,quotient(10,3))

is allowable and which, after the arguments are evaluated, is effectively the call

quotient(6,3)

returning the value **2**.

5.4 The function remainder

remainder behaves in a very similar way to **quotient**. The remainder is calculated by successive subtractions. Using the same names **a**, **b** and **r**, with the remainder **r** now being returned as the result of the function **remainder** we have

```
int remainder(int a,int b)
{
    int r = a;
    while (r >= b)
        r - = b;
    return r;
}
```

Since it is not necessary to calculate the quotient this is not done and the variable **q** is therefore not needed in **remainder**.

quotient and **remainder** use the same names (**a**, **b** and **r**) for formal parameters and local variables. The two sets of names refer to entirely different objects. The formal parameters **a** and **b** for example declared in **quotient** have nothing to do with those declared in **remainder**. Because in each case the names are local to their corresponding functions there is no ambiguity.

C, like most other programming languages, allows the use of the same name for different objects where the language rules ensure no ambiguity.

5.5 Calling quotient and remainder from main

The function **main()** below makes use of **quotient** and **remainder** to calculate and output the quotient and remainder for two input values.

```
main()
{
    int a = getint(),b = getint();
    if (b > 0)
        printf("quotient = %d remainder = %d",quotient(a,b),
        remainder(a,b));
    else printf("The second input must be positive and non-zero");
}
```

Note that **main()** has local declarations for two integers which are given the names **a** and **b**. Once again these names have nothing to do with the formal parameters declared in the functions **quotient** or **remainder**.

We could have made use of the variable names **x** and **y** instead as in

```
main()
{
    int x = getint(),y = getint();
    if (b > 0)
        printf("quotient = %d remainder = %d",quotient(x,y),
        remainder(x,y));
    else printf("The second input must be positive and non-zero");
}
```

By combining **quotient, remainder, main** and **getint** in one or more **.c** files an executable program can be created in the usual way through compilation and linking.

5.6 The allocation of memory to variables and parameters

The original program to calculate quotient and remainder consisted of a single function **main** which made use of four variables **quotient, remainder, a** and **b**. When the program is loaded into memory, memory is set aside for these variables. Let us assume that the C compiler allocates four bytes for each integer. (Note that the number of bytes allocated to integers, and indeed other types, may vary from system to system. The use of two bytes for integers is quite common.) Figure 5.1 shows how memory might be allocated to the for variables in **main**. Four bytes starting at address 16192 are set aside for **quotient**, four starting at address 16196 for **remainder** and so forth. Of course which bytes of memory are allocated to which variables is very much system dependent.

When a function is called, memory is set aside for any parameters and local variables before the function executes. For example in our new version of the program when it is loaded space will be set aside for the variables declared in **main** before **main** starts to execute. When **main** calls **quotient** (via **printf**), memory will be set aside for its two parameters and two local variables.

Figure 5.2 shows the state of memory immediately after **quotient** has carried out the initialisation of its two variables **q** and **r,** assuming **main** took as input the two values **10** and **3**. These values were assigned to the variables **a** and **b** in **main**. On

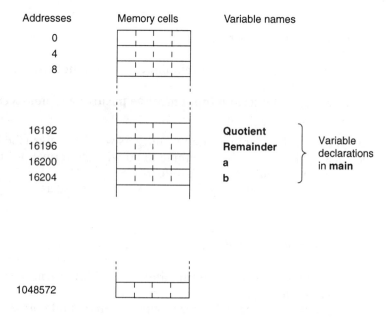

Figure 5.1 *The allocation of memory to variables in* ***main***

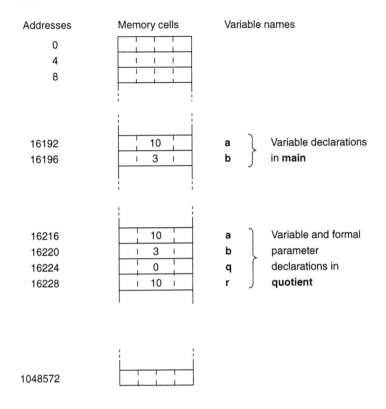

Figure 5.2 *The allocation of memory to variables in* **main** *and* **quotient**

calling **quotient** its formal parameters (also called **a** and **b**) were assigned values from the arguments given to the call. Thus the formal parameters **a** and **b** took the values **10** and **3** respectively.

5.7 Pointers

We saw in Chapter 1 that memory addresses could be treated as values. C supports this but constrains their use in a number of ways. In particular it classifies addresses into different types depending on the value that they point at. So for example the address of an integer is treated as being of a different type to that of a character. For this reason C refers to such addresses as pointer to **int**, pointer to **char** and so forth. Pointers play a central role in C and a clear understanding of this role is essential. One use of pointers is seen in a particular form of parameter sometimes called a reference parameter and we will once again employ our **quotient remainder** program to illustrate this form. In principle what happens is that an address is passed as an argument. The function is then able to use the address to change the value at that address. How do we know that the value given as an argument should be treated as an address? We need some extra notation to indicate this which is given below.

In the last program the functions **main** and **quotient** communicate through function arguments and function results. **quotient** computes both quotient and remainder but returns only the quotient. We can declare functions with as many arguments as we like. They will however return a single result. For **quotient** this result is of integer type which means that only one integer value can be returned from the function. Later we will examine **structured** types and values. These allow us for example to treat a pair of integers as a single value and C allows functions to return such structured values as results. Thus we could return both the quotient and remainder as a single value.

A second way of returning values computed within one function to another is through the use of **pointers** as arguments. The calling function gives the **addresses** of the variables that are to take results as arguments to the called function. The called function places results in the caller's variables by making use of these addresses.

Suppose **main** contains the declaration

int a = getint(),b = getint(), q,r;

where, as before, **a** and **b** hold the dividend and divisor and **q** and **r** are set aside for the quotient and remainder. Since our function is now going to generate and return both the quotient and remainder we will call it **quot_rem**. **quot_rem** will take four arguments, the values in **a** and **b** and the addresses of **q** and **r**. It will place the quotient in **q** and the remainder in **r**.

Figure 5.3 shows how memory might look qiven that **main()** has just called **quot_rem**. It is assumed that **main()** has read the values **10** and **3** into its variables **a** and **b** and that its variables have been allocated memory starting at address **16192**. In particular the variable **q** is at address **16200** with **r** at **16204**. These two addresses provide the last two arguments to **quot_rem**. The formal parameters declared with **quot_rem** are **a, b, q_ptr** and **r_ptr**. These last two have as values the addresses of (or **pointers** to) **q** and **r**. On entry to **quot_rem** no values have been assigned to **q** or **r**. In Figure 5.3 this is indicated by the use of '?'.

The formal parameters **q_ptr** and **r_ptr** take addresses of integer values not integer values themselves and we need to indicate this in the parameter declarations.

The form

variable_type * variable_name

introduces both variables and formal parameters as pointers. The '*****' preceding **variable_name** determines that the variable will be a pointer. When declaring pointers in C not only do we need to indicate that they are pointers but also the type of value that they should point to. A variable declared in this way is assumed to take as its value the addresses of values of type **variable_type**.

The declaration

int * i_ptr

introduces a variable **i_ptr** which takes as values the addresses of **int** values.

The declaration

char * ch_ptr

introduces a variable **ch_ptr** which takes as values the addresses of **char** values.

Pointer values in C are thus not simply addresses but have associated with them the type of the value they point at. Normally this makes no difference to the way

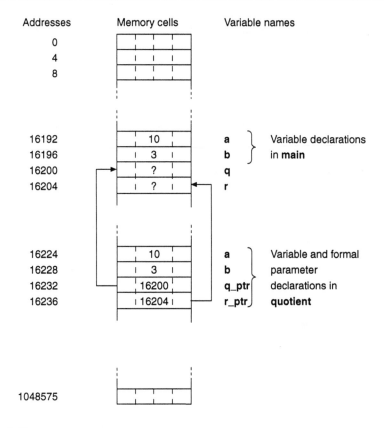

Figure 5.3 *Addresses as arguments to quot_rem*

addresses are dealt with when the program executes. The address of character value and the address of an integer value would probably not differ in any fundamental way. This cannot however be assumed. Where pointers are used in an inconsistent way the C compiler will generate a warning. For example if the address of a character variable is assigned to a variable declared as an integer pointer this will be flagged by most compilers.

5.8 The address and indirection operators & and *

A variable declaration such as

    int q;

introduces **q** as a variable of type **int**. Because it is a variable, memory is allocated for it and therefore there is a value of type pointer to **int** associated with it corresponding to the address of that memory. If a function takes as an argument pointer values we need to be able to write down expressions which describe such values. We also need to be able to use pointer values either to access or change the value at the corresponding address. For example if we want a function to change the value associated with **q** first we must pass its address as an argument to the function and then, within the function, we must use that address to change the value of **q**.

Pointer variables are used in exactly the same way as other variables. For example they can be assigned addresses as values, where the expression on the right of the assignment evaluates to an address. If **i_ptr** and **j_ptr** are both pointers to integers then the assignment

i_ptr = j_ptr;

makes sense. The assumption is that **j_ptr** contains the address of an integer value and that this address is assigned to **i_ptr**.

Since all variables have addresses associated with them and pointer variables take addresses as values, C provides an operator '**&**' which obtains the address of a variable as its result. Indeed we have already used this operator in our first program in its use of the library function **scanf**.

The call

scanf("%d",&i);

reads a sequence of digits corresponding to an integer from the keyboard assigning that value to **i**. Its second argument is an address and it will use that address to determine where the input integer value should be placed. Contrast this with the call

printf("%d",i);

which prints out the value in **i**. Its second argument is the value in **i** not its address and this difference is reflected in the different forms the arguments take.

We noted in Chapter 3 that for an expression such as

i = j;

the context in which a variable occurs determines whether we use its address or its value. An address is used if the variable appears to the left of an assignment and its value is used otherwise. This contextual consideration only applies to the operands within an expression. For expressions themselves no contextual information is taken into account. The form the expression takes completely determines its value. The expression **i**, as an argument, would always yield the value associated with **i**. The expression **&i** would always yield its address.

The use of the address operator '**&**' is not restricted to arguments. The declarations

int i, ∗ i_ptr;

introduce a variable **i** of integer type **int** and a variable **i_ptr** of type pointer to **int**.

The assignment

i_ptr = & i;

assigns the address associated with **i** to **i_ptr**. Note that

i_ptr = i;

has quite a different meaning. Here the value not the address of **i** is assigned to **i_ptr**, and again such an assignment would cause a warning to be generated by most C compilers because **i_ptr** should take values of type pointer to **int** whereas **i** has a value of type **int**.

The form of declaration given here is similar to say

int i, j;

where the occurrence of the comma indicates that both **i** and **j** are of type **int**. Without it we would have to write

    int i; int j;

The declaration of **i_ptr** above uses type **int** since it is part of a list of variables associated with this type. The symbol '*' which precedes **i_ptr** indicates a type pointer to **int** rather than **int**. Again we could have written

    int i; int * i_ptr;

If we can create variables that hold the addresses of values we should be able to get at the values themselves and C provides a second operator, '*' , to do just this.

In the assignment

    i = * i_ptr;

the value pointed by the address in **i_ptr** is assigned to the variable **i**. Appearing as it does to the right of the assignment operator *, **i_ptr** is an expression that evaluates to an integer value. Since it represents an integer value it can be used wherever other integer values are allowed. For example the expression

    * i_ptr + i + 1

is allowable and evaluates to an integer.

    '**&**' is called the **address** operator and '*****' the **indirection** operator.

    The symbol '*****' is used both in declarations to indicate that the variable following it is a pointer type and as an operator in expressions to obtain a value indirectly via a pointer. These two uses are quite distinct.

    Given the above declarations for **i** and **i_ptr** Figure 5.4 shows how the value of both variables are affected by the sequence of assignments

        i = 0;
     i_ptr = & i;
    * i_ptr = 10;

A common misconception in the declaration of pointers is that space will be allocated not only for the pointer variable introduced in the declaration but also for a value of the associated type. As Figure 5.4 indicates this is not the case. On declaration the value of the pointer variable is undefined unless the declaration includes an initialisation. It is the programmer's responsibility to ensure that any value assigned to it makes sense.

5.9 The Function quot_rem

We will now make use of the concepts discussed in Section 5.8 to implement a function **quot_rem** which returns the quotient and remainder usirg pointer variables passed as arguments. It does not make use of **return** and this influences both the way its result type is described and the context in which it is called.

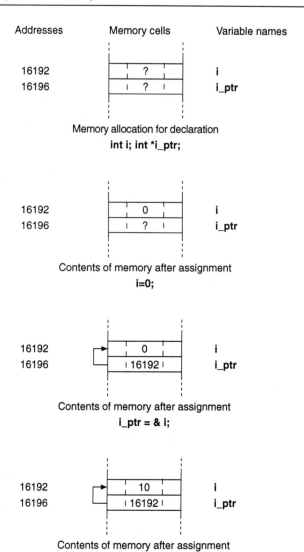

Figure 5.4 *The effect of assignments with * and &*

5.10 Function calls as statements and type void

All the functions other than **main** that have been developed so far have returned values using **return**. The type of a function's result is given as part of the function declaration. We are going to organise **quot_rem** in such a way that it does not return a result, its effect being achieved through the use of pointer arguments. What result type should be given as part of its declaration? Most C systems provide a type **void** which is used to indicate that a function does not return a value. (This was not provided in the earliest versions of C. Since a function can be called in contexts where its result is discarded the use of **void** is optional. However using it in a function declaration makes clear how the function is to be used.)

Using **void** and pointers in the list of parameters, the declaration of **quot_rem** starts with

void quot_rem(int a,int b, int * q_ptr,int * r_ptr);

A call to **quot_rem** requires four arguments. The first two should evaluate to the dividend and divisor used in computing quotient and remainder. The second two should evaluate to values of type pointer to **int**. The first of these gives the address at which the quotient should be stored with the second giving an address for the remainder.

The formal parameters **a, b, q_ptr** and **r_ptr** will be initialised to these values.

A call to **quot_rem** in **main** takes the form of a statement rather than an expression. (Strictly it is still an expression. However it generates no result. **quot_rem** has result type **void** and makes no use of **return** and anyway is used in a context where any result would be discarded.) In

```
main()
{
    int a = getint(),b = getint(), q,r;
    if (b >0)
    {
        quot_rem(a,b,&q,&r);
        printf("quotient = %d remainder = %d",q,r);
    }
    else printf("The second input must be positive and non-zero");
}
```

the call **quot_rem(a,b,&q,&r)** following the declarations of **a, b, q** and **r** takes as its arguments the values associated with **a** and **b** and the addresses associated with **q** and **r**.

The body of **quot_rem**,

```
{
    * q_ptr = 0; * r_ptr = a;
    while (* r_ptr >= b)
    {
        * q_ptr + = 1;
        * r_ptr - = b;
    }
}
```

follows the same pattern as **quotient** except that it uses the indirection operator to identify where the quotient and remainder are to be stored.

The assignment statements

* q_ptr=0; * r_ptr = a;

use indirection to give initial values to the quotient and remainder. For the call to **quot_rem** in **main** above the effect of these assignments is to intialise the variables

q and **r** declared in **main** to **0** and whatever value value gets passed through to **quot_rem** in the parameter **a**. (This is of course the value assigned to **main**'s variable **a** from the call to **getint** in its declaration.) **q_ptr** and **r_ptr** have been initialised to these addresses through the third and fourth arguments to the call.

Note that in the assignment

> **q_ptr = 0;**

the address of **q_ptr** would be used to determine where the value **0** should be assigned. We want to assign **0** to the address held by **q_ptr** not to **q_ptr** itself. Thus we write

> *** q_ptr = 0;**

The indirection operator '*****' takes the value held by **q_ptr** as the required address.

5.11 Extent, Scope and Linkage

So far we have used parameters and function results as a method of communication between functions. This is almost always the best way to interface functions. Very occasionally it is more convenient to allow functions to share access to a variable. This can be done by placing variable declarations at the same level as function declarations in a **.c** file.

Since compound statements can themselves contain compound statements (normally as part of an iterative or conditional statement), blocks can contain blocks. Note that this nesting of blocks is textual in the sense that it is to do with the form the written program takes and not how it executes. We will view the declarations in nested blocks as occurring at different textual levels. Functions are declared at the top level. Declarations that occur within functions are at the next level down and so forth.

C allows variable declarations at the top level. Consider a **.c** file containing

```
int a,b,q,r;
void quot_rem()
{
    q = 0; r = a;
    while (r >= b)
    {
        q + = 1;
        r - = b;
    }
}
main()
{
    a = getint(); b = getint();
    if (b > 0)
    {
        quot_rem();
        printf("quotient = %d remainder = %d",q,r);
    }
```

>   **else printf("The second input must be positive and non-zero");**
> }

Neither **main** nor **quot_rem** contain variable declarations. Four variables of type **int** are declared at the top level along with **main** and **quot_rem**. Both **main** and **quot_rem** can access these variables and they thus provide a way of communicating between the two functions. **main** initialises **a** and **b** using **getint** and **quot_rem** then computes **q** and **r** from **a** and **b**.

We have seen variable declarations within blocks.For example in

```
main()
{
    int s = 0;
    while (s <= 100)
    {
        int i;
        scanf("%d",&i);
        s + = i;
    }
}
```

a variable **i** is declared local to the block forming the body of the while statement. The while statement reads and sums input until the sum is greater than **100**.

The variable **s**, declared at the start of the function, is accessible throughout the function. It is created on entry to the function and ceases to exist on exit. The variable **i** is accessible throughout the body of the while statement. It is created on entry to the body of the while statement and ceases to exist on exit. That is on each cycle of the while statement **i** is re-created.

The accessibility of every variable declared in a .c file has two important properties

- the stage in the execution of a program at which memory is allocated to the variable (i.e. when the variable is created) and the period for which this memory remains allocated (**extent**)
- the section of the .c file from which the variable can be accessed (**scope**).

Variables declared at the top level are created at the start of the program's execution and exist until the program terminates. They can be accessed by functions that appear after them. In the above .c file both functions can access **a**, **b**, **q** and **r**. If we organised the file so that the declaration for **a,b**, **q** and **r** came between that for **quot_rem** and **main** they would not be accessible from **quot_rem**.

A third consideration comes into play when programs are built from a number of .c files. Both functions and variables declared in one .c file can be accessed from different .c files. We saw this with function prototypes in Chapter 4. The term **linkage** is used to describe cross file access.

The rules for extent, linkage and scope are rather complex in C and a simplified version of them will be presented here. Further, the linkage and scope rules for functions and for variables differ. We will introduce those for variables, explaining where necessary how they differ from those for functions.

5.12 Extent

Both variables and functions have memory allocated to them. Extent is to do with when that memory is allocated and when it released. At the start of a program's execution the functions that make up that program will be allocated memory. This allocation will remain throughout the execution of the program. Because of this functions are said to have **static extent.**There are three types of extent associated with C objects (functions,variables,etc.), called **local, static** and **dynamic.**

5.13 Static extent

Objects with static extent have memory allocated on program startup and released when the program stops. Functions always have static extent. Variables with static extent can be created in two ways

- by declaring the variable at the outermost level
- by preceding variables declared within blocks by the keyword **static**.

Variables declared at the top level have static extent.

If a variable declaration within a block is preceded by the keyword **static** then it has static extent associated with it. Such variables behave like those declared at the outermost level but can only be accessed from within the block in which they are declared. Their use is uncommon.

5.14 Local extent

Memory is allocated to the variables on entry to the block in which they are declared and released on exit. Variables declared within a block have local extent unless their declaration is preceded by the keyword **static**.

5.15 Dynamic extent

Memory for data values can be obtained directly by the programmer through the use of C library functions. The programmer can also choose when this memory is released. Such objects are effectively un-named variables and are accessed through the use of pointers. This type of extent is described as dynamic. A detailed description is given in Chapter 6.

5.16 Scope and linkage

The scope and linkage of an object define the accessibility of the object from the rest of the program. Static objects declared at the top level can be accessed throughout the program but there are a number of considerations that determine that access. Programs are typically distributed over several files. Scope is to do with the accessibility of an object within a file and linkage is to do with its accessibility across files.

The scope of a variable declaration is that part of the program text within a file that follows the declaration up to the end of the block in which it is declared. Declarations at the top level have scope that extends to the end of the file. A variable can be made use of anywhere within its scope.

The same name can be declared at different textual levels in which case they introduce different variables. The scope of a lower level declaration takes precedence over the scope of a higher level declaration.

The function

```
main()
{
    int s = 0,i = 0;
    while ((i + = 1)<10)
    {
        int i;
        scanf("%d",&i);
        s + = i;
    }
}
```

reads nine integers printing out their sum.

The scope of the first declaration of **i** does not include the statements following the second declaration of **i**. The **i** used in the while condition refers to the first declaration. The **i** used in the call to **scanf** and the assignment that follows **scanf** refer to the second declaration.

This example illustrates how the use of the same name at an inner level affects the scope of an outer level declaration. You should use the same name to stand for different variables only where there is no danger of confusing the two. Here there is that danger and so the example also illustrates poor programming practice.

Scope rules for functions are similar to those for variables except that

- functions can only be declared at the top level
- functions can be referenced before their declarations.

Restricting function declarations to the top level means that we cannot nest function declarations. We cannot declare within a function **f**, functions **g** and **h** known only to **f**. Pascal and Ada, along with many other programming languages do not impose this restriction. In the main the sort of control over program structure this form of nesting gives you can also be achieved using **.c** files.

When a function reference appears before its declaration, some assumptions are made about its type. For example the result type is assumed to be integer. Errors will result if the types given with the function declaration are inconsistent with these assumptions. In Chapter 4 we used prototypes as a way of interfacing separate **.c** files. A function prototype and a function declaration can appear in the same **.c** file and where it is convenient or necessary to call a function before its declaration a prototype declaration should precede the call.

5.17 Function prototypes

If a function needs to be referenced before it is declared a function prototype declaration should be provided before the reference. Function prototypes give the function name, the result type and the types of the formal parameters. They look very much like function headers, except that the names for formal parameters may be dropped.

Either

void quot_rem(int a,int b, int ∗ q_ptr,int ∗ r_ptr);

or

void quot_rem(int ,int , int ∗ ,int ∗);

would be acceptable prototype definitions for the function **quot_rem**. If parameter names are given these are simply for documentation purposes. A comment may be included with the function prototype declaration describing the purpose of each of the formal parameters, the actions carried out by the function and the nature of its result. In such a case being able to refer to the formal parameters by name is clearly useful.

The full declaration of the function can make use of different formal parameter names, although this could well cause confusion.

The following **.c** file illustrates a function call (to **quot_rem**) before its full declaration with a prototype declaration preceding the call.

```
void quot_rem(int ,int , int *,int * );
main()
{
    int a = getint(),b = getint(), q,r;
    if (b > 0)
    {
        quot_rem(a,b,&q,&r);
        printf("quotient = %d remainder = %d",q,r);
    }
    else printf("The second input must be positive and non-zero");
}
void quot_rem(int a,int b, int * q_ptr,int * r_ptr);
{
    * q_ptr = 0; * r_ptr = a;
    while (* r_ptr >= b)
    {
        * q_ptr + = 1;
        * r_ptr - = b;
    }
}
```

5.18 Defining declarations and referencing declarations

Up to now we have assumed that declarations cause the creation of an object. A function declaration causes the creation of a function and a variable declaration a variable. The introduction of function prototypes complicates things because we now have to deal with two types of declaration. In the last example above **quot_rem** is declared twice. The first declaration provides the C compiler with information about **quot_rem**. The second gives a full description and it is this second declaration that ensures the creation of the function. Declarations that cause the creation of an object are called **defining** declarations. Those that do not but nevertheless give attributes of the object are called **referencing** declarations.

5.19 External references

Finally we look at the way objects with defining declarations in one file are accessed from a second. There are two considerations here. The C compiler treats **.c** files separately. If it encounters a reference to either a variable or a function that is defined in a different file it needs some help in interpreting it. For example in the case of a variable reference it needs to know its type. The second consideration concerns the linker which has to make sure that the link between the reference and the declaration is correctly established. Referencing declarations support both compilation and linkage here.

We have already seen a number of examples of external references. The collection of **.c** files used for the expression evaluator described in Chapter 4 contained cross file function calls.

In principle all top level variables and functions can be accessed throughout the program (that is from all the **.c** files used to build the program) unless they are explicitly hidden. (How this can be done is described below.) However functions and variables are treated differently.

If a variable with a defining declaration on one file is referenced in a second, a referencing declaration is needed in this second file. Such declarations look exactly like defining declarations except that they are preceded by the keyword **extern**.

Given the defining declaration

>   **int i;**

in one file the occurrence of

>   **extern int i;**

in further files gives access to **i** from those files. We can split the **.c** file given in Section 5.10 into two. The first would contain:

```
int a,b,q,r;
    main()
    {
        a = getint();
        b = getint();
        if (b > 0)
        {
```

```
                    quot.rem();
                    printf("quotient = %d remainder = %d",q,r);
               }
               else printf("The second input must be positive and non-
zero");
          }
```

We would need to include **extern int a,b,q,r** in the second part, which would thus take the form

```
          extern int a,b,q,r;
          void quot_rem();
          {
               q = φ; r = a;
               while (r >= b)
               {
                    q + = 1;
                    r - = b;
               }
          }
```

Functions with defining declarations in one file can be accessed from a second without any referencing declarations. It is however good practice to make use of prototype declarations. A prototype declaration for the function in the first file should be given in the second file prior to any use of the function. Without this the compiler will not know the parameter and result types. It will make assumptions about these that could lead to difficulties.

Where library functions are used we normally include an appropriate **.h** file. For example, if we make use of input and output functions we include **stdio.h** which contains among other things the prototype declarations for these functions. (**stdio.h** contains more than just function prototypes. For example we made use of the stream **stdin** in a call to **ungetc** in the expression evaluator developed in Chapter 4. The meaning of **stdin** is defined in **stdio.h** and to use it we do need to include the **.h** file so it is sensible always to include it whenever input or output is used in a program.)

In Chapter 4 we placed prototypes in **.h** files and included these as necessary in order to introduce them into **.c** files. This practice is consistent with the way library function prototypes are made available and should be used where cross file function calls are needed.

5.20 Restricting accessibility using static

All functions and variables declared at the outermost level are potentially accessible from everywhere within a program. Access can however be restricted to the file in which the defining declaration appears by preceding the declaration with the keyword **static**. The role of **static** here is entirely different from that seen earlier where it caused a variable that would normally have local extent to have static extent. All variables and functions declared at the outermost level automatically have static extent. The use of the keyword at this level restricts the accessibility of the defined objects to the file in which it occurs.

In Chapter 4 we illustrated how the modules in a structure chart might map onto
.c files. At that stage we did not concern ourselves with how external references
were handled since there were no difficulties in implementing the modules as
separate **.c** files. It is worth noting however that typically a module will be
implemented in part by functions and variables that are used by other modules and
in part by entirely local ones. By placing appropriate function prototypes and
referencing variable declarations in a **.h** file associated with the module's **.c** file and
using **static** to restrict the accessibility of any remaining functions and variables we
can view the **.h** file as the interface to the module and the **.c** file as its implementation.

Suppose we have the following in a file **qr.c**

```
static int q,r;
static void quot_rem(int a,int b);
{
    q = 0;r = a;
    while (r >= b)
    {
    q + = 1;
    r – = b;
    }
}
int quotient(int a,int b)
{
    quot_rem(a,b);
    return q;
}
int remainder(int a,int b)
{
    quot_rem(a,b);
    return r;
}
```

The two functions **quotient** and **remainder** are accessible from anywhere within a
program that makes use of **qr.c**. Both these functions make use of the function
quot_rem and the variables **q** and **r**. Because **quot-rem**, **q** and **r** are there simply
to support **quotient** and **remainder** their use is entirely local to **qr.c**. Access to them
is therefore restricted through the use of **static**. It is now not possible to make use
of them outside this file whether or not function prototypes or **extern** are used
elsewhere.

qr.c can be thought of as providing a utility – the calculation of quotient and
remainder – with two functions to do just that. It also contains functions and
variables that are used in the calculation but are not made available for external use.
This separation of objects into visible and hidden objects is an important strategy in
the development of software. A module may turn out to have a complex internal
structure but presents a simple and clean interface to other modules that call on its
services. The separation allows a distinction to be made between the functions that
the module provides to other modules and the implementation of those functions.
The advantages of this are twofold. First the separation makes the design easier to
understand and implement. Second implementations can be changed without

affecting the interface. Recent languages such as Modula and Ada provide good support for this separation. The support provided by C is somewhat cruder but is nevertheless worth making use of.

The interface with **qr.c** can captured by the two prototype declarations

>   **int quotient(int ,int);**

and

>   **int remainder(int,int);**

By placing these prototype declarations in a **.h** file associated with the file containing the defining declaration we can then include it wherever the functions are made use of. The **.h** file acts as the interface to its associated (**.c**) file.

In dealing with external objects we have had to look at extent, scope and linkage, covering them in general terms but leaving out some detail.The meanings of the three are inter-related and complex and certainly this aspect of C can be extremely confusing.To use C effectively they have to be understood. Experimenting with simple programs built from a small number of **.c** and **.h** files is a good way of gaining insights into what is going on.

Exercises

1. Write a function **max** that takes two integer arguments and returns the larger of the two.

2. Write a program that reads a sequence of positive numbers and which outputs the largest of these. Assume that the end of the sequence of positive numbers is indicated by the occurance of a negative number in the input. Your program should make use of **max**.

3. Given the sequence of declarations and assignments

    >   **int i ; int j; int * i_ptr; int * j_ptr;**
    >   **i_ptr = &i;**
    >   **j_ptr = &j;**
    >   **i = 10;**
    >   ***j_ptr = * i_ptr;**

    show the values of each of the variables after each assignment statement. You will need to assume values for the addresses of the memory associated with the variables **i** and **j**.

4. The concept of a pointer is general in C. For example the declaration

    >   **int * * i_ptr_ptr**

    associates type pointer to pointer to **int** with the variable **i_ptr_ptr**.

    Given the sequence of declarations and assignments

    >   **int i, j, * i_ptr, ** i_ptr_ptr;**
    >   **i = 3;**
    >   **i_ptr = &i;**
    >   **i_ptr_ptr = &i_ptr**
    >   **j = ** i_ptr_ptr;**

show the values of each of the variables after each assignment statement. Again you will need to assume values for the addresses associated with the variables **i** and **i_ptr**.

5. Modify the function **max** of question **1** so that it takes pointers to integers as arguments and returns a pointer to the larger of the two integer values as its result.

6. Given

```
main()
{
    int x,y;
        .
        .
        .
}
int a;
static int b;
static int f()
{
    int i,j,x;
        .
        .
    while (i > 0)
    {
        int x;
            .
            .
            .
    }
}
int g()
{
        .
        .
        .
}
```

give the extent and scope for each of the declarations. Given that these declarations are in the same file which would be accessible from different files.

6

Structured data types

So far we have made use of integers, characters and pointers. These were manipulated as single indivisible objects. Such values are described as unstructered **scalar** values. Most programs however deal both with scalar values and with more complex **structured** values.

For example, suppose we wanted to provide a computerised telephone directory for an internal company telephone system. Company employees would use it to look up the telephone numbers of other employees. As new employees join the company the directory would be extended and entries would be deleted when employees leave. Such a system would need access to a table of name,number pairs in order to work. Such a directory structure would consist of a collection of values, with each such value itself being made up of a pair of values.

Pictorially we might be dealing with

Name	Number
Adams E	1937
Anderson K	8281
Brown W	2305
Davies K	4478

This directory is an example of a structured value with component values also being structured. Indeed each of these component values is built from yet another structured value (a string) and a scalar value (an integer) representing the telephone number.

We need to access such an object at a number of levels. We would like to treat it as a single value if we are reading it from a file, copying or printing it out. If we are adding entries to it then it appears as a collection of pairs. Finally if we are looking up a number then we are dealing with it at the level of names and numbers. Thus we can think of a directory as a single value or as a collection of values, depending on what we are doing with it. As we will discover C provides support for such structured objects which include their creation, and language features that allow the programmer to access the component values that make up the structured value. To some extent C allows such values to be manipulated at various levels although the limitations on doing this are fairly severe.

In this chapter we will develop a program that supports such a computerised directory. In developing the program we will make use of

- arrays
- structures
- objects with dynamic extent
- files.

The first three of these support the use of structured values within a program, with the fourth allowing for their preservation between program executions. It would not be very practical to insist that the telephone directory be typed in manually each time the program is executed.

6.1 Arrays

The directory is made up of a collection of pairs. These pairs are effectively all of the same type in that they are made up of a name and an integer. Collections of values all of the same type are so common in programming that all programming languages provide a special way of dealing with them. Because the values have the same type they always take the same amount of memory to store. (Names of course vary in length. However the way they get dealt with will ensure that these pairs do indeed occupy the same amount of memory.) This has a number of advantages in the way individual values are accessed.

Before looking at the way arrays get used we need to define a few terms.

6.2 Array elements

As with scalar variables, arrays will have memory allocated to them to hold the values that make up the array. The amount of memory set aside with depend on how much memory is needed to hold the individual values and the number of values in the array. An array can be thought of as a collection of variables all of the same type. These variables are called array **elements**. For example, an element of an array of integers is treated in exactly the same way that an integer variable is treated. The only difference comes in the way the array element is declared (as part of an **array declaration**) and the way it is accessed, through array **indexing**.

6.3 Array declarations

Array declarations look exactly like scalar variable declarations, except that the array name introduced in the declaration is followed by the number of elements in square brackets.

For example

    int scores[10]

declares an array of **10** integer numbers. **scores** is made up of the **10** elements

    scores[0], scores[1], ... , scores[9]

The number of elements must be given as a **constant** expression. That is the compiler must be able to evaluate the expression. This limitation on the use of arrays (which incidentally C shares with many other programming languages) is sometimes inconvenient because programs do arise that need arrays to take different sizes from execution to execution. The limitation means that the programmer has to decide on the largest size that the program is ever likely to need and use that in his array declaration.

Arrays that have their size calculated when the program is executing are called **dynamic** arrays. The programming language Ada for example supports dynamic arrays as does one of the earliest languages, Algol. We will see later that, where dynamic arrays are the most appropriate for an application, C does provide ways of simulating their effect. Indeed we will make use of this in dealing with the names that appear in the telephone directory.

6.4 Array initialisations

As with other variable declarations array declarations can include initial values for the array elements. This is expressed as a series of constant expressions separated by commas and enclosed in '{' and '}'.

A constant expression should appear for each of the array elements that needs to be initialised.

The declaration

int numbers[10] = {0,1,2,3,4,5,6,7,8,9};

creates an array **numbers** of **10** elements with the first element initialised to **0** and the last to **9**.

Where all the array elements have initial values specified a size specification is unnecessary. The above declaration can be written

int numbers[] = {0,1,2,3,4,5,6,7,8,9};

6.5 Array indexes

In C array elements are always numbered starting with **0**. Element numbers are called array **indexes**. Although in some ways similar to memory addresses, indexes differ in two important respects. First they reference within the area of memory allocated to the array. Second they take account of the size of elements. There is however a strong link between array indexing and pointers, as we shall see later. Arrays have names and array elements are referenced using a combination of array name and the index.

Indexing takes the general form

<array_name> [<expression>]

where **<array_name>** is the name of the array and **<expression>** generates an integer value corresponding to the index. If the array has **n** elements then this should be a value in the range **0 ... n − 1**. That we are able to make use of expressions to produce array indexes is one of the main advantages of using arrays. For example, we are able to reference every element of the largest of arrays using a small number of C statements as is illustrated by

```
int index = 0;
while (index < 10)
{
    printf("%d\n",scores[index]);
    index += 1;
}
```

or, taking advantage of assignment within the index expression,

```
int index = - 1;
while (index < 9) printf("%d\n",scores[index += 1]);
```

which prints out successive values from the array **scores**. In indexing arrays great care has to be taken to ensure that the indexes are in the index range determined by the array declaration. In each case above the expression used to index **scores** takes values in the range **0** ... **9**. The effect of the array reference

scores[10]

is unpredictable and possibly disastrous. It is the programmer's responsibility to ensure that this does not happen. Other languages such as Pascal ensure that such illegal references are caught and reported on during program execution. The program is terminated with some information about the error. C systems give no such help, so programmers must exercise great care in the use of arrays. In dealing with arrays within loops always check that the last cycle of the loop carries out a legal reference. Index values must be at most one less than the number of elements since elements are numbered from **0**.

Where an isolated array reference is made, the generated index value should be checked and if it is illegal approriate action taken.

For example if an index is input as in

```
int i;
scanf("%d",&i);
printf("score for %d is %d",i,scores[i]);
```

there is no guarantee that what is typed in is a valid index so a check is necessary as in

```
int i;
scanf("%d",&i);
if (i < 0 || i > 9) printf("input value should be in the range 0 .. 9\n");
else printf("score for %d is %d",i,scores[i]);
```

6.6 Accessing arrays using the for statement

Although array elements can be accessed in any order very often they are accessed in sequence within a program loop as above. Although we could always use a while statement to do this the C for statement is more convenient to use. This takes the form

$$\textbf{for } (<\textbf{expression}_1>_{opt};<\textbf{expression}_2>_{opt};<\textbf{expression}_3>_{opt}) <\textbf{statement}>$$

If **<expression₁>** is present it is evaluated and its value is discarded. Normally this expression will involve an assignment.

If **<expression₂>** is present it is evaluated. If its value is equal to **0** the for statement terminates. If **<expression₂>** is not present or its value is not equal to **0** **<statement>** is executed.

If **<expression₃>** is present it is evaluated and its value is discarded. Again an assignment of some form would normally take place here.

The cycle is then repeated from the stage where **<expression₂>** is evaluated if it is present.

Note both that all the expressions are optional and that semicolons, which should always appear, separate the three expressions.

The **for** statement

for (;;) printf("hello world\n");

prints 'hello world' unceasingly.

The first expression is normally an initialisation of a variable that is used to control the execution of the loop. The second is normally a comparison which when it no longer holds causes the termination of the loop. The third normally increments the control variable.

As a first example, the for statement equivalent of the while statements that output the contents of **scores** given above is

```
int index;
for ( index = 0; index < 10; index += 1) printf("%d\n",scores[index]);
```

This behaves in the following way.

1. The variable **index** is assigned the value **0**.
2. The comparison **index < 10** is carried out. If it holds then the execution of the for loop continues. If it does not (**index** is greater than or equal to **10**) then its execution ends.
3. Where execution continues the **printf** statement is executed.
4. **index += 1** is executed, incrementing **index** by **1**.
5. Execution continues at step **2**.

Although for statements are very useful in processing arrays they are general and can be used whenever we can calculate the number of times a loop has to execute.

For example the program

```
main()
{
    int i,j;
    scanf("%d",&i);
    if (i < 2 || i > 12)
        printf("Only two to twelve times tables are generated");
    else
        for (j = 1; j <= 12; j += 1 ) printf("%2d * %2d = %d\n",j,i,i * j);
}
```

uses a for loop to display times tables. The program takes as input the table number which must be between **2** and **12** and produces the corresponding times table as output.

Given **9** as input it will for example generate

1	*	9	=	9
2	*	9	=	18
3	*	9	=	27
4	*	9	=	36
5	*	9	=	45
6	*	9	=	54
7	*	9	=	63
8	*	9	=	72
9	*	9	=	81
10	*	9	=	90
11	*	9	=	99
12	*	9	=	108

We have made use of a new feature in the format directive. The directive **%d** causes an integer to be displayed on the screen as a sequence of digits. Only as many digits as are necessary with be output with no preceding or following spaces.

The print statement

printf("%d %d",237,56);

outputs the two integer values **237** and **56** as the sequence of digits **23756**. We need to write

printf("%d %d",237,56);

if we want the two values to appear separated.

Because the number of digits output for a given integer will vary if we are generating tables of numbers we need some way of ensuring that columns of numbers are lined up. If a number appears between the '**%**' symbol and the integer output format indicator '**d**' this number gives the minimum number of positions that must be used for the output value. If the output integer requires fewer digit positions than specified that minimum number will be made up by preceding it with as many spaces as are necessary.

In the table the first column of numbers is aligned to the last digit position of the largest number (which we have ensured will require at most two digits) whereas for the last column, where no minimum number of positions was specified, the first digit position is used.

6.7 Increment and decrement operators

In the for statements seen so far the control variable has been incremented using compound assignment. It is common practice in C to increment or decrement control variables using the **post-increment** or **post-decrement** operators. Their effect is determined in part by the type of the operand that they are applied to and we will see later how they are used in what is called **address arithmetic**. Where they are applied to integer variables they simply increment or decrement the variable by **1**.

   If we write

> **index ++; (or index– –;)**

its effect is to add **1** to (or subtract **1** from) the value of **index**.

   We have seen that

> **index = index + 1;**

can be expressed more compactly using compound assignment as

> **index += 1;**

We now have a further compaction in

> **index ++;**

An argument against the use of C as a vehicle for the study of programming is that it includes features such as the postincrementing of variables. Their use, the argument goes, makes programs more difficult to read. The opposite is probably true. They are not difficult to get used to since they do not introduce any new ideas and when used sensibly they reduce textual clutter.

   Using it our very first example of the use of a for loop becomes

> **int index;**
> **for (index = 0; index < 10; index ++) printf("%d\n",scores(index));**

In an expression such as

> **k = i + j;**

the values associated with **i** and **j** are used as operands for the addition operation. Post-increment and post decrement operators can be applied to variables anywhere within an expression.

   In

> **k = i +++ j ++;**

i +++ j ++ generates the same value as **i + j** and this value gets assigned to **k**. However, once the value in **i** has been obtained as an operand for the addition, **i** is incremented. In a similar way **j** is updated after its value has been obtained as a second operand.

   The post-increment and post-decrement operators have higher precedence than addition. Thus **i +++ j ++** reads **(i ++)+(j ++)**.

   If **i** and **j** have the values **10** and **20** before this last assignment, **k** will have the value **30** with **i** and **j** having the values **11** and **21** after it. Hence the terms post-increment and post-decrement.

   As a second example, if **i** has the value **10** before the expression **i +++ i ++** is evaluated it will end up with the value **12** and the value of the expression itself will be **21**. We have already observed that with binary operators we cannot assume that the operand to the left of the operator is dealt with first. The order in which the two operands are processed is left to the compiler writer. However since both operands in **i +++ i ++** apply post-increment to **i,** one will yield **i**'s original value **(10)** with the other yielding its incremented value (**11**).

By placing the operators '**++**' or '**--**' **before** a variable the variable is incremented or decremented before it is used. The operators are then referred to as **pre-increment** and **pre-decrement** operators.

With **i** and **j** taking the above values

$$k = --i + --j;$$

assigns the value **28** to **k** with **i** and **j** having the values **9** and **19**.

6.8 Arrays and pointers

An array declaration will at some stage cause the allocation of enough memory for the elements of the array. In particular the elements follow one another in memory. The array name itself is a pointer **constant**. It represents a pointer value in much the same way that the integer constant **1024** represents an integer value. Just as we cannot change the integer value associated with an integer constant we cannot change the pointer value associated with an array name. We can however use this pointer value in exactly the same way as any other pointer value of the same type.

The declaration

int scores[10], * i_ptr;

introduces an array of integers and a pointer variable. Figure 6.1 illustrates a possible allocation of memory to the array **score** and to the pointer variable **i_ptr**. **scores** has associated with it the address **16192**. 10 4 byte areas of memory have been set aside for the integer elements of **scores**. These elements can be thought of as having the variable names **scores[0]**, **scores[1]**, ... **scores[9]**.

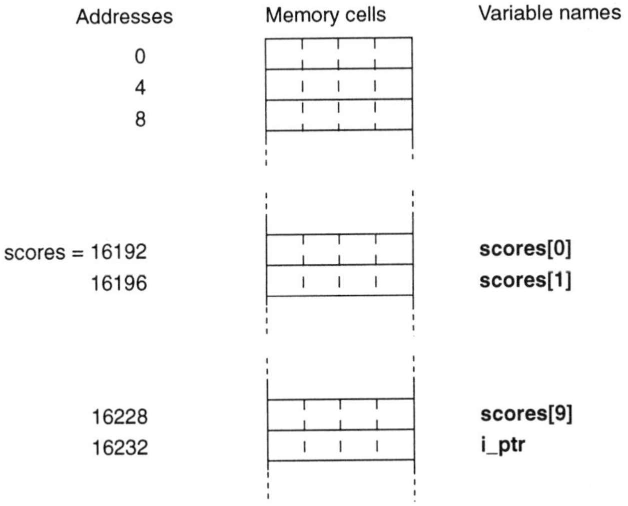

Figure 6.1 *The layout of arrays in memory*

The assignment

i_ptr = scores;

assigns as a pointer value the address **16192** to **i_ptr**.Now **i_ptr** can be used wherever **scores** can be used. For example

for (i = 0;i < 10;i++) printf(" %d\n",scores[i]);

is equivalent to

for (i = 0;i < 10;i ++) printf(" %d\n",i_ptr[i]);

They are not interchangeable however since **i_ptr** is a variable whereas **scores** is not. We can change the pointer value associated with **i_ptr** but we cannot change the one associated with **scores**.

6.9 Array arguments and array results

The fact that an array is a pointer with memory associated with it is important for a number of reasons.

When an array is passed as an argument to a function or returned as a result it is the array's pointer value not the values of the elements that is used.

If a function takes an array as an argument this argument must be declared as being of type pointer. We can do this in one of two ways. For example if we have a function which sums an array of integers the formal parameter for this array could be declared as **int * arr** or as **int arr[]**. Both describe a parameter of type pointer to **int**. In making a call to such a function the formal parameter would be assigned a pointer value.

The size given with an array declaration determines the amount of memory allocated for its elements. However no size information is held at run time. This means that when an array is passed as a parameter its size should also be passed as a separate argument or the function code should be written taking into account the array size. This second approach is unsatisfactory since it means that the function can only deal with arrays of that specific size.

The following function sums **size** integers starting at **array**:

```
int sum_elements(int * array, int size)
{
    int sum = 0,i;
    for (i = 0;i < size;i ++) sum + = array[i];
    return sum;
}
```

Given an array declaration

int numbers[] = {0,1,2,3,4,5,6,7,8,9};

then

s=sum_elements(numbers,10);

assigns the value **45** to s.

6.10 Strings

The C function library includes a function, **malloc**, that will obtain unused memory and allocate it to the calling program. It returns as its result a pointer to that memory. Dynamic arrays can thus be created by declaring a pointer variable of an appropriate type and using this function to find space for the array. We will make use of this feature to handle names in our telephone directory.

The obvious way to hold the telephone directory in memory is as an array. We need somehow to make its elements look like pairs, the first being a name with the second a telephone number. We have already decided that these numbers will be held as integers.

We will first deal with the problem of representing employee names and then the problem of pairing the name with the telephone number.

We will hold names as arrays of characters. We could use something like

    char name[20];

to hold a name of up to **20** characters.

The name '**Smith A**' might then be stored in the array as

name

| S | m | i | t | h | | A | | | | | | | | | | | | | |

with space characters placed in those elements not occupied by letters.

There are a number of disadvantages with this approach. The first is that all the processing of names has to be carried out in terms of array elements. For example when two names represented in this way are compared for equality the individual letters will need to be compared as character values. This is of course possible to do. However the use of C strings here makes the programming considerably easier since there are several C library functions that provide such operations as comparison. We have already seen string constants used as format strings for input and output. String variables do not exist as such. Strings are held in character arrays. The characters making up the string are held in successive elements with the last character followed by an 8 bit zero value.

'**Smith A**' would be written as a string constant in the form **"Smith A"** the character '**"**' being used to delineate the string. It would be held in memory as

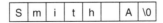

where '**\0**' is the (non-printable) ASCII character with ASCII code **0**, which we shall refer to as the string **terminator**. Recall that the ASCII character codes are in the range **0 ... 127**. In writing down a character constant we can either place the character in single quotes as in '**a**' or we can use the escape character '****' followed by the ASCII code for the character. Because there is no a printable character that corresponds to the ASCII code **0** we write it '**\0**'.

The string library functions include functions for copying strings, obtaining their length, joining strings together and comparing them. The functions work on character arrays which hold strings and which are passed to or returned from the functions as values of type pointer to **char**.

A second disadvantage in using character arrays for names in the way originally suggested arises because the telephone directory we are trying to construct will contain many names. We could decide that no name required more than **20** characters and create as many **20** character arrays as are needed. Each pair in our directory would then consist of such a **20** character array and an integer. This creates a problem with names longer than **20** characters, and, since names are normally much smaller, would waste memory. These difficulties can be overcome if dynamic arrays are used. When a name is inserted in the directory a dynamic array is created for it. We will look at how this can be done simplifying the problem at this stage to a collection of names rather than pairs of names and telephone numbers.

Let us assume that the directory contains at most **1000** entries. We therefore want to contruct a **1000** element array to hold employee names. Each name is held as a string in a character array with the lengths of these arrays varying.

We want to create a data structure with something of the form of Figure 6.2.

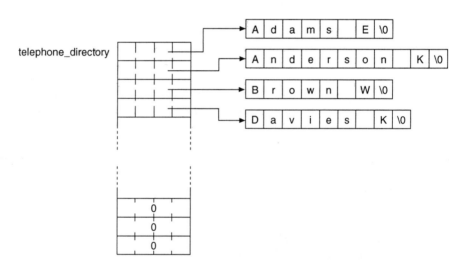

Figure 6.2 *The telephone directory without numbers*

Figure 6.2 shows an array of pointers with the first four pointers addressing four character arrays each containing a string. The last three pointer values shown in the diagram are **0**. A pointer value of **0** is taken to mean that the pointer does not point anywhere. It is sometimes called the null pointer.

We have to be careful not to treat the null value as an address. It is perfectly legal to do this since memory addressing starts at **0**. However it is very unlikely that a C program would make use of memory address **0** and in all probability its use would cause the program to fail. (The low address area of memory is normally dedicated to the operating system). Thus it can be used as a way of indicating that a pointer variable has not been assigned a sensible address. In a condition a value of **0** is interpreted as false, with all other values interpreted as true. In making use of a pointer variable the organisation of the program may be such that we know it has some sensible address assigned to it. Where this is not the case the variable should be initialised to **0** on declaration. If the address is now used as a condition the condition will be false if no assignment has taken place (it retains its initialisation value **0**) and true otherwise.

The declaration

int * i_ptr;

creates a pointer variable but it will not point anywhere sensible. This is analogous to what happens with other declarations. If we declare an **int** variable all we get is space for an integer. The programmer is responsible for ensuring that variables have sensible values in them and with pointer variables these values will be addresses.

The array **telephone_directory** is created by the declaration

char * telephone_directory[1000];

The element type of this array is **char *** and there are **1000** elements. Such a declaration creates a collection of **1000** pointers.

The for statement

for (i = 0;i < 1000;i ++) telephone_directory[i] = 0;

initialises each element to the null value.

A useful directory will have most of these pointers associated with employee names. Even though the directory will normally be held as a file and read in when needed it must have entries inserted into it at some stage. The directory system that we develop will provide the insertion of new entries as one of its features, so we will look at how a name is added to the above structure.

Let us assume that the name is typed in at the keyboard. Here some upper limit will be applied to the length of the name. Three things will happen.

- The name will be read in.
- A character array of suitable size will be created and its address will be assigned to a free entry in **telephone_directory**.
- The name read in will be copied into that character array.

6.11 Reading in a new name

We will read the name into character array using **getchar()**. The input will be terminated by an 'enter' (which is seen in the C program as the character '\n'). A maximum of **20** characters will be allowed for a name. If more characters are typed in these will be ignored. The characters will be held as a string by adding the character '\0'.

This is accomplished by the following

```
while (ch != '\n')
{
    if (i < 20) new_name[i ++] = ch;
```

```
    ch = getchar();
}
new_name[i] = '\0';
```

using the declarations

```
char new_name[21],ch = getchar();int i = 0;
```

The array **name** is used to hold the input. The number of elements specified makes allowance for the extra '\0' character. **i** is used as an indexing variable and **ch** (initialised to the first character of input) is used to hold the characters as they are read in.

The **while** loop continues until the character '\n' (generated by 'enter') is encountered. The conditional statement within the while loop ensures that at most **20** characters are moved into **new_name**.

The use of the postincrement operator here simplifies the code in that a compound statement under the conditional is avoided. Without its use the conditional becomes

```
if (i < 20)
{
    name[i] = ch;
    i += 1;
}
```

6.12 Creating a dynamic array

The built in function **malloc** allocates memory to an executing program, returning a pointer to the start of the area allocated. It takes as its argument the size of the memory area to be allocated.

The pointer values assigned to elements of **telephone_directory** should be character pointers.

malloc can be used to allocate space for any type of value. This means that we want it to return values (which will always be pointer values) with a type determined by the context in which it is being used. ANSI C allows this and C systems based on the ANSI standard provide a version of **malloc** that can be used in this way. Originally **malloc** was defined to return a character pointer value. Thus non ANSI systems may cause problems if **malloc** is used to create space for types other than characters. Throughout we are assuming ANSI C thus avoiding this difficulty.

The operator **sizeof** takes either a type specification such as **int** or an expression such as **3.15** and gives the number of bytes taken by values of the given or implied type.

After a new name has been read in the variable **i** above holds a count of the number of characters input (other than the 'enter'). Since we need to include the string terminator the number of elements required to hold the word as an array of characters is **i + 1**.

Assuming that new names are inserted into **telephone_directory** in order and the variable **next** indexes the next unused entry then

```
telephone_directory[next ++] = malloc(sizeof(char) * (i + 1));
```

- obtains enough memory for an array to hold the new name
- assigns the address of this area of memory as a pointer value to the next free element of **telephone_directory.**

In making use of **malloc** the **.h** file **stdlib.h** should be included.

6.13 Copying strings

C does not provide a way of dealing with arrays as single values. We cannot for example assign the value of one array variable to another. We would have to carry out such an assignment element by element. C does however provide a number of library functions to manipulate strings. We will use three of these, **strcpy** which copies strings, **strcmp** which compares strings and **strlen** which gives the length of a string. In all cases the arguments are character pointers. Recall that strings are held in character arrays and that arrays are always passed to functions by passing the pointer value associated with the array. We will describe how each of these functions works when we come to make use of them. We will need the first function to copy the contents of **new_name** to the area created for it by our call to **malloc**.

strcpy takes two character pointer arguments. The first gives the destination of the copy and the second the source.
Our call to **strcpy** takes the form

> **strcpy(telephone_directory[next],new_name);**

Both **telephone_directory[next]** and **new_name** are character pointers.

Since we have produced most of the C code needed to read and insert a new entry into the directory we will bring it all together into the function **insert_new_name**. Chapter 7 presents a number of functions all manipulating the telephone directory. We need to decide whether the directory should be passed as an argument to these functions or whether it should be declared at the top level. Declaring it at the top level at the start of a program makes it (potentially) accessible from anywhere within the program, and we could adopt this approach here. In Chapter 7 we demonstrate an alternative strategy making use of arguments.

Both **telephone_directory** and **next** will be declared using **static** to limit their accessibility to the file in which they are declared.(Because they are both top level they have static extent anyway. The keyword **static** here has its second meaning to do with limiting accessibility.)

```
static char * telephone_directory[1000];
static next;
void insert_new_name()
{
    char new_name[21],ch = getchar();int i = 0;
/* Read in the new name storing the first 20 characters*/
    while (ch != '\n')
    {
        if (i < 20) new_name[i ++] = ch;
        ch = getchar();
    }
    new_name[i] = '\0';
```

```
/* Obtain space for this new name */
      telephone_directory[next] = malloc(sizeof(char) * (i + 1));
/* and move the new name into that space */
      strcpy(telephone_directory[next],new_name);
}
```

The directory structure is incomplete since telephone numbers are not included. We could build the directory as two arrays, each with the same number of elements. The first array holds the names with the second holding the telephone numbers. By ensuring names and numbers correspond positionally in the arrays the same index value could be used to access a name and its corresponding number.
If we added the declaration

int telephone_numbers[1000];

telephone_directory[next] gives the element that is used for the next name and **telephone_numbers[next]** gives the element that is used for its associated number.

Since the name and number are logically related it would be nice if we could contruct a value that captures that relationship. This is possible in C through the use of **structures**.

6.14 Structure types and structured values

Arrays allow values of the same type to be grouped together. Groupings of values of different types are also allowable. For example

struct {char ∗ name; int number;} directory_entry;

creates a variable **directory_entry** with a value made up of a character pointer and an integer.

In this declaration the variable is preceded by

struct {char ∗ name; int number;}

This is called a **structure type definition**. Here the keyword **struct** is followed by what look like normal declarations within brackets. They have a different interpretation, however. Structure type definitions introduce templates for values but do not cause any space to be allocated. It is the occurence of the variable **name** in the above declaration that causes this to happen. They should be thought of as introducing a new type of object with the context in which the type definition appears determining how the new type is used. In a variable declaration above it is used to describe the structure of the variable.

In

sizeof(struct{char ∗ name;int number;})

it is used to describe a type for which **sizeof** will calculate the memory requirements. No variables are created in this context.

A variable introduced using a structure type definition is made up from a number of components, each component having associated with it a component name. The type of the component and its name appear in the structure type definition. As with normal variable declarations several components can be introduced with the same type specifier. Thus if we wanted two **char** pointers associated with a telephone number, one giving the name of the employee with the second giving his department our declaration might look like

struct {char * name, * department; int number;} directory_entry;

Each sequence of component names introduced under a specific type is terminated by a semicolon including the last. A common syntax error is to miss out this last semicolon.

6.15 Structure initialisations

As with arrays structures can be initialised on declaration. Such initialisations follow the form taken by array initialisations. The values to be assigned to the structure components appear between curly brackets to the right of the assignment operator. The values should correspond in type to the components in the structure type definition.

In the declaration

struct {char name[20]; int number;} directory_entry = {"Adams E", 1937};

a variable **directory_entry** of type **struct{char name[20]; int number;}** is declared with component **name** initialised to **"Adams E"** and component **number** initialised to **1937**.

Note that the character array in **directory_entry** has a string assigned to it which means that the first eight elements of the array are initialised, the eighth being initialised to '\0'.

The following declaration is better in two ways:

struct {char * name; int number;} directory_entry = {"Adams E", 1937};

The compiler has to make sure that any constants that appear in a program are available when the program executes. Both **"Adams E"** and **1937** will be held somewhere as part of the compiled code. If this were not the case then the above initialisation could not take place. With the first declaration this string is copied to the array **directory_entry.name**. With the second declaration a pointer value of type pointer to **char** is copied. Thus with the second declaration less space is used and less copying takes place.

Given the second declaration what is the effect of the assignment

directory_entry[0].name[0] = 'B';

The area of memory created by the compiler to hold **"Adams E"** is changed via **name**. Some implementations do not allow this making such memory 'read only'. Where it is allowed there is a risk. The same string constant may appear in several different places in a program. The compiler may recognise that these occurrences are the same and create only one instance of the constant in memory. The sort of assignment given above will thus affect all uses of the constant.

For example

printf("%s","Adams E");

would output **Bdams E** if it were executed after the above assignment. The lesson here is never assign to string constants.

6.16 Accessing the components of a structured variable using the selection operator

We need a way of 'breaking into' structured objects to use or change their component values. This is the purpose of those component names that appeared between the brackets. To access a component of a structured value the reference to the structured value is immediately followed by the **selection operator** '.' followed by the component name.

> **directory_entry.name**

references the character pointer in the structure and

> **directory_entry.number**

the integer. Referenced in this way the values of the components of a structure can be used directly. If the structure is a variable then its components can be treated as variables.

Since structure type definitions appear where the standard types can appear we can declare arrays of structured elements.

The declaration

> **struct {char * name; int number;} telephone_directory[1000]**

declares an array of **1000** structured values. Using this as our final directory structure we need to modify **insert_new_name** where it inserts the employee name and add the insertion of the telephone number.

> **telephone_directory[next] = malloc(sizeof(char) * (i + 1));**

becomes

> **telephone_directory[next].name = malloc(sizeof(char) * (i + 1));**

and

> **strcpy(telephone_directory[next],new_name);**

becomes

> **strcpy(telephone_directory[next].name,new_name);**

Let us assume that input to **insert_new_name** takes the form of a name followed by the associated number on the next line and that the number is followed by an 'enter' (indicating the end of the line). **insert_new_name** is extended by adding

> **scanf("%d",&(telephone_directory[next ++].number));**

as its new last line. The format directive '**%d**' will ensure that the next integer typed in is read into **telephone_directory[next].number**. The index **next** is postincremented to move it to the next free directory entry.

telephone_directory is now an array of structured objects. To get one of these we simply index the array as in **telephone_directory[next]**. This structured value is further broken into as in **telephone_directory[next].name** and **telephone_directory[next].number** by using component names. Structured objects can have arrays or other structured objects as their components. There is no limit to the complexity of such structures in C. However there should be no difficulty in constructing the right sequence of indexing and selection operations. At each stage in decomposing a structured object the value generated will have a type that can be determined from the object's declaration. If the type is an array and further decomposition is required then the next operation is an indexing operation. Otherwise it is a selection.

We have covered enough of the data structuring features of C to deal with our telephone directory. We want to turn finally to the subject of preserving the directory as a file. Before doing this we will look at some of the other useful things we can do with structures.

6.17 Treating structures as single entities

ANSI C allows structures to be treated as single entities. They can be copied, using assignment, passed as arguments or returned as results. Recall that with arrays we had to do this sort of thing using pointers. We have said that structure type definitions introduce new types. Unlike types **int, char** and so forth these new types are created by the programmer using existing types.

The declaration

>   **struct {float real,imag;} c;**

introduces a new type which we can write **struct {float real,imag;}** and declares a variable of this type. There are a number of contraints on the way the values associated with these types can be used.

Each structure type definition introduces a new type. Even if the structures defined by two separate such definitions look exactly the same they will be treated as different and incompatible.

The variables declared using

>   **struct {float real, imag;} c1; struct {float real, imag;} c2;**

are treated as being of different types even though the structures look the same. An assignment such as

>   **c1 = c2;**

is illegal.

There are two ways round this difficulty.

The first is to include the variables **c1** and **c2** under the same structure type definition as in

>   **struct {float real, imag;} c1,c2;**

Only one type structure type definition appears and both **c1** and **c2** take that type. This does require that all the variables taking the same structured type are declared together. If variables, formal parameters and function results need to use the same structured type this is not possible. The second way round the difficulty which allows for this is to associate a name with the type itself and with further declarations make use of that name.

When a structure declaration is being made the keyword **struct** may be followed by a name which is then the name of the new type created by the structure type definition. This name is called a structure **tag**.

The definition

struct complex {float real, imag;};

associates the name **complex** with the structured type **struct {float real,imag;}** . We can now use **complex** in much the same way that we use **int, char** and so forth with the proviso that its use is always preceded by the keyword **struct**.

We write

struct complex c1,c2;

rather than

complex c1,c2;

We can combine tagged structure type definitions with variable declarations as in

struct complex {float real, imag;} c1,c2;

This declaration introduces two variables of type **struct {float real,imag;}** giving this new type the name **complex**. We can use the names of structured types in all the contexts that types like **int** are allowed. For example, suppose **complex** is intended to represent complex numbers and that the structure definition appears at the top level in a **.c** file. We may then use it for example to declare a function **add** which adds together the components of two complex numbers returning the result of these additions as a complex number.

This would be declared as

```
struct complex add(struct complex a,struct complex b)
{
    struct complex result;
    result.real = a.real + b.real;
    result.imag = a.imag + b.imag;
    return result;
}
```

where both the result type and the argument types are declared as complex. Given two **complex** variables **c1** and **c2**

c1 = add(c1,c2);

updates **c1** by adding to it the component values of **c2**. The function **add** returns a value of type **complex** which is assigned to **c1**.

If a tagged structured type is needed in several different **.c** files then its definition should be repeated in each of the files. Provided that the definitions have the same tag name then they will be treated as the same type. C systems tend to be trusting. If you describe two structures in different **.c** files at the outermost level and give them the same tag they will be accepted as describing the same structure. If they differ in shape then the program using them will behave unpredictably. This is at odds with the constraints on the use of structured types **within** a **.c** file. Here we saw that for two structured variables to be treated as of the same type they must be declared under the same structured type definition or the structured type should be given a name with that name being used in declarations.

It is good practice to name structure types and introduce structured variables in separate declarations and where a structure is used in different **.c** files place the declaration that names its type in a **.h** file.

For example we might want to make use of complex numbers in many different programs. We would place functions such **add** above in a **.c** file (**complex.c** say) and place the definition

> **struct complex {float real, imag;};**

along with prototypes for **add**, etc. in a **.h** file (**complex.h** say). We would then include this **.h** file whenever we needed to make use of complex numbers.

As a simple example

```
#include "complex.h"
main()
{
    struct complex c1,c2;
    c1.real = 1.1;c1.imag = 2.2;c2.real = 3.3;c2.imag = 4.4;
    c1 = add(c1,c2);
    printf("%f %f",c1.real,c1.imag);
}
```

adds two complex numbers together printing out the result of this addition. It is always a good idea to try out C programs given as examples. With this example bear in mind first that ANSII C is assumed and that a compiled form of the file **complex.c** should be available to the linker. You will have to make sure both this compiled form and **complex.h** are in the right place in the file store (normally the current working directory).

6.18 Using array types and structure types in arrays and structures

All the examples of arrays and structures that we have seen have been built from scalar types. Array elements have been integers or characters or pointers. Structure components have been integers or pointers. Any of the standard types provided by C can be used as element or component types.

Structure type definitions add to the possible types that can be used in this way. We have already seen arrays of structures. Structures can themselves have structured components.

If, for example, we wanted to include with a telephone number a room number one of the ways we could do this would be to pair the telephone and room as a substructure within the structure associated with directory entries.

The structure type definition

struct directory_entry{char * name; struct {int number,room;} addr;};

achieves this. There is considerable flexibility in the way new types can be introduced and mixed.

We could for example create the same effect with the following

struct address (int number,room;};
struct directory_entry{char * name; struct address addr;};

The choice we make will depend to some extent on how we make use of substructures throughout the program in which the declarations occur.

Structures can have arrays as components. We could have chosen to model directory entries using the structure type definition

struct directory_entry{char name[21];int number;};

the directory itself then being declared as

struct directory_entry telephone_directory[1000];

where a thousand **21** character arrays are allocated for employee names by the declaration.

This difference between this approach and the way we have chosen to do it is that here space for arrays is generated by the declaration rather than it being obtained through the use of **malloc.** References such as

telephone_directory[i].name

are to pointer constants here and to pointer variables in the chosen approach.

Arrays can takes arrays as elements. Such arrays are called **multi-dimensional** arrays. The declaration

int matrix[4][3];

introduces an array **matrix** with four elements each of which is a three element integer array.

In mathematics a matrix is a collection of numbers which can be thought of as arranged in rows of equal length.

For example

$$\begin{bmatrix} 1 & 5 & 2 \\ 0 & 3 & 9 \\ 3 & 6 & 9 \\ 2 & 2 & 4 \end{bmatrix}$$

is a matrix made up of four rows and three columns. A number of operations are defined on matrices, including matrix addition which applies to pairs of matrices with the same number of rows and columns. The result of adding two matrices is a matrix whose numbers result from the addition of the corresponding numbers of the two matrices being added together.

Thus

$$
\begin{bmatrix} 1 & 5 & 2 \\ 0 & 3 & 9 \\ 3 & 6 & 9 \\ 2 & 2 & 4 \end{bmatrix} + \begin{bmatrix} 8 & 2 & 6 \\ 9 & 4 & 0 \\ 2 & 6 & 1 \\ 8 & 7 & 7 \end{bmatrix} = \begin{bmatrix} 9 & 7 & 8 \\ 9 & 7 & 9 \\ 5 & 12 & 10 \\ 10 & 9 & 11 \end{bmatrix}
$$

The array **matrix** defined above models a matrix with four rows and three columns.

C allocates memory to arrays row by row as Figure 6.3 illustrates, each row being an array of integers.

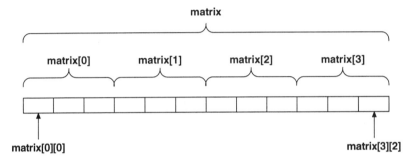

Figure 6.3 *The memory allocation for the elements of matrix*

We have seen that array names are interpreted as pointer constants. Where an array is indexed the address of the indexed element is calculated using the pointer value associated with the array, the given index and the amount of memory needed to hold an array element. A pointer value is not simply an address – the type of the value it points at is significant. As we have seen if we declare a pointer variable it is of type pointer to **int** or **char** or whatever.

One reason then for this is that C compilers can carry out consistency checks. With

      int * i_ptr; char ch;

the assignment

      i_ptr = &ch;

assigns a value of type pointer to **char** to a variable of type pointer to **int**. Almost all C compilers would generate a warning that the types are inconsistent, although it would be possible to execute the resultant program.

A second reason is to do with arrays. A reference to an array name is a pointer reference. The type associated with that pointer takes into account the array element size. When an array is indexed this element size must be used in locating the indexed element.

We know that for

      int scores[10]

scores is of type pointer to **int**. If **int** values occupy two bytes and the array **scores** starts at address **1024** then the address of the element **scores[3]** is given by **1024 + 2 * 3**.

In fact we can achieve the effect of array indexing through operations on pointers. We can add an integer to a pointer. The result is a pointer. (We can also subtract an integer from a pointer giving a pointer.) This addition takes into account the amount of memory needed to hold values of the type the pointer points at.For example, **scores+3** will generate a pointer value addressing the fourth element (**scores[3]**) of **scores**. We can then use indirection on this pointer value.

$$* \, (\mathbf{scores} + 3) = 11;$$

has exactly the same effect as

$$\mathbf{scores[3]} = 11;$$

We can also use increment and decrement operations on pointer variables and again these operations take into account value sizes.

Given

int scores[10], * i_ptr;

the assignment

i_ptr = scores;

assigns the address of the array **scores** to **i_ptr** and

for (i = 0;i < 10;i++) *(i_ptr++) = 0;

has exactly the same effect on **scores** as does

for (i = 0;i < 10;i++) scores[i] = 0;

In the first for statement the assignment *(i_ptr++)=0; works as follows. The indirection operator '*' takes the contents of **i_ptr** as an address to which the value **0** is assigned. After **i_ptr** has been accessed the post_increment operator '++' is applied, updating **i_ptr** by the number of bytes needed to hold a vlaue of type **int**.

These ideas extend to multidimensional arrays. The array **matrix** above will have a pointer constant associated with it. The type of value pointed at by this will be an array because the elements of **matrix** are arrays.

The reference

matrix[2]

is to an array of integers and as such has type pointer to **int**.

The reference

matrix

is to an array of arrays. Its type is effectively pointer to **3** element array on **int**. Its type has to take into account the size of the arrays that it addresses in order that the indexing mechanism described above works.

Since **matrix[2]** is of type pointer to integer and the type of **matrix** is pointer to something it is tempting to treat it as having type pointer to pointer to integer. This is however incorrect – the elements of **matrix** are themselves arrays not pointers.

Given the declarations

    int m1[4][3], m2[4][3], m3[4][3];

The addition of **m1** and **m2** with the result placed in **m3** would be achieved by

```
for (row = 0;row < 4;row++)
    for (col = 0;col < 3; col++)
        m3[row][col] = m1[row][col] + m2[row[col];
```

Multi-dimensional arrays and nested for loops go together. The above statement deals with **m1, m2** and **m3** row by row, the inner for loop dealing with each row and the outer for loop moving from row to row. For each cycle of the outer for loop the inner for loop executes three times.

There is no restriction in C on the number of dimensions an array may have. **matrix ,m1, m2,** and **m3** are two dimensional but any number of dimensions is allowable. However arrays with more than one dimension are of limited use because of their static nature. For example it would be nice to be able to write a general addition function which added the corresponding elements of two two-dimensional arrays to produce a third. The only way this can be done is to fix the size of the second dimension.

The function

void add_matrices(int opand1[][3],int opand2[][3],int result[][3],int rows)
```
{
    int i,j;
    for(i = 0;i < rows;i++)
        for (j = 0;j < 3;j++)
        result[i][j] = opand1[i][j] + opand2[i][j];
}
```

will add together the corresponding elements of the first two arguments assigning the result to the third. The arguments are arrays whose elements are themselves three integer arrays.The element size is needed in order that the array indexing can be correctly carried out. Whenever arrays are specified as formal parameters it must be possible to work out the element size at compile time, although the number of elements in any actual array argument may vary.

With any call to **add_matrices** the array arguments are treated as pointers. If a function generates an array as a result it must either use space for the array that has already been created in which case it is either declared at the top level, or a pointer to that space is passed as a further argument, or it must find the space itself using **malloc**. In either case its interface with any caller will be through pointers. It could not for example return an array as a result. Here we have chosen to pass to **add_matrices** a pointer to the result matrix.

Although **add_matrices** will work with arrays with any number of elements, each element has to be an array of three integers. The purpose of the fourth argument is to specify the number of elements in the arrays involved. There is no way using multidimensional arrays that a more general matrix addition function can be written.

A more general function can however be written if we make the array elements pointers rather than 3 integer arrays.

The declaration

> **int ∗ matrix[4]**

can be used to model a two dimensional array of four rows. Since the elements of our new version of **matrix** are integer pointers they can be treated as integer arrays. The declaration does not create space for the rows themselves. This needs to be done using **malloc**. The length of each row can vary, since it will depend entirely on how much space we ask **malloc** to allocate.

The loop

> **for (r = 0;r < 4;r++) matrix[r] = malloc (sizeof(int) ∗ 3);**

will allocate space for each row assigning the row addresses to the elements of **matrix**. See Figure 6.4.

The reference

> **matrix[2]**

is again to an array of integers. Where we had a multidimensional array such a reference yielded a pointer constant. Here we get have a pointer variable.

In the function declaration

> **void add_matrices(int ∗ opand1[],int ∗ opand2[],int ∗ result[],int**
> **rows,int cols)**
> **{**
> **int r,c;**
> **for(r = 0;r < rows;r++)**
> **   for (c = 0;c < cols;c++)**
> **   result[r][c] = opand1[r][c] + opand2[r][c];**
> **}**

the arguments are arrays of pointers to integers. The row length is now no longer bound to the formal parameters **opand1**, **opand2**, and **result**. It thus becomes a further argument to a more general function.

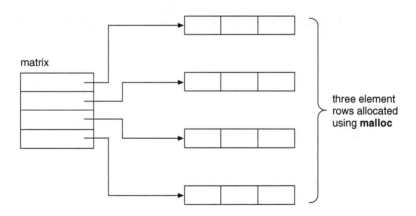

Figure 6.4 *Memory allocation for matrix using malloc*

The following illustrates how our new **add_matrices** might get used:

```
main()
{
    /* declare three four element arrays of pointers */
    int * a[4],*b[4], * res[4],r,c;
    /* allocate space for the rows for each array */
    for(r = 0;r < 4;r++)
    {
        a[r] = malloc(sizeof(int) * 3);
        b[r] = malloc(sizeof(int) * 3);
        res[r] = malloc(sizeof(int) * 3);
    }
    /* assign values to the elements of a and b */
    for(r = 0;r < 4;r++)
        for(c = 0;c < 3;c++)
        {
            a[r][c] = r;
            b[r][c] = c;
        }
    /* use add_matrices to add a and b into res*/
    add_matrices(a,b,res,4,3);
    /* output the rows of res on separate lines*/
    for (r = 0;r < 4;r++)
    {
        for (c = 0;c < 3;c++)
            printf("%d ",res[r][c]);
        printf("\n");
    }
}
```

Because **a**, **b**, and **r** are four element arrays of integer pointers they can be used as four row matrices with the rows on any length. Here **malloc** is used to allocate enough space for three integers for each row creating the effect of four by three matrices.

To demonstrate the function **add_matrices a** and **b** are assigned values. For **a** each element is assigned its row number and for **b** each element is assigned its column number.

After **add_matrices** has been called the matrix **res** is output.

Arrays may be declared with any number of dimensions. For example

int aaa[2][3][4]

declares an array of two three by four matrices. **aaa** is an array of arrays of arrays.

- The reference **aaa** is to an array of arrays of arrays.
- The reference **aaa[1]** is to an array of arrays.
- The reference **aaa[1][1]** is to an array of integers.
- Finally the reference **aaa[1][1][2]** is to an integer.

Figure 6.5 gives the layout of **aaa** in memory. It is assumed to contain the values **0 ... 23**.

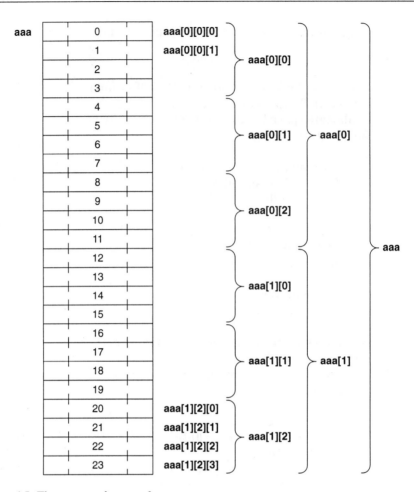

Figure 6.5 *The memory layout of aaa*

6.19 Files

In the previous sections we have looked at how data structures are declared and used. In all cases the data structures exist only while the program is running. The telephone directory program will be executed whenever a telephone number is needed. On termination all the data held in program variables is lost, including the directory held in **telephone_directory**. Therefore at the start of each execution the data in this array must be established. There are two ways of doing this.

We can initialise the array **telephone_directory** on declaration as in

> **struct directory_entry telephone_directory[1000] =**
> **{{"Adams E",1937},**
> **{"Anderson K",8212},**
>
> .
> .
> .
>
> **};**

given that the type name **directory_entry** is introduced by

struct directory_entry{char ∗ name; int number;};

This approach has efficiency benefits but it is inflexible. Where data do not change it works well. Telephone directories do change. Employees leave or new employees join the company. With data that is likely to change it is better to separate the data from the program.

A second approach then is to read the directory into the array **telephone_directory** at the start of the program's execution. Making the program and the directory separate means that we can use different directories with the same program and changing directories becomes easier. We need to hold the directory as a file on either a hard or a floppy disk in order to do this. As a result our directory will exist between executions of programs that makes use of it and entries can be added to or removed from the directory by making modifications to the file. Indeed if we need several different directories this can be achieved simply by creating several different files.

6.20 Files and streams

We have seen in Chapter 1 that files are named collections of data maintained by the operating system. Through the use of C library functions we can create and access files.

We need to be aware of the two ways in which a file is identified

- as a named object within a directory of the file store
- as an object being accessed from an executing program.

The way in which files in the file store are named varies from operating system to operating system. However such names can always be represented as C strings. Recall that files are accessed from C programs via streams. A file is linked to a stream using the library function **fopen**. This function takes two arguments, the first being the operating system file name and the second giving information on how the file is to be accessed. It returns as a result a pointer value which identifies the steam linked to the file. Access to the file is then made using this pointer. The pointer is to a structured object of type FILE which is used to control access to the file. Type FILE is declared in **stdio.h** which should always be included if files are to be accessed.

Both C and the operating system UNIX were developed together and there is a close link between the two. The UNIX operating system provides access to files through file descriptors. It also provides what are called UNIX **system calls** which provide operations at the operating system level similar to those provided by the C library. A UNIX **open** will create a file descriptor for a file and UNIX provides input and output via these descriptors.

The management of files takes place at two levels. As far as the C programmer is concerned he will almost always open and access files using the standard C library. These library functions however call on operating system functions to achieve their effect.

Whatever operating system is used to support an implementation of C, the two levels of file access, operating system and standard library, will exist. It is almost always the case that C programs can directly access operating system functions. For example, C programmers using UNIX can access files either using streams and the standard library functions or they can use the UNIX system calls to open files and access them using file descriptors. That is they can deal with files at either level.

Unless there are very good reasons otherwise the C library should always be used. The chances are that a program that only uses the standard library can more easily be moved from system to system.

We have seen that when a C program is executed a number of streams are set up automatically. These include the stream linked to the keyboard (**stdin**) and the stream linked to the screen (**stdout**). Whenever **scanf** and **getchar** are used the stream **stdin** is assumed and with **printf stdout** is assumed.

There are a large number of library functions which may be used to access files linked to streams using **fopen**. The three that we shall use here allow us to treat files as streams of characters. Reading from a file is similar to reading from the keyboard and writing to a file is similar to writing to the screen. The functions are **fprintf**, **fgetc** and **fscanf** and take the same sort of arguments as **printf**, **getchar** and **scanf**, except that there is an extra argument giving the stream to be associated with the input or output. The steam is given as the first argument.

The call

fprintf(ints," %d",100);

for example writes out the value **100** as a sequence of digits to the file opened on the stream **ints**.

There is no real difference between the streams **stdin** and **stdout** set up automatically and streams created by the programmer using **fopen**. The functions **printf** and **scanf** can always be replaced by calls to **fprintf** and **fscanf**, where the streams **stdin** and **stdout** are given explicitly and are provided in the library for convenience.

The call

fprintf(stdout," %d",100);

has exactly the same effect as

printf(" %d",100);

In particular the call

ch = getchar();

is equivalent to

ch = fgetc(stdin);

The operating system is responsible for checking that the named file actually exists and can be accessed from the requesting program. It also carries out the actual input and output on behalf of the executing program. Functions such as **printf**, **scanf**, **fprintf**, **fscanf** and **fopen** will call on the operation system to carry out the operations associated with these functions. Where the operating system cannot carry out the specified operation the library function will return as its result something that indicates that an error has occurred. For example if **fopen** successfully opens a file it returns the stream that the file has been opened on. If it fails to for example because the file does not exist it returns the null pointer.

Files may be accessed in several ways. **fopen** allows six different types of access to be specified, of which three are of interest as far as the file containing our telephone directory is concerned. These are read access (**"r"**) in which case only input operations are allowed from an existing file; write access (**"w"**) where only output operations are allowed on a new file or which overwrites an existing file; and append access (**"a"**) where the file is open for output in such a way that the file is extended.

The function **fgetc** reads single characters. The function **fscanf** reads sequences of characters as directed by the given format string. In either case characters are read from the file in order and there may come a point where there are no more characters to read. A further attempt to read causes an **end of file** signal to be generated. Both functions return integer results. If an attempt is made to read beyond the end of the file the end of file signal manifests itself as a system dependent integer result. Because it is system dependent it is defined under the name EOF in **stdio.h**.

Note that the result from **fgetc** is normally a character. Since characters are actually small integers in C there is no inconsistency here. Because **fscanf** may input into a number of variables and each input may consume a number of characters the end of file may be encountered after **fscanf** has successfully completed some but not all the input requests. EOF is only returned if **fscanf** found the file exhausted on the very first input. Otherwise it returns a count of the number of successful inputs.

Note that an attempt to input a value may fail for a number of reasons. For example integer input may be specified in the format string but the characters to be read in next from the file may be letters. The value returned from **fscanf** gives the number of successful inputs. It is perfectly possible that in a call to **fscanf** all the inputs fail yet the file is not exhausted. In this case **fscanf** returns **0**.

To illustrate the use of files we will develop two simple programs the first of which allows us to create a file of integers with the second reading the file summing its contents.

6.21 Creating a file of integers

fopen takes as its first argument the name by which the file is known within the file store with the second giving the type of access required. Both arguments should be strings and are thus of type pointer to char. If the file name is always the same then it can be given as a string constant. The access mode will almost always be specified as a string constant. If the file is called **numbers** and **ints** is a variable of type pointer to FILE then

    ints=fopen("numbers","a");

will open the file **numbers** so that values can be added to the end of the file. **"a"** specifies this access mode which is called **append** mode. If the file 'numbers' does not exist then a new file will be created with that name.

Using the string constant "numbers" in **fopen** works but limits the program to a single file. The arguments to **fopen** are both of type pointer to **char** so any expression that evaluates to a pointer to **char** value can be used for either argument.

In particular if a file name is read in by the program and placed in a **char** array as a string this array could be used as an argument. For example if **file_name** holds the name of a file then

ints = fopen(file_name,"a");

would open that file.

In reading in a file name we will use the directive **%s** which reads in a line of text from the keyboard as a string as in

scanf("%s",file_name);

The program will read numbers from the keyboard and place them in the opened file. Because the access mode is **append** if the file already exists it will be extended and if not a new file with the given name will be used.

The input of numbers must be terminated in some way. We will assume that the file name and numbers are all typed in on separate lines with the last line of input being the character '*'.

Thus for the input

> **numbers**
> **1234**
> **5678**
>   *

the program would place the numbers **1234** and **5678** at the end of the file 'numbers'. If **printf** is used to output two successive numbers as in

printf("%d%d",1234,5678);

these will be output without any separating spacing. If we want such spacing this needs to be specified in the format string. To ensure that they are separated we would need something like

printf("%d %d",1234,5678);

The same is true for **fprintf**. To ensure that the numbers are separated in the file created by the program it should explicitly output separating spaces. If this is not done the file will appear to hold a single very large number and it is then impossible to identify the numbers that have been used to create the file.

Since each line apart from the first and last is assumed to start with a digit, the end of input is recognised by the occurrance of the character '*'. To check for this the first character of each line has to be read. We are going to read integers using the format control '%d', so the digit needs to be made available again using **ungetc**.

The call

ungetc(ch = getchar(),stdin);

will return to **stdin** the value obtained by the call **getchar**. This value is also asigned to **ch.**

The expression

ch = getchar()

causes a value to be placed in **ch** and has as its result that value. Two things happen when the expression is evaluated. An assignment is carried out and a result is generated.

The first argument to **ungetc** is an expression involving assignment. This both updates the variable **ch** and also provides a value to be returned to **stdin**.

The call to **ungetc** is equivalent to

```
ch = getchar();
ungetc(ch,stdin);
```

Expressions involving the assignment operator normally appear as statements as in

```
ch = getchar();
```

with the effect that the assignment is carried out but the result of the expression is discarded. It is sometimes useful to make use of the value associated with an assignment as we do here.

The term **side effect** is often used to describe a secondary effect of an operation. The primary effect of the first expression in the call to **ungetc** is to provide an argument value. Its secondary effect is to assign that value to the variable **ch**. (The assignment is carried out first however.) Assignment as a side effect is used widely in C programs. The use of side effects is viewed by many as poor programming practice. Certainly where a side effect is hidden within the body of a function the program is more difficult to analyse and such side effects should be avoided. For example if a variable is declared at the top level it can be modified by any function within its scope. A function with some primary role may as a side effect also change the value of that variable. If there is no relationship between the primary purpose of the function and the variable then such a change would indeed be an example of poor practice. Sometimes such side effects are useful and in fact many of the input/output library functions make use of them. They are however best avoided. The type of side effect involving assignment seen above is a different matter because it is localised. Very often such assignments appear as function arguments, eliminating the need for a separate assignment statement. Their effect is restricted to a small section of the program in which they appear and because of this there is no hidden effect which might cause confusion. In such situations their use is more a matter of taste than principle.

The main program loop uses **scanf** to read numbers until the character '*' is input. The format string used, `"%d%c"`, takes in a number and the end of line character.

The input value is then output using **fprintf**. The first argument to **fprintf** gives the stream through which output is directed to the file. The second argument is the format string which includes spaces to separate the numbers in the file. The third argument is the value to be output.

Putting all this together we have

```
main()
{
    char file_name[20],ch;int i;
    FILE * ints;
/* Read in the file name for the file of integers moving to the next
line of input. */
    scanf("%s%c",file_name,ch);
/* Open it for appending. */
```

```
        ints = fopen(file_name,"a");
/* get and unget the first character on the line */
        ungetc(ch = getchar(),stdin);
/* read and output numbers until an '*' is encountered */
        while (ch != '*')
        {
            scanf("%d%c",&i,&ch);
/* Output the number followed by a space */
            fprintf(ints,"%d ",i);
            ungetc(ch = getchar(),stdin);
        }
}
```

6.23 Accessing a file of integers

The following program demonstrates how a file of integers may be read. As with the earlier program the name of the file is input. This name is then used in a call to **fopen**. An existing file is to be read so the access mode given in the call is **"r"**.

In the program an integer and a character are read in by **fscanf**. Because the program which creates files of integers always outputs an integer followed by a space, each call to **fscanf** will either read in two values (and return as its result **2**) or, where the file is exhausted, will fail to find any and return **EOF**.

In the program the result from **fscanf** is used directly as a condition for the while statement. Again a primary and a secondary effect can be observed. The primary effect is that the result returned from **fscanf** is used to control the execution of the loop. The secondary (side) effect is that input takes place.

```
    main()
    {
        FILE * ints;char file_name[21],ch;int i,tot = 0;
        scanf("%s%c",file_name);
        ints = fopen(file_name,"r");
        while(fscanf(ints,"%d%c",&i,&ch) != EOF) tot += i;
        printf("sum of file values = %d",tot);
    }
```

We have looked at almost all the features of C that support the creation and manipulation of data structures. These will all be employed in one way or another in writing the telephone directory management system which we will do in the next chapter.

Exercises

1. Construct a program that reads **10** integers into an array. The array should then be reordered to ensure that the largest integer is in the first element of the array.

2. Construct a program that reads **10** integers into an array. It should then reorder the array so that the largest integer is in the first element, the next largest in the second and so forth. Equal integers will appear in adjacent elements.

3. A fares table is to be constructed for a bus route which has **30** stops and for which the route itself is divided up into **8** fare zones. Assuming the stops are numbered **0 . . 29** the fares table is to indexed by the two stop numbers between which the fare is required. Thus for a fare between stop **i** and stop **j** , **i** and **j** would be used as an index into the table. The fare a passenger pays is given by **10 * (b + 1)** where **b** is the number of zone boundaries that the passenger crosses on his journey. Because stops are not evenly distributed along the route and because fare zones are intended to be of approximately equal distances, different fare zones may contain different numbers of stops. A program should be constructed that generates a suitable fares table. The program should take as input the size in terms of the number of stops in each of the eight fare zones.

4. Construct a program that will read in an **n** by **n** matrix **M** and output a matrix derived from **M** by swapping corresponding elements about the diagonal M_{11}, M_{22}, ... M_{nn}.

5. Given two matrices **A** and **B,** the first consisting of **p** rows and **n** columns with the second of **n** rows and **r** columns, a third matrix **C** with **p** rows and **r** columns can be formed by taking their product. The value in the ith row and j^{th} column of **C** is given by the sum

$$C_{ij} = \sum_{k=1}^{k=n} A_{ik} * B_{kj}$$

construct a program which will read in the matrices **A** and **B** and output **C**.

6. Devise a structure suitable for representing fractions. Write functions which add, subtract, multiply and divide fractions and that ensure that the resultant fraction is expressed in its simplest form.

7. Construct a program which will create a file of decimal numbers. Assume that the decimal numbers are input at the keyboard.

8. At first sight constant expressions other than simple integer constants would appear to be of little use. There is no point in expressing an array size for example as an expression involving integer constants and arithmetic operators.
    The declaration

    float ages[23 + 37];

    although allowable, would be better written

    float ages[60];

    However C allows names to be associated with constant values using **#define** For example suppose the array **ages** is used to hold the ages of employees within a company and that there were 23 female employees and 37 male employees.
    The definitions

    #define NUMBER_OF_FEMALES   23
    #define NUMBER_OF_MALES   37

associate the name **NUMBER_OR_FEMALES** with the number **23** and the name **NUMBER_OF_MALES** with the number **37**.

There are two reasons why **#define** is useful.

First we can give meaningful names to constant values and in doing so make our programs more readable. If the number **23** appears in a program its significance has to be determined from context. If **NUMBER_OF_FEMALES** is used instead then there is no doubt.

Second the program is easier to modify. A program may make use of the count of the number of males and females in several places. If integer constants are used, then if these counts change each occurrence of the integer constants will need to be changed. If the constants are defined and the defined name used then only the definition needs to change.

As with **#include**, **#define** must start at the start of a line. Provided that nothing else appears on the line **#define**'s can appear anywhere within a **.c** or **.h** file. After their definition any use of a defined name is replaced by whatever constant is associated with that name.

Here we are following the common practice of using upper case names in making definitions.

The array declaration

float ages[NUMBER_OF_MALES+NUMBER_OF_FEMALES]

declares an array of **60** elements because the constant expression giving the array size evaluates to **60**.

Extend the expression evaluator developed in Chapter 4 to allow the use of defines. It should accept a sequence of lines with each line taking the form

#define <identifier> <constant_expression>

apart from the last. The last line gives the expression to be evaluated. Thus for example

```
#define NUMBER_OF_CHILDREN    25
#define NUMBER_OF_ADULTS  14
#define ADULT_FARE        180
NUMBER_OF_ADULTS * ADULT_FARE +
NUMBER_OF_CHILDREN * ADULT_FARE/2
```

should give a value **4770**.

Allow expressions used to bind names with values to make use of names that have already been introduced. Thus for example

```
#define C   25
#define A   14
#define S   75
#define P   S – (C + A)
```

should bind the value 36 to P

7

A telephone directory management system

The system developed here is intended to provide a way of obtaining employee telephone numbers by giving their names. However, for the system to be of use we need to be able to update the telephone directory as personnel changes occur. At the program level these two operations will have much in common. For example, both will make use of the directory itself. In designing the system such commonality should be identified and made use of, leading to a system made up of some components that are specific to an operation and others which are shared by several different operations. Looking up a telephone number and deleting an entry from the directory require that the directory is loaded into the array set aside for it (which we have called **telephone_directory**) and that the position of a specific entry in the array, identified by an employee name, is located. The code for both loading the directory from file store and locating a specific entry should be used by the two operations.

A software system can usually be organised in many different ways. Here for example we could write a single program which both interrogated and updated the directory. It would require the user to select which operation was needed. An alternative would be to write separate programs for each of these tasks. This is very much a 'packaging issue'. In carrying out the system design we will identify a number of modules that will be implemented as **.c** files. We can then use these files to build a single program or build separate programs for each task. Here we will construct two separate programs, the first supporting telephone number **look up** and the second providing for directory modification. The modifications will be either the **addition** of entries to the directory or their **deletion**.

We will assume that names appear in the directory only once, although telephones may be shared. Such properties of the directory would normally be given as part of the specification of the system.

We will also assume that a directory name must be supplied by the user of the system. That is the name is not hard wired into the program. This allows for more than one directory but means extra work on the part of any user of the system since he has to type in this directory name.

7.1 Directory lookup

The directory lookup program will first load a specified directory into **telephone_directory** and then look up and display the number of a specified employee. Figure 7.1 gives the module chart for the **Look up** program. The main module **Look up** makes use of the two subordinate modules **Load Directory** and **Look up Number**. The first of these reads the name of the file containing the directory from the keyboard, opens the file containing the directory and reads its contents into the array **telephone_directory**.

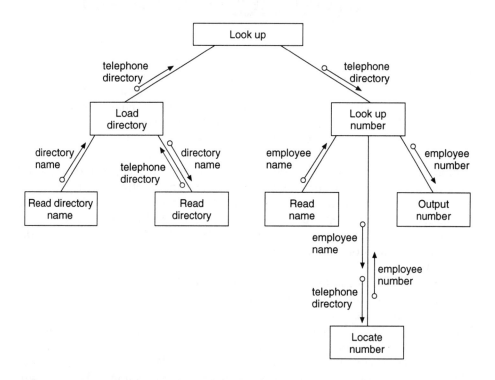

Figure 7.1 *The telephone number look up module chart*

The module **Load Directory** also has two subordinate modules, namely **Read Directory Name** and **Read Directory**. The first of these reads the directory name from the keyboard which the second then reads into memory.

The module **Look up Number** has three subordinate modules, **Read Name** which obtains the employee name from the keyboard The second module,**Locate Number**, locates the number and the third, **Output Number**, outputs it.

We need to decide the form that input and output take. Again this would be made explicit in the specification. We will adopt a line oriented approach in that each piece of data input to the program from the keyboard will be on a separate line. The directory name will be input on a separate line as will the employee name. (For the directory modification program, where the directory is being extended, employee names and employee numbers will also be input on separate lines.)

7.2 Directory update

Figure 7.2a gives the module chart for the **Update** program. The module **Update Directory** has two subordinate modules. The first of these, **Read Operation,** determines the type of update and the second, **Apply operation** , carries out the update. There are two modules subordinate to **Apply operation**, the first of which handles additions to the specified directory with the second deleting entries.

Add Entries first reads the name of the directory to be extended and then reads a sequence of names and numbers from the keyboard, adding them to the directory. The design assumes that the entries are added to the end of the file containing the directory and that this can be done directly using open append.

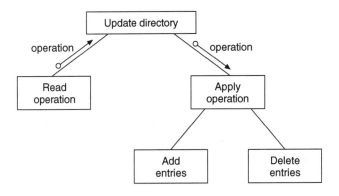

Figure 7.2a *Directory update*

Delete Entries first reads the name of the directory, which it then reads into memory. It then reads a sequence of names, removing the corresponding entries from the directory. Finally it writes the updated directory to a file with the same name as the original file. **Add Entries** takes advantage of the file operations available to the C programmer which allow files to be added to. There is no easy way of deleting sections of a file directly, so the approach adopted for **Delete Entries** is to read the whole file in to memory, find and mark in some way those entries that are to be deleted and finally write out the unmarked entries to a file with the same name as the original file. Effectively the original file is overwritten.

The structure chart for **Update Directory** is given as three separate diagrams simply as a matter of convenience. The first diagram takes the chart to the modules **Read Operation**, **Apply operation**, **Add Entries** and **Delete Entries**. The second and third diagrams develop the last two of these modules.

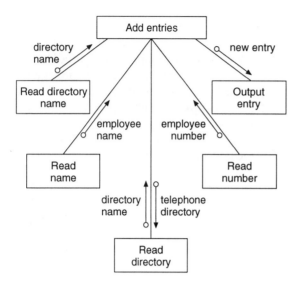

Figure 7.2b Add entries

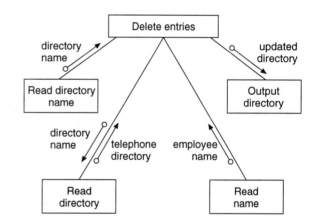

Figure 7.2c Delete entries

7.3 Module implementations

The standard way forward from a structure chart is to construct pseudo code descriptions for each module and develop code from the pseudo code. In practice whether this is done or not is very much application dependent. Where a programming task is complex the programmer gets a better understanding of what he is trying to do by developing a structure chart and pseudo code than would be the case if he went straight from specification to code. He also provides important language independent documentation on the program by doing so.

Documentation can however be overdone. Pseudo code and the program code itself can sometimes be so close that the pseudo code adds little to the overall system description. Its presence can be unnecessary representing pointless effort both in its creation and to anyone studying the program. Whether this is so depends very much on the context in which the program is being developed and the standards by which the programmer is expected to operate. Within a large software house where programmers make use of many different programming languages it is likely that a standard form of pseudo code will be required across all projects. In such an environment pseudo-code should be developed even where the pseudo-code and the program code are very close. If the same programming language is used for all projects the argument for always writing pseudo code is less strong.

Here we will give the code for each module, providing pseudo code descriptions only where the complexity of the corresponding module demands it.

The reader is advised to try out the code given here using the functions described in the following text to build the program for himself.

A second consideration when making use of a structure chart is to do with the relationship between chart and code. There should of course be a correspondence between the two. Variables and functions that correspond to data couples and modules in the chart should have the same or similar names. One way of ensuring such a correspondence is to implement each module as a separate collection of functions and variables in separate .c files. There is a danger in this approach that we end up with an unnecessarily large number of .c and .h files. This number can be reduced by placing subordinate modules in the same file as their superordinate module. For example, each of the charts in Figures 7.2a, 7.2b and 7.2c could be placed in different .c files with appropriate .h files provided as interfaces. How a structure chart is mapped onto .c files is very much a matter of judgement and again is influenced by the context in which the program is being developed. Both implementation and maintenance considerations will influence the choice.

We will present an implementation of **Look up** which maps each chart module onto a function and each data couple onto a variable. We will then modify the implementation to produce a more efficient program. We will end up with a program that preserves the correspondence between structure chart and code but one where this correspondence is less obvious.

Structure charts do not always say everything about a design. The telephone system will need to read lines of text both from the keyboard and from file store. A single function, **read_line**, will be written to do this job. This function will take as an argument the stream it should use to read the line. In the structure chart for **Lookup** all of the modules **Read Dir Name**, **Read Directory** and **Read Name** will make use of this function but this is not shown in the chart. A judgement has always to be made about what should be left to the implementor. Should we have extended the chart? For example, should the module **Read Dir Name** have a subordinate module as in Figure 7.3.

We want to express the design as clearly as possible through structure charts. Too much detail can cloud it.

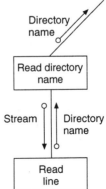

Figure 7.3 Extending the structure chart

7.4 Look up

The module **Look up** is implemented as the function

```
void look_up()
{
    struct directory_entry * telephone_directory = load_directory();
    look_up_number(telephone_directory);
}
```

This makes use of the functions **load_directory** and **look_up_number,** which are implementations for the two modules **Load Directory** and **Look up Number**. The structure chart data couple **Telephone Directory** corresponds to the pointer variable **telephone_directory**.

The function **load_directory** obtains the name of the directory to be used and then loads it into an array using **read_directory**. The array is declared as **static** within **read_directory** to ensure that it is preserved on exit from **read_directory**. C does not allow functions to return complete arrays as results. We cannot therefore conveniently model the data couple (the interface between **Look up** and **Load Directory**) directly as an array. Making the array local to **load_directory** and static allows us to model the data couple as a pointer which we can return as **load_directory**'s result.

We saw in the last chapter that an array declaration introduced a pointer constant along with the space needed for the array elements and that we could treat pointer variables as if they were arrays, provided that they held sensible values. The array used to hold the directory will consist of elements described by the structure

```
struct {char * name; int number;} directory_entry;
```

The declaration

```
struct directory_entry * telephone_directory = load_directory();
```

in **look_up** introduces a pointer variable which can be used to address values of type **directory_entry** or arrays of such values. It is initialised to the result returned from **load_directory**. **load_directory** returns the array pointer it obtains from **read_directory** and is defined as

```
struct directory_entry * load_directory()
{
    char * directory_name = read_dir_name();
    return read_directory(directory_name);
}
```

which again faithfully reflects the structure chart itself.

The function **read_dir_name** requests and reads in the name of the file containing the directory. This name will be read into a character array and a pointer to that array returned from **read_dir_name**. It is defined as

```
char * read_dir_name()
{
    printf("input directory name\n");
```

```
        return read_line(stdin);
    }
```

read_line reads a line of text via the stream specified in the argument. A character array declared as static within **read_line** is used to hold the line read in and a pointer to this array is returned as the function's result. A description of **read_line** is left until later.

read_directory takes as its argument the file name read in by **read_dir_name**. It opens and reads this file into an array, returning a pointer to the array. The array is actually declared within this function. **look_up** makes use of the array – it passes it to **look_up_number**. It is made available to **look_up** by a pointer value returned to it from **read_directory** via **load_directory**.

Algorithmically, **read_directory** can be described as follows

> **attempt to open the argument file name for input;**
> **if the open fails**
> > **output an error message;**
>
> **else**
> > **while there are lines in the file**
> > > **read employee names and telephone numbers and store them**
> > > > **in successive elements of the array telephone_directory;**
> >
> > **mark the next unused element of telephone_directory;**
> > **return a pointer to telephone_directory;**

The corresponding C function is

```
struct directory_entry * read_directory(char * directory_name)
{
    char ch, * line; int next = 0;
    static struct directory_entry telephone_directory[1000];
/* Open the file directory_name for input */
    FILE * directory = fopen(directory_name,"r");
    if (!directory)
        printf("open failure\n");
    else
/* read all the file entries */
        while(line = read_line(directory))
        {
/* allocate enough space for the line using malloc assigning the pointer value
returned from malloc to telephone_directory and copying the line to this
space using strcpy */
            telephone_directory[next].name = malloc(sizeof(char) * (strlen(line) + 1));
            strcpy(telephone_directory[next].name,line);
            fscanf(directory," %d%c",&(telephone_directory[next ++ ].number),&ch);
        }
    telephone_directory[next].name = 0;
    return telephone_directory;
}
```

There are a number of reasons why an open might fail. The most likely is that no file with the argument name can be found, either because the file does not exist or it is not in the directory **fopen** has searched. We have already noted that **fopen** returns a null pointer (**0**) on open failure. We can therefore use the result from **fopen** as a condition to determine if an open failure has occurred. A null pointer value as a condition is treated as false (since it is **0**), with any other value treated as true.

The operator **!** is used for negation. If **directory** is assigned the null pointer value, as a condition its value will be interpreted as false, with **!directory** interpreted as true.

The while statement makes use of the function **read_line** to read lines of text via the stream **directory**. This function is developed in Section 7.5. It is written in such a way that it can read input typed in from the keyboard and from file store. Its argument determines the source of the input.

Both the update operations on the directory involving the addition or removal of entries will take as input from the keyboard a sequence of lines. For example, to delete three names from the directory the names are input on three separate lines. We need a way of indicating that there are no further lines of input. An empty line (consisting only of the end of line character) is used for this. **read_line** reads names in for both operations and needs to take this into account.

The directory itself is held in a file as lines of text and **read_line** is used to read the employee names from the file. Here the end of input is indicated by the occurance of the EOF value.

read_line is written so that it returns a null pointer if it encounters either an empty line or EOF. Since **read_directory** is reading a file in file store the while statement should terminate on EOF. The value returned from **read_line**, as a condition, will be 0 only when EOF is encountered so we can use it as a condition in the while statement.

In the last chapter we saw how assignments could be used as values. If we make the while condition an assignment we can use its value to control the loop and take advantage of its side effect (the assignment itself) in the body of the while statement.

Each element of the array **telephone_directory** is made up of a character pointer and an integer. We need to find space for each name read in, copy the name into that space as a string and set a pointer to the string in **telephone_directory**. The first two lines of the body of the while statement use **malloc** and **strcpy** to do this, with the last line reading in the associated telephone number.

Notice that the format string for the call to **fscanf** includes **%c**. This ensures that the end of line character following the digits that make up the telephone number is read.

The entries read in should not completely fill **telephone_directory**. The size of the array is chosen to be just larger than the largest directory the system is likely to be requested to load. (Although this is not included in **read_directory** a check should be made that the directory being read in is not too large. This is left as an exercise.) So that only valid entries are examined when the array is searched the element immediately following the last valid entry is marked by assigning the null pointer to its character pointer component.

Apart from **get_line**, we have dealt with all the functions needed to implement the module **Load Directory** so we will turn our attention to **Look up Number** which is implemented as

```
void look_up_number(struct directory_entry * telephone_directory)
{
    char * employee_name = read_name();
    int employee_number =
        locate_number(employee_name,telephone_directory);
    output_number(employee_number);
}
```

The function

```
char * read_name()
{
    printf("input employee name\n");
    return read_line(stdin);
}
```

makes use of **read_line** returning as its result the character pointer value obtained from **read_line**.

A line is read via the stream **stdin** and stored as a string by **read_line** with a pointer to the string returned as its result. Since **stdin** is associated with the keyboard this is where the line is read from.

The function

```
int locate_number(char * employee_name,struct directory_entry *
telephone_directory)
{
return telephone_directory
    [find(employee_name,telephone_directory)].number;
}
```

takes as its arguments a pointer to the employee name and a pointer to the telephone directory.

find(employee_name,telephone_directory) locates the position of **employee_name** within the array **telephone_directory,** returning this position as its result. In **locate_number** this value is then used to index **telephone_directory** for the corresponding employee number. Note that the indexing operation on telephone_directory is given above on a separate line.

The function

```
void output_number(int employee_number)
{
    printf("The telephone number is %d\n",employee_number);
}
```

simply outputs the employee's telephone number.

7.5 The function read_line

The nature of **read_line** has been almost fully described already. It will read a line of text from a specified stream, convert it into a string and return a pointer to the string. If **read_line** encounters an empty line or EOF a null pointer is returned.

There is an upper limit, **LINE_SIZE**, on the number of characters in a line and **read_line** outputs an error message if that limit is exceeded.

The behaviour of **read_line** is described algorithmically as follows:

> **read a character from the argument stream;**
> **if at end of line or end of file return the null pointer;**
> **while not at end of line**
> > **if the number of characters read is less than LINE_SIZE**
> > **{**
> > > **add the last character read in to the input line;**
> > > **read a character from the argument stream;**
> >
> > **}**
> > **else**
> > **{**
> > > **output an error message to the screen;**
> > > **return the null pointer;**
> >
> > **}**
>
> **make the character sequence a string;**
> **return a pointer to the string;**

We need space to store the line and this will be declared within **read_line** as a **static** array **line**. Because it is declared as **static** its contents are preserved between calls to **read_line**. The string read into this array must of course be dealt with before a further call to **read_line** is made.

The C code corresponding to the above algorithm is

```
/*  read_line reads a line of characters from stream.
    If the line is non-empty the line is read into LINE
    and made a string by the addition of the string terminator.
    A pointer to LINE is returned as the function's result.
    If an empty line or EOF is encountered the null pointer is
    returned. If more characters than LINE_LENGTH appear on
    the line an error message is output with the null pointer
    returned.
*/
char * read_line(FILE * stream)
{
    int i = 0;
    int ch = fgetc(stream);
    static char line[LINE_SIZE];
    if (ch == '\n' || ch == EOF ) return 0;
    while (ch != '\n')
    {
        if (i < LINE_SIZE)
        {
            line[i ++ ]=ch;
            ch=fgetc(stream);
        }
```

```
            else
            {
                    printf("error-line to large\n");
                        return 0;
            }
        }
        line[i] = '\0';
        return line;
    }
```

7.6 The function find

find searches **telephone_directory** for a specific employee name, returning as its result the corresponding telephone number. If the name is not found an error message is output and the value **–1** is returned. Expressed agorithmically we want

> **next = 0;**
> **while telephone_directory[next].name points to a valid name**
> **{**
> > **if the name pointed at by telephone_directory[next].name**
> > **and the argument name are the same return next;**
> > **next ++;**
> **}**
> **output an error message and return – 1**

Two conditions appear in the algorithm.

If **telephone_directory[next].name** does not point to a valid name it will have as its value the null pointer (the value **0**). This **read_directory** ensured. The while condition can therefore be expressed

> **telephone_directory[next].name != 0**

Since a non-zero value is treated as true and the above condition is true when the left hand side of the comparison is non-zero we can use

> **telephone_directory[next].name**

for the while condition.

The function **find** uses the library function **strcmp** to compare the name searched for with successive names in the telephone directory. **strcmp** takes two pointer to **char** arguments which should reference strings and returns an integer result. The two strings are compared for lexicographical ordering. Lexicographical ordering is similar to the ordering found in most dictionaries except of course C strings may contain characters other than letters. It is governed by the character codes (ASCII on most systems) that are used to represent the characters that may appear in strings. If the first string precedes the second string lexicographically then a negative value is returned. If the two strings are the same a zero value is returned. Otherwise a positive value is returned.

The call

> **strcmp(name,telephone_directory[next].name)**

will return the value **0** if the two strings match. As with the first condition that appeared in the function **read_directory** the condition

strcmp(name,telephone_directory[next].name) == 0

can be written

!strcmp(name,telephone_directory[next].name)

If we implemented the algorithm directly, our code for the while loop would look something like

```
while (telephone_directory[next].name)
{
    if (!strcmp(name,telephone_directory[next].name))
    return next;
    next ++;
}
```

where **next** is initially **0**. By initialising **next** to **–1** and making use of the pre-increment operator we can write the loop more compactly as we have done in the following final form of the function.

```
/* The telephone_directory is searched for the occurrence of name.
   If found its index is returned. If not found an error message
   is output and – 1 is returned.
*/
int find(char * name)
{
    int next = – 1;
    while (telephone_directory[++ next].name)
        if (!strcmp(name,telephone_directory[next].name))
            return next;
    printf("name not in directory");
    return – 1;
}
```

The above implementation of **Look Up** follows the structure chart reasonably faithfully. In practice an implementor may simplify the structure as displayed in the structure chart where it is convenient to do so.

For example our function

```
void look_up()
{
    struct directory_entry * telephone_directory = load_directory();
    look_up_number(telephone_directory);
}
```

simplifies to

```
void look_up()
{
    look_up_number(load_directory());
}
```

by making the call to **load_directory()** the argument to **look_up_number**. The data couple **Telephone Directory** that interfaces **Look Up** with **Load Directory** and **Look up Number** now has no associated variable.

Simplifying

```
void look_up_number(struct directory_entry * telephone_directory)
{
    char * employee_name = read_name();
    int employee_number =
        locate_number(employee_name,telephone_directory);
    output_number(employee_number);
}
```

to

```
void look_up_number(struct directory_entry * telephone_directory)
{
    output_number(locate_number(read_name(),telephone_directory));
}
```

gives a further illustration of how a function can be simplified by the removal of unnecessary variables.

When programs are transformed in this way the relationship between program and structure chart may become less clear although the chances are the code itself is easier to follow.

A second type of simplification involves the merging of modules. A module is implemented as a sequence of statements within the code for its superordinate module rather than as a separate function.

For example if we implement **Look Up** as

```
void look_up()
{
    look_up_number(read_directory(read_dir_name()));
}
```

the module **Load Directory** is not explicitly implemented as a function but corresponds to the argument to **look_up_number**.

Having constructed a structure chart we often find it convenient to make the sort of modifications illustrated above. It should however always be possible to map the structure chart onto the program in some sensible way.

7.7 Update directory

Given the functions **read_operation** and **apply_operation** as implementations of the modules **Read Operation** and **Apply Operation** the module **Update Directory** is implemented as

```
void update_directory()
{
    apply_operation(read_operation());
}
```

The data couple **Operation** corresponds to the function result from **read_operation** and argument to **apply_operation**. **apply_operation** takes a character argument indicating the type of operation to be carried out. This is determined by **read_operation** which returns it as a character result.

apply_operation calls either **add_entries,** or **delete_entries** depending on the value of its character argument and has the form

```
void apply_operation(char operation)
{
    if (operation == 'a') add_entries();
    else delete_entries();
}
```

read_operation determines the type of operation required by the user by requesting it as input. The user will type in a character indicating the operation, followed by an end of line character. Both characters need to be read in. **read_operation** is coded

```
char read_operation()
{
    char op;
    printf("Input 'a' for add operation and 'd' for delete\n");
    op = getchar();
/* Discard end of line character. */
    getchar();
    return op;
}
```

The modules **Add Entries** and **Delete Entries** are implemented as the functions **add_entries** and **delete_entries**. No data couples appear in the structure chart interfacing **Apply Operation** with these modules. Thus the functions take no arguments and return no results.

add_entries is based on the following algorithm.

> **read the name of the file containing the directory, opening it append;**
> **while there are names and telephone numbers to add**
> > **read a name and telephone number from the key board writing**
> > **it out to the end of the file containing the directory;**

add_entries makes use of two functions that have already been described, namely **read_dir_name**, and **read_name**. It makes use of a third function, **read_number** which corresponds to the module **Read Number,** which is described later. Although it would of course be possible to write one there is no function that corresponds to **Output Entry:** the code for this is merged into the code for the **Add Entries**.

For **add_entries** we have

```
void add_entries()
{
    char * name; int new_number;
    FILE * directory;
/* Read in the name of the file and open the file for appending */
```

```
directory = fopen(read_dir_name(),"a");
if (!directory) printf("open failure\n");
else
{
```
/* Read new entries from the keyboard appending then to the directory file */

```
    while( name = read_name())
    {
        fprintf(directory," %s\n",name);
        fprintf(directory," %d\n",read_number());
    }
  }
}
```

Note that entries in the file are line oriented with names and telephone numbers on separate lines.

To complete **add_entries** we write the function **read_number** as

```
int read_number()
{
    int number;char eoln;
    printf("input employee number\n");
    scanf(" %d %c",&number,&eoln);
    return number;
}
```

The function **delete_entries** follows the algorithm

read in the name of the file containing the directory;
read the directory into the array telephone_directory;
while there are entries to delete
{
read the name associated with an entry to be deleted;
locate the element in telephone_directory associated with the
name and mark it deleted;
}
create a file with the same name as the original directory file;
write out all undeleted directory entries to the file;

Reading in the name of a file and loading the directory held there makes use of exactly the same functions employed by **look_up**.The function **find** is used to locate the position of an entry for a given name. An entry in the loaded directory is marked deleted by setting its telephone number to –1. By closing the file containing the directory and re-opening it for output the original file contents can be overwritten.

The code for **delete_entries** is

```
void delete_entries()
{
    char * name, * dir_name, * directory_name = read_dir_name() ;
    int next = 0;
```

```
    struct directory_entry * telephone_directory;
    FILE * directory;
/* Save the name of the directory for later output.
    The file containing the original directory is overwritten. */
    dir_name = malloc(sizeof(char) * (strlen(directory_name) + 1));
    strcpy(dir_name,directory_name);
/* Read in the original directory. */

    telephone_directory = read_directory(directory_name);

/* Read the names of entries to be deleted and locate them marking
    their positions in the directory*/
    while (name = read_name())
        telephone_directory[find(name,telephone_directory)]. number = - 1;

/* Create a new file with the same name with this entries removed */
    fclose(directory);
    directory = fopen(dir_name,"w");
    while (telephone_directory[next].name)
    {
        if (telephone_directory[next].number != - 1)
        {
            fprintf(directory," %s\n",telephone_directory[next].name);
            fprintf(directory," %d\n",telephone_directory [next].number);
        }
        next++;
    }
}
```

7.8 Linked lists

read_directory uses an array to hold the directory. Because C arrays cannot be dynamic some upper limit on the size of a directory has to be incorporated into the program. Since we can allocate memory dynamically using **malloc** we could allocate space for each entry in the directory as we encountered it in the directory file. We would then not need an array at all. We do in fact already allocate some of the memory needed because we use **malloc** to obtain space for the employee names.

Programming such an approach involves quite extensive use of pointers. The type of structure that we need is illustrated in Figure 7.4.

Directory entries hold three values. The first, **name**, is a character pointer to the employee name held as a string. The second, **number**, gives the employee telephone number. The third, **next**, is a pointer to the next entry in the directory. If there is no next entry then this will be null. In Figure 7.4 the last entry is that for **Young S** and its **next** component is null.

Linked lists are important in C programming. They take a little getting used to so we will look at a simpler use of the ideas associated with them first.

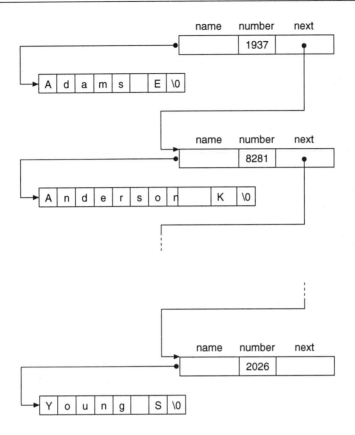

Figure 7.4 *The directory as a linked list*

7.9 A linked list of integers

If we make the declaration

struct int_list{int i; struct int_list ∗ next;};

we introduce a structure type with two component fields, the first holding an **int** value and the second holding a pointer value of type pointer to **struct int_list**. The first component is straightforward to understand. The second can at first sight be a little confusing since it appears to be in some way circular. We are using the type defined by the declaration to describe the type of one of its components! A good way of understanding what is happening is through the following diagrams.

A declaration of the form

struct int_list first_int;

introduces a variable **first_int** which we can represent as in Figure 7.5.

The first component **first_int.i** of **first_int** is an integer, the second, **first_int.next,** is a pointer. The two question marks in the diagram indicate that we do not know the values of the two components.

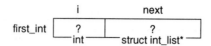

Figure 7.5

With

struct int_list second_int

again we can represent **second_int** as shown in Figure 7.6.

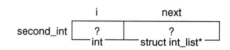

Figure 7.6

The effect of the assignment

first_int.next = &second_int;

can be represented as shown in Figure 7.7.

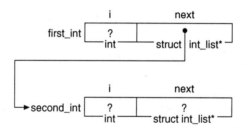

Figure 7.7

first_int.next has been assigned the address of **second_int**. The two variables have been linked together. No other values have changed. If we make the assignments

```
first_int.i    = 10;
second_int.i   = 20;
second_int.next  = 0;
```

the new state of affairs can be represented by the diagram in Figure 7.8.

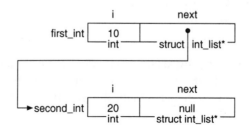

Figure 7 8

The two integer values **10** and **20** are linked together via **first_int.next**, with the null pointer assigned to **second_int.next**. The two variables form a linked list of integers. This can be generalised to any number of variables with each variable linked to the next via its **next** field with the last variable's **next** field assigned the null pointer. In practice such linked lists are constructed using **malloc** to obtain space for each value of type **struct int_list**.

The code sequence

```
struct int_list * linked_list = 0;
int i;
scanf("%d", &i);
while (i >= 0)
{
    struct int_list * temp = linked_list;
    linked_list = malloc(sizeof(struct int_list));
    (* linked_list).i = i;
    (* linked_list).next = temp;
    scanf("%d",&i);
}
```

will read a sequence of non-negative integers from the key board building a linked list of integers using them. The while statement will terminate at the input of a negative value. **linked_list** will end up pointing at a value of type **struct int_list** created for the last non-negative integer input. **malloc** is used to create space for each entry in the linked list. **linked_list** is initialised to null indicating an empty list. Each time an entry is created **linked_list** is set to the address of that entry with the entry's **next** field set to the old value of **linked_list**. The result of taking as input the sequence of integers 9, 8, ... 0, – 1 is illustrated in Figure 7.9.

Note that since **linked_list** points to a value of type **struct int_list**, using indirection (as in * **linked_list**) gives us a value of that type and (* **linked_list**).i and (*linked_list).next give us access to that value's components. This rather clumsy notation can be improved on as we shall see later but the syntax provided by C for the manipulation of pointers is always hard on the eye. What it describes is however straightforward and, with care, expressions involving pointers can be unravelled. Drawing diagrams such as those given above can help.

The linked list created by the above code can be accessed via **linked_list**. For example the list can be input as in

```
while(linked_list)
{
    printf("%d\n",(* linked_list).i);
    linked_list= (* linked_list).next;
}
```

In our telephone directory the original declaration for **entries**

```
struct directory_entry{char * name;  int number;}
```

becomes

```
struct directory_entry{char * name; int number;  struct
directory_entry * next;};
```

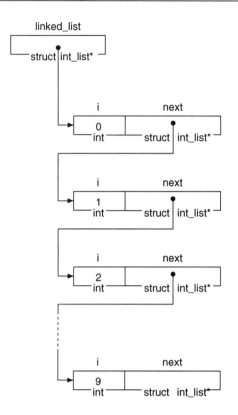

Figure 7.9

A third component has been added which takes pointers to values of type **directory_entry** The values themselves have exactly the structure seen in Figure 7.4.

Adopting this approach means of course that we need to change some of the functions that deal with the directory. We will look at the changes necessary for **Update Directory**, leaving those for **Look Up** as an exercise.

The functions **find**, **read_directory** and **delete_entries** all deal with the directory as an array and so will need to be modified. Before doing this we will introduce some further C notation.

7.10 Structure component selection using –>

We have seen that given a value **d_e** of type **directory_entry** for example we access its components using the selection operator '.'. **d_e.name**, **d_e.number** and **d_e.next** reference each of the components of **d_e**.

If we have a pointer to a structure we can still select components but we first need to de-reference the pointer.

Thus if **d_e_ptr** is of type pointer to **directory_entry** and points at an actual value of that type, we can access its components using (∗ **d_e_ptr).name**, (∗ **d_e_ptr).number** and (∗ **d_e_ptr).next**.

Because the selector operator '.' has a higher precedence than the indirection operator '*' we need the brackets. Without them the selection operator is applied first, which means that *** d_e_ptr.name** attempts to select a component of **d_e_ptr** before the indirection is applied; since **d_e_ptr** is not itself a structured value (although it points to a structured value) the selection would be illegal.

C provides a shorthand for this in the selection operator '->'. The expression **(* d_e_ptr).name** can be written **d_e_ptr->name**. Thus where we see **(* d_e_ptr).name**, **(* d_e_ptr).number** and **(* d_e_ptr).next** we can write **d_e_ptr->name, d_e_ptr->number** and **d_e_ptr->next**.

We also met a third way of doing this. Since array indexing is really a combination of pointer arithmetic with dereferencing, we could achieve the same effect with **d_e_ptr[0].name, d_e_ptr[0].number** and **d_e_ptr[0].next**. It would be unusual to do so.

7.11 The function find

Our original version of **find** took an employee name and the telephone directory as its arguments and returned the name's position in the directory as an index. The arguments to **find** do not change, but the result will be a pointer to the entry for the employee name rather than an array index. For example, using Figure 7.4 if the first argument to **find** is **Anderson K** then a pointer to the entry for **Anderson K** is returned. This is the same value as the value taken by the **next** component of the entry for **Adams E**. We therefore make **find**'s result type **struct directory_entry ***

The structure of **find** is unchanged. The only changes are those to the way components are referenced (using '->') and the way **find** moves through the linked list searching for the required entry. A pointer to the first entry in the linked list is passed to **find** as its second argument. It will move to the second entry using the assignment

>   **telephone_directory = telephone_directory->next;**

As the function iterates, this assignment moves **telephone_directory** through the directory. If the name is not in the directory, **telephone_directory** will eventually be assigned the null pointer value. Since this is zero and zero is treated as false in a condition the loop terminates.

```
struct directory_entry * find(char * name,struct directory_entry *
    telephone_directory)
{
    while (telephone_directory)
    {
        if (!strcmp(name,telephone_directory->name))
            return telephone_directory;
        else telephone_directory=telephone_directory->next;
    }
    printf("name not in directory");
    return 0;
}
```

7.12 The function read_directory

The argument and result types remain unchanged. The name of the file containing the directory is passed as an argument, with a pointer returned as the result. In the original function this pointer addressed an array. Now it must address the first entry in a linked list built by the function.

next is used as an array index. Since we no longer use array indexing it will not be needed in our revised function so we remove its declaration.

In Section 7.9 we saw how a linked list of integers could be built. The first entry in the list turned out to be the last entry created. Ensuring that the first entry is the first entry created is a little more difficult. Given

struct int_list * linked_list;

and   **scanf("%d",&i);**

then the sequence of assignments

linked_list=malloc(sizeof(struct int_list));
(* linked_list).i = i;
(* linked_list).next = 0;

will build a structure something like that in Figure 7.10.

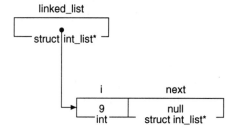

Figure 7.10

To extend this to the structure shown in Figure 7.11 we need to assign the result of a call to **malloc** to the first entry's **next** component and then assign values to the components of the second list entry created in this way.

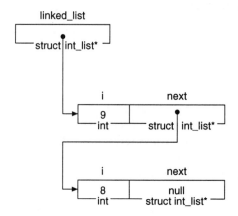

Figure 7.11

This can be done by either by introducing an extra level of indirection or by treating the creation of the first entry as a special case. Here we use double indirection. A variable (**linked_list_ptr**) of type **struct int_list ∗∗** (pointer to pointer to **int_list**) is initially pointed as **linked_list**. All access to structures created in **malloc** is made using **linked_list_ptr**. Each time an entry is created, **linked_list_ptr** is changed so that it points at the **next** component of the most recently created entry.

The way the list develops can be seen in the following sequence of diagrams.

After the declarations

        struct int_list ∗   linked_list=0;
        struct lint_list ∗∗ linked_list_ptr=&linked_list;

we have the structure shown in Figure 7.12.

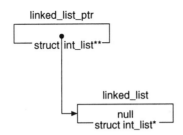

Figure 7.12

After the first list entry hase been constructed **linked_list_ptr** would address the **next** component of this entry as in Figure 7.13.

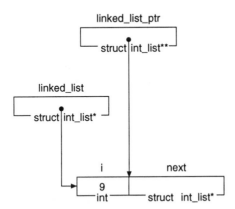

Figure 7.13

Assuming that an integer variable **i** contains the value to be added to the list the assignments

        ∗ linked_list_ptr = malloc(sizeof struct int_list);
        (∗∗ linked_list_ptr).i = i;
        (∗∗ linked_list_ptr).next = 0;
        linked_list_ptr = &((∗∗ linked_list_ptr).next);

These can be written

> *** linked_list_ptr = malloc(sizeof struct int_list);**
> **(* linked_list_ptr) –>i = i;**
> **(* linked_list_ptr)–>next = 0;**
> **linked_list_ptr = &((* linked_list_ptr)–>next);**

using the combined dereference and select operator '–>'. There is little to choose between the two forms.

link_list_ptr points at an object of type **struct int_list ***. The first assignment uses indirection to get at that object and assign to it the pointer value returned from the call to **malloc**.

The second assignment uses double indirection. The first application of '*' gives an object of type **struct int_list ***. The second application uses the value of that object to get an object of type **struct int_list**. The second assignment asigns its **i** component an **int** value with the third assignment assigning the null pointer value to its **next** component. The last assignment uses double dereferencing and component selection to access the **next** component of this entry. The address operator is then used to obtain its address, which is assigned to **linked_list_ptr**.

The same sequence of assignments can be used to extend the list a second time as illustrated by Figure 7.14.

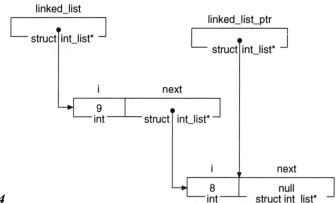

Figure 7.14

The sequence can be used in a while statement similar to that given in Section **7.9** to construct a list of arbitrary length in such a way that **list_ptr** always addresses the first entry created.

Using these ideas to construct our telephone directory, we replace

> **static struct directory_entry telephone_directory[1000];**

by

> **struct directory_entry * telephone_directory, ** t_d;**

On exit from **read_directory, telephone_directory** will point at the first entry in a linked list of telephone entries created by the function. **t_d** is used in much the same way as is **linked_list_ptr** above.

The assignment

t_d = &telephone_directory;

is placed at the start of the function. Its effect is illustrated in Figure 7.15.

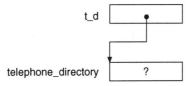

Figure 7.15

The body of the while statement is replaced by

* t_d =malloc(sizeof(struct directory_entry));
(* t_d)–>name = malloc(sizeof(char) * (strlen(line) + 1));
strcpy((* t_d)–>name,line);
fscanf(directory," %d %c",&((*t_d)–>number),&ch);
t_d = &((* t_d)–>next);

The first line uses **malloc** to find space for an entry and sets the address of that space into whatever **t_d** is pointing at.

The second,third and fourth lines are much as in the original while loop except that indirection is used to get at the pointer to the entry's structure ((*** t_d**)) and the pointer form of component selection is then applied.

For the last line (*** t_d)–>next** selects the component **next** and **&((* t_d)–>next)** then generates its address which is assigned to **t_d**.

(*** t_d)–>next** is of type pointer to **directory_entry** and thus **&((* t_d)–>next)** is of type pointer to pointer to **directory_entry** which is what we need for **t_d**.

The state of the variables after the first cycle of the while loop is shown in Figure 7.16, with Figure 7.17 illustrating the state of the variables on the second.

When the file has been read **t_d** points at the **next** component of the last entry. This should be assigned the null value. To ensure this we replace

telephone_directory[next].name = 0;

by ***t_d=0;**

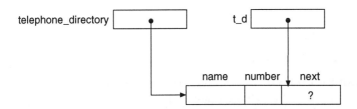

Figure 7.16

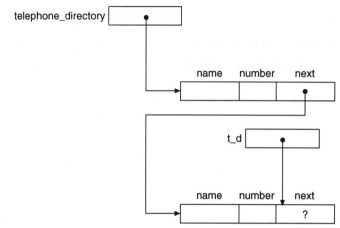

Figure 7.17

Taking all these changes into account, our revised version of **read_directory** looks like:

```
struct directory_entry * read_directory(char * directory_name)
{
    char ch, * line;
    struct directory_entry * telephone_directory, ** t_d;
/* Open the file directory_name for input **/
    FILE * directory=fopen(directory_name,"r");
    t_d=&telephone_directory;

    if (!directory) printf("open failure\n");
    else
/* read all the file entries */
    while(line=read_line(directory))
    {
        * t_d = malloc(sizeof(struct directory_entry));
        (* t_d)->name = malloc(sizeof(char) * (strlen(line) + 1));
        strcpy((* t_d)->name,line);
        fscanf(directory,"%d%c",&((*t_d)->number),&ch);
        t_d = &((*t_d)->next);
    }
    *t_d = 0;
    return telephone_directory;
}
```

7.13 delete_entries

Since indexing is not used, the declaration of the variable **next** is removed. **find** now returns a pointer to the located directory entry, so

telephone_directory[find(name,telephone_directory)].number = – 1;

becomes

> **(∗ find(name,telephone_directory)).number = – 1;**

Our first version of the system had the end of the directory in memory marked by a final entry, with a null valued name component. Here the last entry has a null **next** component set up by **read_directory**. In our second version of **delete_entries** we use the variable **telephone_directory** to point at successive entries as they are written out to file store in the second loop. This is achieved by replacing

> **next ++ ;**

with

> **telephone_directory = telephone_directory–>next;**

Eventually **telephone_directory** will take the null value so the condition

> **telephone_directory[next].name**

in the second loop is replaced by

> **telephone_directory**

The only other changes we need to make are to replace indexing operations such as

> **telephone_directory[next].number**

by **–>** as in

> **telephone_directory–>number**

With these changes to our original version of **delete_entries** we get

```
void delete_entries()
{
        char * dir_name, * directory_name = read_dir_name(), * name;
        struct directory_entry * telephone_directory;
        FILE * directory;
/*      Save the name of the directory for later output.
        The file containing the original directory is overwritten. */
        dir_name = malloc(sizeof(char) * (strlen(directory_name) + 1));
        strcpy(dir_name,directory_name);
/*      Read in the original directory. */

        telephone_directory = read_directory(directory_name);
/*      Read the names of entries to be deleted and locate marking their
        positions in the directory*/
        while (name = read_name())
            (*find(name,telephone_directory)).number = – 1;
/*      Create a new file with the same name with this entries removed */
        fclose(directory);
        directory = fopen(dir_name,"w");
        while (telephone_directory)
            {
```

```
            if (telephone_directory->number != - 1)
            {
                fprintf(directory," %s\n",telephone_directory->name);
                fprintf(directory," %d\n",telephone_directory->number);
            }
            telephone_directory = telephone_directory->next;
        }
    }
```

Exercises

1. The system assumes that each employee is allocated only one number. Add checks to **append_entries** to ensure that a name does not appear twice in the directory.

2. **Look Up** takes an employee name and returns the telephone number allocated to the employee. Given that a new operation **Look Up Name** is required which takes a number and returns the employee name on that number develop both a module structure chart and corresponding code for the operation. Assume that telephones are not shared.

3. Extend your solution to Question 2. above to allow for shared telephones. The look up operation will now return a list of names on a given number.

4. The declaration

    struct linked_list(int i; struct linked_list * next;};

    can be used to create a linked list of integers using **malloc**. Construct functions which sum the integers that appear in a linked list of integers, which write out the integers five to a line and which add new integers to the end of a linked list of integers

5. Section 7.12 described how double indirection could be used in such a way that the list head was the first entry created on the list. Double indirection can be avoided by using two variables which point at the last entry created and the current entry. To do this the creation of the first entry has to be treated differently from the creation of subsquent entries. This differentiation can be made within the while statement that builds the list using an appropriate conditional statement. How can this be done?

6. The declaration

    struct binary_tree{int i; struct binary_tree * left_tree;
    struct binary_tree * right_tree;};

    can be used to build ordered binary trees of integers. An ordered binary tree of integers is a set of nodes with each node holding an integer value **i** and a pointer **left_tree** to a binary tree with integers all less than **i** and a pointer **right_tree** to a binary tree with integers all greater than or equal to **i**.

    Such trees might be depicted graphically, as for example,

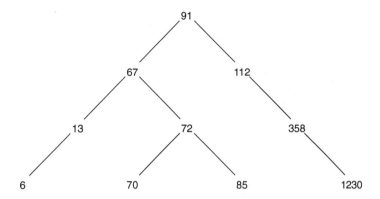

Each node of the tree can be represented by values of type **struct binary_tree** with each value suitably linked through either **left_tree** or **right_tree**. Construct functions that insert an integer into an ordered binary tree and locate the position of a node holding given integer value.

7. In searching a telephone directory for a given name, a sequential search from the start of the directory is made. For large directories this unsatisfactory. A more efficient approach is to ensure that the directory is ordered alphabetically and that looking up an entry entails a binary search.

    The original version of **add_entries** simply adds new entries to the end of the directory file. If the file is alphabetically ordered then this ordering can be preserved by reading the file into memory, adding new entries in positions that take into account order and writing out the modified directory. If the directory is held as an array then it is necessary to find the entry in the array that should immediately follow the new entry, shift down this and later entries to make space for the new entry and copy the new entry into the freed array element. If a linked list is used then updating is easier, since the entry that should immediately follow the new entry can be uncoupled from its predecessor, with the new entry inserted between the the two.

    Modify **add_entries** so that it creates an updated file with alphabetical order preserved.

    In searching for a given name the alphabetical ordering can be taken advantage of by carrying out what is called a binary search. The midpoint of the ordered array is located. If the entry searched for is the midpoint entry then the entry has been found. If not the same process is applied either to the first or the second half of the array. The first half is chosen if the given name is lower in the ordering then that at the midpoint. If it is not the second half of the array is chosen This process is repeated until either the given name is found or it is not possible to divide the array any further in which case the given name does not appear in the directory. Using this strategy, modify **lookup** to take advantage of array ordering.

8. A robust piece of software is one that deals sensibly with invalid input. Identify in what ways the directory software can be given invalid input and add approriate actions to deal with this.

9. A group of students take six examinations and that the set of marks for each examination is stored in a separate file. Draw a structure chart giving the modular structure of a program which locates and displays the mark obtained by a given student in a given examination. The name used to identify an examination and the name of the file containing the marks for that examination are not necessarily the same. Your structure chart should include data couples showing the interface between each module.

A single file is to be created containing all the marks for each student along with his average mark. Draw a structure chart for a program which will create this file of combined marks.

Develop programs from each of your structure charts.

8

An assembler case study in C

In this chapter we will examine how to construct an **assembler** for a simple **assembler language**. Although C is appropriate for a wide range of programming tasks, the main application area that its designers had in mind was that of **systems programming**. Systems programs are those programs such as compilers and operating systems that sit between the machine and the user hiding much of the hardware detail that the user would otherwise have to contend with. They form an integral part of the computer system. In Chapter 1 we looked briefly at hardware concentrating on main memory but also touching on the role of machine code. Computer processors execute machine code programs and programs written in high level languages such as C first have to be compiled into equivalent machine code programs before they can be executed. It is sometimes (though rarely) necessary to write in machine code. For example if very compact code is required this is sometimes more easily achieved using machine code rather than a high level language such as C. Again if speed of execution is critical the use of machine code may be justified. A given processor will normally have associated with it an assembler language which will correspond closely to the machine code for that processor but will be a little easier to use than machine code itself. For example mnemonics for machine instructions are provided in the language and labels can be used to label instructions and areas of memory used to hold data values. This assembler language is used to write machine code programs. It allows the programmer to write such programs without him having to know the bit patterns for each instruction or how instruction operands are held in memory. Assembler programs are translated by a program called an assembler into machine code instructions.

Assemblers tend to be rather large, complex programs, partly because of the complexity of the machines that they are designed to generate machine code for and partly because of the range of facilities they provide. We will keep things as simple as possible, first by keeping the machine language simple and second by providing only a small number of the features normally found in an assembler.

The instruction set of a simple machine is described first. Much of the detail found in real machines has been discarded. However the essential characteristics of such machines have been retained. In describing the machine, the assembler language will be introduced with examples of assembler instructions and programs.

The primary task of the software described here is to take programs written in assembler language and convert them into machine code programs. Since there is no hardware to run our machine programs on, a program which behaves like the hardware of our simple machine will also be provided This steps through the machine code instructions of a machine code program, carrying out the actions associated with each instruction. Such programs are called **interpreters**.

The overall structure of the assembler/interpreter will be described using module structure charts. This is followed by descriptions of the various functions and data structures developed for each module.

Appendix **2** gives a listing of the final program. This chapter contains a considerable amount of detail both on the target machine that code is assembled to and the structure of the assembler/interpreter itself. This may seem daunting on first reading but the effort needed to get to grips with the material will yield dividends.

8.1 The target machine

The main features of our machine are

- **32** bit words
- **8 32** bit general purpose registers **R0** ... **R7**
- **5** address modes
- **15** machine instructions of which **7** are to do with branching and **2** are for input and output.
- a stack for sub-routine entry and exit
- unsigned integer arithmetic
- a two bit register condition code register **CC** which is used to hold the result of a comparison.

Each separately addressable memory word is **32** bits in size (rather than the more common **8** bit size), with an address range from **0** to **65535**. The word size has been chosen to allow **32** bit instructions to be used in a straightforward way. The only types of value recognised by the machine are instructions, addresses and unsigned numbers held in **32** bit words.

The **8 32** bit registers may be used either to address memory or to hold numbers on which arithmetic operations are carried out.

Each instruction takes either **0**, **1** or **2** operands. For example the **MOVE** instruction takes two operands. The first indicates a source value and the second indicates a memory location that that value is to be moved to. We will use this to illustrate the five address modes supported by the machine.

Each operand takes one of five possible address modes. The address mode taken by an operand determines how the hardware will deal with the operand. For example, the operand may be an address of an area of memory or it may be a literal value. The five address modes are **absolute, literal, register, indirect** and **indirect with offset**.

Absolute addresses are actual addresses such as **1024, 0, 65535** etc. Because using numbers for absolute addresses is inconvenient all assemblers allow the programmer to **label** memory locations with identifiers. Where these labels are used, the assembler will substitute the corresponding memory address. Without them the programmer would have to keep track of the addresses of instructions and any locations used to hold numeric values. Labels are used both to label locations which hold instructions and locations set aside for numeric values.

Literals are used where values rather than addresses or their contents need to be given as an operand.

If **1024** appears as an operand in an instruction it is treated as an absolute address. It refers to a memory location. The instruction may either change or use the value at that location in some way. If we need the value **1024** itself as an operand we use literal address mode which is indicated by preceding **1024** by a '#'.

Registers are used in a similar way to addresses. We can change or use their contents. The names **R0,R1, . . R7** are set aside to refer to registers (address mode **register**).

Both **indirect** and **indirect with offset** make use of registers. For **indirect** a register appears as an operand and its contents are treated as an address. Either the address or the value at that address will then be used in the instruction. To indicate that a register is being used in this way it is enclosed in brackets. If **indirect with offset** is used, the offset (either a label or an absolute address) precedes the indirect reference. Here the address used by the instruction is obtained by adding together the offset and the contents of the specified register.

Given that **TABLE** labels a location in memory. the following illustrate these address modes.

(a) **MOVE 1024,R0** – move the value at location **1024** into register **R0**.

The first operand,**1024,** has address mode **absolute** with the second, **R0**, having address mode **register**.

(b) **MOVE #1024,R0** – move the value **1024** into register **R0**.

The first operand,**#1024,** has address mode **literal** with the second, **R0**, having address mode **register**.

(c) **MOVE (R0),R1** – move the value at the address held in **R0** into **R1**.

The first operand,**(R0)**, has address mode **indirect** with the second**R1**, having address mode **register**.

(d) **MOVE TABLE(R0),R1** – move the value at the address obtained by adding together the address associated with **TABLE** and the contents of **R0** to **R1**.

The first operand, **TABLE(R0)**, has address mode **indirect with offset** with the second, **R1**, having address mode **register**.

(e) **MOVE R3,TABLE** – move the value in **R3** to the address associated with **TABLE**.

The first operand,**R3**, has address mode **register** with the second, **TABLE**, having address mode **absolute**.

Note that in the above examples one of the operands always has address mode **register**. This is true for all two operand instructions. It is a constraint typical of most processor instruction sets and is included here because of that. A memory address requires at least **16** bits to code. If both operands could take any address mode then at least **32** bits would be needed just for operand addressing. An instruction encodes not only the operands but the operation itself. If each operand required **16** bits then instructions could not be encoded in **32** bits. By restricting one operand to address mode **register** only **32** bits are needed.

Table 8.1 *The attributes of each instruction*

Instruction mnemonic	Number of operands	Allowable Address Modes	
		First Operand	Second Operand
ADD	2	any	memory/register
CMP	2	any	any
SUB	2	any	memory/register
BRA	1	memory	
BEQ	1	memory	
BNE	1	memory	
BLT	1	memory	
BLE	1	memory	
BGT	1	memory	
BGE	1	memory	
JSR	1	memory	
RTS	0		
MOVE	2	any	memory/register
WRI	1	any	
READ	1	memory/register	

Table 8.1 lists the instructions available, giving the instruction assembler mnemonic, the number of operands and the allowable address modes for each operand.

memory refers to those modes that correspond to a reference to main memory, namely absolute, indirect and indirect with offset.

Where an instruction takes two operands the first is referred to as the **source** and the second the **destination**. For **ADD**, **SUB** and **MOVE** the second operand is always either a memory location or a register that is changed by the instruction.

For **CMP** only **CC** is effected.

The address modes given for the instructions **ADD**, **SUB**, **MOVE** and **CMP** are subject to the contraint that one must be **register**. It does not matter which. The other can take any of the address modes indicated in the table.

Table 8.2 describes the effect of each instruction. A C like notation is used to describe that effect. For example with **ADD s,d** the expression **d = d + s** used to describe the effect of **ADD** indicates that the value associated with **d** and the value associated with **s** are added together, with the result placed in the memory location or register indicated by **d**.

The letters **s**, **s1**, **d** and **m** are used to indicate operands. Where either **s** or **s1** appears the operand can take any of the allowable address modes. **d** is used to indicate that the address mode must specify either an address in memory or a register (it cannot be **literal**). **m** is used to indicate that the address mode must specify an address in memory (it cannot be **literal** or **register**).

The two bits of the condition code register **CC** are referred to in Table 8.2 as **cc_eq** and **cc_lt**. Only the comparison instruction effects this register. If the compared values are equal then **cc_eq** is set to **1**. Otherwise it is set to **0**. This is described in the table by the expression

cc_eq = s1 == s;

Table 8.2 *The effect of each instruction*

Instruction	Effect
ADD s,d	d = d + s
CMP s,s1	cc_eq = s1 == s; cc_lt = s1<s
SUB s,d	d = d - s
BRA m	branch to m
BEQ m	if (cc_eq) branch to m
BNE m	if (!cc_eq) branch to m
BLT m	if (cc_lt) branch to m
BLE m	if (cc_eq || cc_lt) branch to m
BGT m	if (!cc_eq && !cc_lt) branch to m
BGE m	if (!cc_lt) branch to m
JSR m	branch to m saving the address of the next instruction
RTS	branch to the most recently saved instruction address
MOVE s,d	d = s
WRI s	output s
READ d	read in an unsigned number into d

As a C expression the effect would be to assign **1** to **cc_eq** if **s1** and **s** were equal and **0** otherwise.

If the value of the second operand (**s1**) is less than that of the first then **cc_lt** is set to **1**. Otherwise it is set to **0**. Again this effect is described by the expression

cc_eq = s1 < s;

In describing the effect of branching instructions '**branch to m**' means transfer control to the instruction at address **m**. **m** may be any of the address modes that give a memory address.

The instructions **jsr** and **rts** support subroutine calls. Wherever a **jsr** instruction is executed the address of the instruction immediately following it in memory is preserved. Whenever an **rts** instruction is executed the most recently preserved address is retrieved and control is transferred to the instruction at that address. The retrieved address is then discarded. Later in the chapter we will need to examine **how** the effect of these two instructions is achieved. For now assume that the preservation and retrieval of addresses is hidden and automatic, and that the hardware uses a special dedicated memory to hold these addresses. The assembler programmer cannot access this memory. The two instructions work in tandem. A **jsr** instruction should be followed at some stage by an **rts** instruction. An important feature of the way they work is that **rts** makes use of the address associated with the most recently executed **jsr** instruction.

The above description not only covers the underlying machine but in part the assembler language.

8.2 The format of instructions in memory

Instructions are held in **32** bit memory locations during program execution. Figure 8.1 shows how the various bit groupings in a **32** bit location are used to encode an instruction, with the left most bit numbered **31** and the rightmost numbered **0**. This type of layout is typical of most machine code instruction sets although the detail will vary. Part of what an assembler does is to take instructions expressed in a symbol form and construct corresponding machine instructions in the form of bit patterns.

The various bit grouping are used in the following way.

- Bits **31 ... 26** hold the **operation code** for the instruction (**MOVE,ADD** etc). This allows for **64** possible operation codes, although we only make use of **16** of these. The operation codes **0 ... 14** are used for the instructions given in Table 8.1 with the code **15** used to indicate that the program should terminate. The correspondence between operation code and mnemonic follow the order of Table 8.1, with **0** corresponding to **ADD** and **14** corresponding to **READ**.
- Bit **25** is used to indicate which operand is the source and which the destination. For instructions with two operands one has to be a register. This is coded in bits **24 ... 22**. The other can take any appropriate address mode which is coded in bits **21 ... 0**. Bit **25** is set if the first (source) operand is a register. Otherwise it is clear. Note that both the first and second operands can be registers. In this case bits **21 ... 0** are still used to code the second register.
- Bits **24 ... 22** hold the register.
- Bits **21 ... 19** give the address mode of the operand coded in the remaining **19** bits. The modes **register, literal, absolute, indirect** and **indirect with offset** are coded **0 ... 4** respectively.
- Bits **18 ... 16** hold the register associated with the address mode coded in bits **21 ... 19**.
- Bits **15 ... 0** hold the value (absolute, literal or offset) associated with the address mode coded in bits **21 ... 19**.

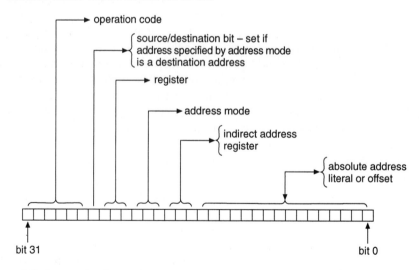

Figure 8.1 *Instruction layout in memory*

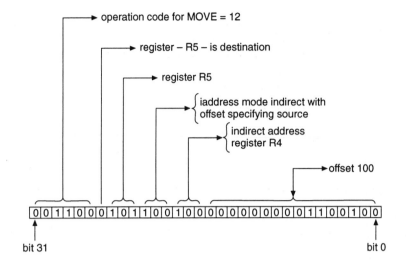

operation code for MOVE = 12

register – R5 – is destination

register R5

iaddress mode indirect with offset specifying source

indirect address register R4

offset 100

```
0 0 1 1 0 0 0 1 0 1 1 0 0 1 0 0 0 0 0 0 0 0 0 0 0 0 1 1 0 0 1 0 0
```

bit 31   bit 0

Figure 8.2 *The machine code form for MOVE 100(R4),R5*

For example our assembler will produce the bit pattern given in Figure 8.2 for the instruction

MOVE 100(R4),R5

8.3 Assembler features

Instructions are written one to a line. If the first character on a line is '*' then the line is treated as a comment. If the first character is a letter then the instruction is assumed to be labelled. Labels are made up from letters, digits and the '_' character but must start with a letter. If the first character is a space then the mnemonic for an instruction should first appear on the line. Spaces should separate the instruction mnemonic from its operand or operands. Where two operands appear, these should be separated by a comma. Spaces may be used freely to separate labels from mnemonics and mnemonics from operands.

Labels may appear on separate lines. That is, a label need not be followed by an instruction on the same line.

As the assembler generates machine code instructions it keeps track of memory addresses. Whenever an instruction is labelled the assember associates that instruction's address with the label. Wherever a label is used in an assembler program it is treated as the numeric value corresponding to that address. Thus a label may appear as an absolute address, or as an offset, or as a literal value. Literals are always preceded by the '#' character and this applies if a label is being used as a literal.

Three further mnemonics called **assembler directives** are provided, namely **END, DC** and **DS**. All three take one argument. For **END** it is an absolute address and for both **DC** and **DS** it is a literal (which requires the use of '#').

END indicates the end of input to the assembler, with its argument indicating where execution should start. To allow the execution of assembler programs the assembler includes an **interpreter** (discussed in Section 8.4) that behaves like the target machine. For convenience **END** is treated as an instruction. On encountering the **END** directive the assembler generates a pseudo instruction with operation code **15**. On encountering an instruction with operation code **15** the interpreter terminates the program.

The **END** directive therefore has three roles:

(i) It indicates to the assember the textual end of the assembler program.
(ii) It gives the address (through its argument) of where execution of the assembled program should start.
(iii) It indicates where the execution of the assembled program should end.

Note that (i) and (iii) are not the same. Most assemblers provide a separate way on indicating where a program should terminate execution, with **END** used only for (i) and (ii).

DC allows the programmer to set up an unsigned number in a memory word. The literal value associated **DC** is used as the unsigned number.

DS allows the programmer to set aside a given number of memory locations for data. The literal value associated with **DC** gives the number of locations required. To illustrate the use of the assembler language a slightly simplified version of the quotient-remainder algorithm given in Chapter 2 is programmed here.

Dropping the check that b > 0 our algorithm becomes

> **quotient = 0;**
> **remainder = a;**
> **while (remainder >= b)**
> **{**
>   **quotient = quotient + 1;**
>   **remainder = remainder – b;**
> **}**

We would write this as an assembler program

```
      * Given the values a and b the sub-routine QR calculates the
      * two values quotient and remainder that satisfy
      * a == b * quotient + remainder with remainder < b.
      *
      * The registers R0,R1,R2 and R3 are used for a,b, quotient
      * and remainder respectively.
      *
QR        MOVE    #0,R2      * quotient = 0;
          MOVE    R0,R3      * remainder = a;
WHILE     CMP     R1,R3      * WHILE (remainder >= b)
          BLT     QRX        * {
          ADD     #1,R2      * quotient = quotient + 1;
          SUB     R1,R3      * remainder = remainder – b;
          BRA     WHILE      * }
QRX       RTS
      *
      * Input a and b into R0 and R1
      *
```

```
START    READ      R0
         READ      R1
*
* Call sub-routine to calculate quotient and remainder
*
         JSR       QR
         WRI       R2        * output quotient
         WRI       R3        * output remainder
         END       START
```

Execution starts at the instruction labelled START. The values for a and b are read into the two registers R0 and R1. The subroutine QR is called. This calculates quotient and remainder, leaving these values in registers R2 and R3. On return these values are output. The comments in the assembler program relate it to the original algorithm.

A number of points about this program a worth making.

The instruction that QRX labels follows the use of that label. The assembler must cater for this, ensuring that the address associated with the BLT instruction is that of the RTS instruction labelled by QRX. This type of forward reference is sometimes unavoidable in assembler programming.

The while statement is implemented by

- a comparison corresponding to the while condition
- a branch to the end of the while statement if the comparison fails
- a branch back to the comparison at the end of each iteration of the while statement.

It is not necessary to be able to program in assembler to make sense of how an assembler generates machine code. It is however important to understand the relationship between assembler code and its corresponding machine code. Figure 8.3 shows in tabular form the machine code instruction generated for each of the assembler instructions in the program. These machine code instructions will follow the form given in Figure 8.1. Figure 8.3 gives the numeric equivalent of the bit pattern that the assembler will generate in each of the fields of each instruction. The reader should convince himself that the values that appear in Figure 8.3 are what he would expect given the codings for the various fields described at the start of Section 8.2. The instructions are assumed to start at address **0** and since the word size is assumed to be **32** bits subsequent instructions are at addresses **1,2, ... 13**. The job of the assembler is to generate a sequence of **32** bit values that encode the sequence of assembler instructions it is presented with. If a real machine existed with the characteristics described here that sequence could be loaded into its memory and its processor could be directed to execute the sequence starting at the instruction at address **8**. No such machine is available, so our interpreter does the job instead. The last instruction in the sequence below is not part of the machine's instruction set. It is included to allow the interpreter to recognise the end of the program's execution. This would be handled within the operating system on a real computer system. The operand generated with the instruction is not used other than by the assembler/interpreter at the end of assembly to identify the address at which execution should start.

Figure 8.3 *Assembler program with instruction codings*

Assembler instruction			Operation code	Source/ destination bit	Operand code Register	Operand code		
						Address mode	Register	Absolute address/ literal
QR	MOVE	#0,R2	12	0	2	1	0	0
	MOVE	R0,R3	12	1	0	0	3	0
WHILE	CMP	R1,R3	1	1	1	0	3	0
	BLT	QRX	6	0	0	2	0	7
	ADD	#1,R2	0	0	2	1	0	1
	SUB	R1,R3	2	1	1	0	3	0
	BRA	WHILE	3	0	0	2	0	2
QRX	RTS		11	0	0	0	0	0
START	READ	R0	14	1	0	0	0	0
	READ	R1	14	1	1	0	0	0
	JSR	QR	10	0	0	2	0	0
	WRI	R2	13	1	2	0	0	0
	WRI	R3	13	1	3	0	0	0
	END	START	15	0	0	2	0	8

8.4 The assembler/interpreter system

Assemblers normally generate machine code into a file which can then be loaded and executed as a program. Because no real machine is available to execute our assembled programs, a program that behaves like our target machine is provided as part of the assembler system. Such programs are called **interpreters**. They interpret instructions that a real machine would execute. Functionally there is not a lot of difference between an interpreter and a machine, except that an interpreter is a piece of software whereas a machine is piece of hardware.

Our case study is intended to show how an assembler might be written in C. By simplifying the target machine we can write an assembler which can be described in a chapter yet which deals with many of the problems that real assemblers have to deal with. The interpreter is provided so that the assembled programs can be observed executing.

Figure 8.4 shows the relationship between the assembler and the interpreter. The assembler takes input from a **source** file which contains the assembler instructions. It produces a machine code program which is passed to the interpreter along with the program start address. Any errors found in the source code will be reported on. Normally the assembled program would be written to a file. Here it is preserved in an array called **assembled_program**. This is copied into the array **mem** by the function **load_program**. **mem** simulates our machine's main memory and **load_program** can be viewed as part of the software provided with the machine. We could have generated machine code instructions directly into **mem**, avoiding the need for the array **assembled_program** and the function **load_program**. The slightly more complicated approach was chosen both because it provides a cleaner interface between the assembly stage and the interpreter and also because it follows

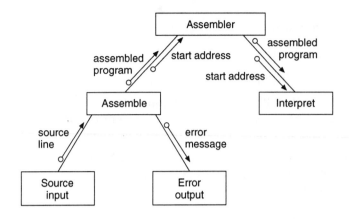

Figure 8.4 *The assembler/interpreter system*

more closely what actually happens with real assemblers and the machine the assembled code executes on.

So far we have provided fairly detailed structure charts to document program designs. In practice such charts would be used to express important design features, with much of the detail left to the coding stage. For example in implementing a module a programmer will almost certainly use functions to structure his code. In analysing instructions the assembler needs to distinguish the registers **R0, R1, ...,** **R7** from labels in operands. The function **read_id** is used to read sequences of letters, digits and underscore characters as strings. Such sequences can be labels, registers or indeed instruction mnemonics. However where a register is expected (for example in the case of indirect operands) the function **a_reg** is used. To include this level of detail in the structure charts that describe the program design would be counter productive.

8.5 The assembler

Assembler programs are assembled a line at a time. First the line is analysed to ensure that it makes sense as an assembler instruction. Is the instruction mnemonic recognised? Do the right number of operands appear and are the forms they take allowable for the instruction? In carrying out this analysis the instruction, including its operands, are coded into an internal form from which the machine code form is then generated, this being the second stage in the assembly process. The task of analysis is thus clearly separated from that of code generation. It would have been possible to merge the two processes and go directly from a line of assembler code to its machine code equivalent. Such a program would have been more difficult to write and to follow once written.

We will use the term **lexical analysis** to cover the analysis process. To describe the type of value produced by this analysis phase we need to make use of a further feature of the C language.

8.6 Enumerations

In C a declaration of the form

$$\text{enum } \text{<id> } \{\text{<}id_0\text{>} , \text{<}id_1\text{>} , ..., \text{<}id_n\text{>}\};$$

is called an **enumeration**. It allows the programmer to give the names $\text{<}id_0\text{>}$, $\text{<}id_1\text{>}$, ..., $\text{<}id_n\text{>}$ to the successive integer values **0, 1, ..., n. enum <id>** can the be used to declare variables that take these values. For example given the enumeration

**enum op_code { add,cmp,sub,bra,beq,bne,blt,ble,
bgt,bge,jsr,rts,move,wri,read,end,ds,dc};**

the declaration

enum op_code o_c;

introduces the variable **o_c** as if it were of type **op_code**. In fact it is merely a notational convenience. **o_c** is of type **int** and can take any integer value and **add, cmp, ..., dc** are simply names for the integer values **0,1 , ... , 17**. It is a useful notation however because it allows us to give names to values that we **represent** in our program as integers. The operation codes of the machine that we are assembling to are introduced by the enumeration above (along with the directives **DS** and **DC**).

We will also make use of the enumeration

enum address_mode {gen_reg,literal,absolute,indirect,offset};

to stand for the possible address modes (**register,literal,absolute,indirect** and **indirect with offset**) that an operand can take.

The task of the lexical analyser is to convert each line of assembler code into a value of the form

**struct instruction {enum op_code o_c;
int no_of_opands;
struct operand opand1, opand2;};**

where the operands themselves have values of the form

struct operand { enum address_mode a_m;int reg,lit_val;};

This encodes the operation code and for each operand its address mode and any register and literal value associated with it. Thus for example the instruction

MOVE #1234,R5

would be converted to the internal form

{move,2,{literal,_,1234},{gen_reg,5,_}}

Here an underscore is used to indicate a particular componant of a structure is not assigned a value.

This value is then used to generate the machine code form of the instruction. How this is done is described in Section 8.10.

8.7 Dealing with labels

Labels would be very straightforward to handle if their introduction always preceded their use. In the assembler program given above this is true for the labels QR, WHILE and START but not for the label QRX. If a label is referred to before its introduction, this reference is described as a **forward reference**. For such references no address can be associated with the label at the point of reference. Only when the label is introduced can this be done. The BLT instruction that references QRX cannot be completely dealt with until QRX has been introduced as a label. The problem is compounded by the fact that a label may be referenced more than once before its introduction. Label handling thus becomes a significant part of the assembly process.

We now see three separate modules that to make up the assembler, namely

- Lexical analysis
- Label processing
- Machine code generation.

Most of the errors that arise are because the assembler statements are ill formed in some way. The wrong number of arguments for instance have been supplied or a non-existant mnemonic has been specified. Such errors are identified during lexical analysis. However errors do arise elsewhere and because of this error handling is treated as a separate component.

As we have seen machine code is first generated in the array **assembled_program**. In filling this array the position at which instructions are generated will need to be maintained. The variable **code_addr** is used for this. In dealing with labels and in particular forward references label processing functions will need to access to both **assembled_program** and **code_addr**. Again we treat the management of this array as a separate component.

A final component is needed to deal with assembler directives such as **END** or **DC**. We therefore add to our list of components

- Error management
- Code management
- Directive processing.

The assembler is organised into six modules corresponding to these six components. Figure 8.5 shows how these six components interact with each other. Note that input into the system from the source file and the output of error messages are not shown.

Each of the six modules is implemented as a collection of functions and data structures, with one or more of the functions corresponding to the module's interface with other modules.

The interfacing functions for each module are

Lexical analysis

- **analyse_instruction,** which returns a value of type **instruction** being the analysis of the next line of assembler code.
- **open_source,** which opens the source file for input.

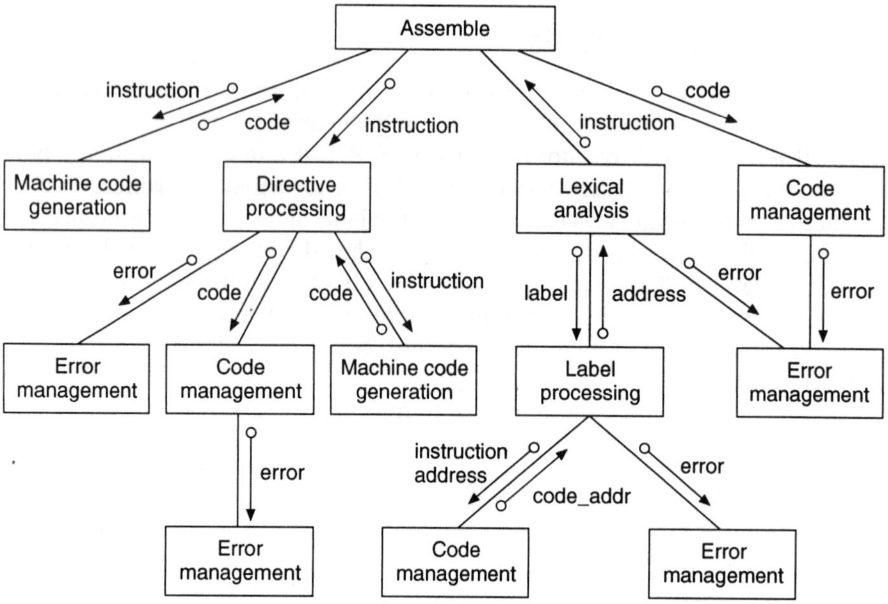

Figure 8.5 *The assembler module structure*

Machine code generation
- **build_code,** which takes an argument of type **instruction** and returns a result of type **unsigned long int.** This result holds the encoded form of the instruction.

Label processing
- **process_label** which takes an argument of type **char.** This should be the first character of a label occurring as a label introduction. **process_label** reads the label. It deals with both the case where this is the first occurrence of the label and where it has been used in a branch instruction or subroutine call prior to this introduction.
- **look_up_label** takes a label as its argument and returns the address associated with the label. If the label has not yet been introduced then **0** is returned.

Error management
- **error,** which takes an error code and outputs a message corresponding to that code.
- **increment_line_count,** which updates the count of the number of lines read in.
- **get_error_count,** which returns the number of errors encountered.

Code management
- **save_code,** which takes a coded instruction and stores it in **assembled_code.**
- **update_code,** which modifies the address field of an instruction already coded in **assembled_code** with the current value of **code_addr.** It takes as its argument the address of the instruction. This is used by **Label Processing** to place the correct address in an instruction where the corresponding assembler

instruction has forward referenced a label.

- **get_code_address,** which returns the current value of **code_addr.**
- **update_code_address,** which takes an integer argument which is added to **code_addr.** This is used in dealing with the directive **DS.**
- **call_load,** which takes the program start address and which calls **load_program,** a function provided as part of the interpreter, to load programs into the interpreter's memory.

Directive processing

- **directive,** which takes an argument of type **instruction** and returns **1 (TRUE)** if it is a directive and **0 (FALSE)** otherwise.
- **process_directive,** which takes an argument of type **instruction** and deals with it as a directive.

The module with the largest number of functions at its interface is Code management. In fact this module is about the simplest to implement and could even be eliminated by accessing the variables **assembled_program** and **code_addr** directly from the other modules. Not allowing such access across modules is a design policy here. By hiding the structure of data behind a functional interface a more flexible system is created. We can change the way assembled programs are held without having to change any of the other modules, so long as we ensure that the functional interface is unchanged. We might for example decide at some stage that it would be better to hold the assembled program in a file rather than in an array. Such a change would only affect Code management. Note that we use the same policy with Label processing. Modules using either of the functions provided at its interface are not influenced in their implementation by the way labels are actually stored.

8.8 Lexical analysis

This module is built from 14 functions, including **analyse_instruction** and is by far the most complex of the six modules. It is primarily concerned with the generation of internal representations (values of type **instruction**) for instructions that appear in assembler programs. This would be very straightforward if such programs could be guaranteed correct. Assembler programmers make errors and an assembler would be of little value if it did not report on such errors. Assemblers, like compilers, must be able to take in any mix of valid instructions and those that contain errors making a useful response to the errors.

There are two types of errors that need to be recognised. First an instruction may be ill formed. For example a programmer may leave out the closing bracket in an indirect specification. Second, the instruction may correctly specify illegal constructs such as address modes. The JSR instruction reguires an operand that specifies a memory address. A literal or register operand would therefore be illegal.

The first type of error is deal with piecemeal. As the characters of a line are read in expected characters are checked for and if they are not found an appropriate error message is generated. The missing bracket above would be picked up in this way.

For the second type of error two data structures are used. The array **mnemonics_table** holds the instruction mnemonic, the operation code, the number of operands and their allowable address modes for each instruction. Both in the text above and in the assembler itself address modes are referred to in two ways. Strictly we mean the five address modes **absolute**, **literal**, etc. In Table 8.1 we also grouped address modes under the classifications **register**, **memory** (covering **absolute**, **indirect** and **indirect with offset**), **memory/register** and **any**. This classification is used in **mnemonics_table** with a second array, **class_table**, used to relate address mode to the operand classification. Table 8.3 shows this relationship. In dealing with an instruction the assembler will determine the address modes of its operands and use this array to see if they are allowable for the instruction.

Because operands may have fewer than two operands the class **none** is added to the classification to classify the allowable address modes for non-existent first and second operands. The classification **literal** is used for the two directives **DS** and **DC**. Each takes a single literal operand.

The directive **END** should have an absolute address as its operand. Rather than making this a further classification, its operand is given the class **memory** and a specific check is carried out when dealing with this directive.

An enumeration **operand_class** is used for these address mode classes with a choice of identifiers different from those that appear in Table 8.3.

Table 8.3 *Address mode/class correspondence*

Mode	Class					
	Register	Memory	Memory or register	Any	Literal	None
Register	✓	✗	✓	✓	✗	✗
Literal	✗	✗	✗	✗	✓	✗
Absolute	✗	✓	✓	✓	✗	✗
Indirect	✗	✓	✓	✓	✗	✗
Indirect with offset	✗	✓	✓	✓	✗	✗

The functions **instruction_properties** and **check_class_ok** access these data structures with the first returning the properties associated with a given mnemonic and the second checking that a given address mode and class are compatible.

There are six functions associated with input from the source file.

- **open_source,** which opens the source file for input.
- **get_next_char,** which returns the next non-space character on a line.
- **move_to_next_line,** which moves input to the next line.
- **next_instruction,** which returns the first character of the next line that contains an instruction. Comment lines and blank lines are skipped.
- **read_id,** which takes as its argument a letter being the start of an identifier (either a label or a mnemonic) and which reads to the end of the identifier returning it as a string.
- **read_int,** which takes as its argument an digit being the start of an integer and which reads to the end of the digit sequence returning the corresponding integer value.

Four functions are used to carry out the analysis of a line of assembler code.

The function **analyse_instruction** reads characters until either an '*' or an end of line is encountered. It first checks that what it finds (label, instruction mnemonic and any operands) make sense as components of an instruction. It then checks that they make sense for the particular instruction found using the properties associated with that instruction in **mnemonics_table**. As it carries out these checks it builds a value of type **instruction**. It makes use of **analyse_operand** to read in and check individual operands.

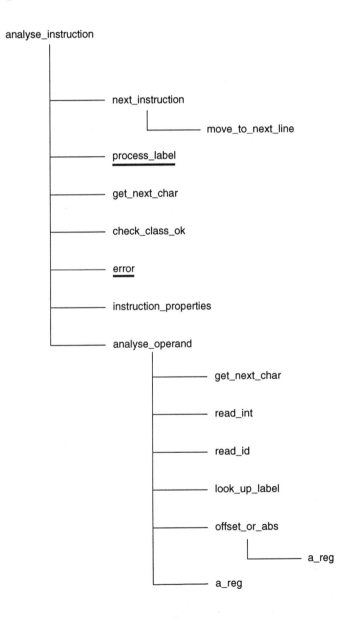

***Figure 8.6** Functions used by analyse_instruction*

The function **analyse_operand** reads an operand. It checks that it is well formed and returns a value of type **operand**. It makes use of the function **offset_or_abs**. If a label or number appears in an operand it may or may not be followed by a register in brackets, depending on whether the address mode is indirect with offset or absolute. **offset_or_abs** deals with this making use of the function **a_reg** which looks for a register in the input. **analyse_operand** also makes use of **a_reg** directly when dealing with register indirect.

Figure 8.6 shows the functions used by **analyse_instruction** and other functions within Lexical analysis. Underlined functions are those associated with a different module.

8.9 Label table management

Labels are held in a linked list much as employee names were in the structure **directory_entry** described towards the end of Chapter 7. The structure used is

> **struct labtab_entry {char * label;**
> **int lab_addr;**
> **struct addr_list_entry * forward_refs;**
> **struct labtab_entry * next;};**

where the type **addr_list_entry** is defined by

> **struct addr_list_entry {int addr; struct addr_list_entry * next;};**

A value of type **labtab_entry** is added to a linked list **label_table** for every label found in the assembler program being assembled. This holds both the label and the address at which the label is introduced. If a label is used before it is introduced then the code address of the instruction referencing the label is preserved in a linked list **forward_references** associated with this value. The address field of this instruction will need to be updated when the address associated with the label is available (at its introduction). Potentially, each entry in the label table may have such a linked list although in most cases they will not. A linked list is used because there may be more than one use of a label before its introduction. Once a label is introduced any associated linked list is used to modify instruction address fields and the linked list is effectively deleted by setting the value **forward_refs** to **0** (the pointer value **null**).

Figures 8.7 and 8.8 show the state of the label table after the fourth and eighth instructions in the assembler program given above.

After the fourth instruction the labels QR, WHILE and QRX have been entered in the label table. For the first two of these the label address is held in the table. For the third there is a linked list consisting of one entry giving the address of the BLT instruction. The value **3** is also assigned to the label address field, but this is of no significance.

After the eighth instruction the label QRX has been introduced. As a result the corresponding entry is modified by assigning the correct label address (**7**) to the entry's address field and removing the linked list **forward_refs** after updating the instruction at address **3**.

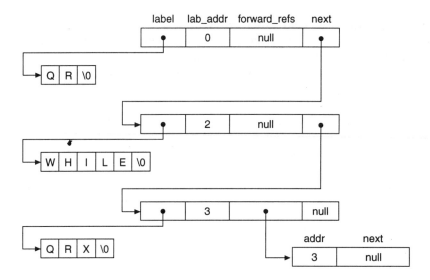

Figure 8.7 *label_table after instruction BLT QRX*

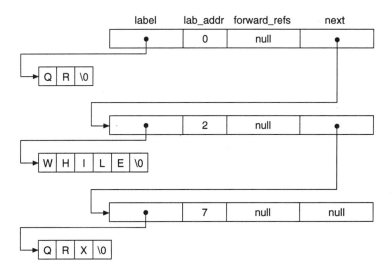

Figure 8.8 *label_table after instruction QRX RTS*

Five functions are used to maintain **label_table**:

- **process_label** which deals with a label introduction. If the label has already been used then there will be an entry for it in **label_table**. The function **find_label_entry** is used to find this entry. (**find_label_entry** either returns a pointer to the label's entry in the table or the value **0** if it is not there.) Its address field is assigned the current value of **code_addr.** It should also have a non_null **forward_refs** value. This is used to modify the instructions referencing the label. If the label has not already been used then **add_label** is used to add the label to **label_table**.

- **look_up_label** uses **find_label_entry** to search for an entry for a label in **label_table**. It returns the value of the entry's address field if the label has been introduced and **0** otherwise. If the label has not been introduced then there are two cases that need to be dealt with. Either the label has already been used in which case there is an entry for it or this is its first use and **add_label** needs to be used to create an entry for it. In either case **add_forward_reference** is used to add the address of the referencing instruction as a forward reference.
- **add_label,** which adds a label to **label_table** assigning the current value of **code_addr** to its address field and **0** to its forward reference field.
- **find_label_entry.** which searches for an occurrence of the label in **label_table**. If the label is there then a pointer to its entry is returned. Otherwise **0** is returned.

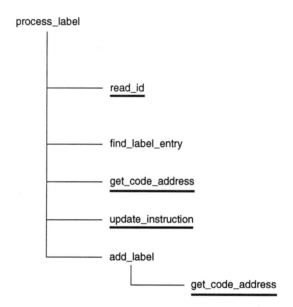

Figure 8.9 *Functions used by process_label*

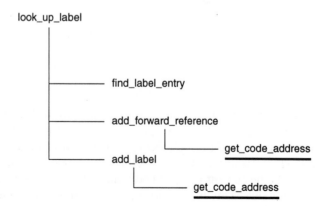

Figure 8.10 *Functions used by look_up_label*

- **add_forward_reference.** which extends the linked list of forward references associated with a specified entry by adding the current value of **code_addr** to the list.

Both **add_label** and **add_forward_reference** use exactly the same technique for dealing with linked lists that we saw used in Chapter 7. Double indirection is used with variables of type pointer to pointer to **labtab_entry** and pointer to pointer to **addr_list_entry**, which are used to address pointer fields in the linked lists **label_tabel** and **forward_refs,** respectively.

Figures 8.9 and 8.10 show **process_label** and **label_look_up** and the functions they use.

8.10 Machine code generation

This module is implemented as five functions.

- **build_code,** which takes as its argument a value of type **instruction** and builds a **32** bit machine code instruction in **code** (of type **unsigned long int**). Calling its argument **i,** its task is to take values from **i** placing them as bit patterns in the correct positions in **code**.
- **set_bit_field,** which takes the argument **code,** a position ,length and value and places the value as a bit pattern in **code** at the specified position. It leaves unchanged the rest of the **code.**
- **set_op_code,** which sets the operation code in **code** using **i.**
- **set_operands,** which sets the operand fields in **code** again using **i.** Recall that an operand may be encoded as a general register in bits **24 ... 22** or as any of the allowable address modes in bits **21 ... 0,** with bit **25** used to indicate which operand is the source and which the destination. These settings are controlled by **set_operands.**
- **build_effective_address** which is called by **set_operands** to set bits **21 ... 0.**

Two C operators so far not encountered are made use of in this module, namely '<<' (shift left) and '|' (bit-wise **OR).**

The result of the expression

$$x << y$$

is the value in **x** bit shifted left by **y** bits. In general, the operator takes two expressions that yield integer values as its operands. The shift is applied to the value of the left operand. The value of the left operand will have a size (**8,16** or **32** bits) associated with it. In shifting left, left-most bits will be discarded with **0** valued bits shifted in from the right.

This operation is used in **set_bit_field** to position a bit pattern in an unsigned long integer.

There is a corresponding 'shift right' operator '>>' which the interpreter uses to extract the value of a bit field from a machine instruction. With this operation rightmost bits will be discarded. If the left operand is unsigned (type **unsigned int, unsigned long int** etc), then **0** valued bits are shifted in on the left. Otherwise the effect is system dependent.

The result of the expression

    x | y

is the value obtained by ORing together corresponding bits of the values associated with **x** and **y**. If both corresponding bits are **0** then the resultant bit is **0**, otherwise it is **1**. In general the operator takes two expressions that yield integer values as its operands.

This operation is used in **set_bit_field** to assign a bit pattern to a field in an unsigned long word without altering the rest of the long word.

The operation should not be confused with '||' .

There are two further corresponding bit-wise operations '**&**' (bit-wise AND) and '**^**' (bit-wise XOR), but since we make no use of them we will leave them aside.

Figure 8.11 shows the function **build_code** and the functions it uses.

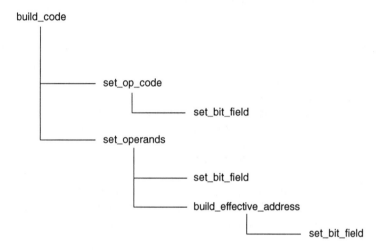

Figure 8.11 The functions used by build_code

8.11 The modules error management and code management

Apart from ouputting error messages error management 'owns' two integer variables, **error_count** and **line_count,** and provides two functions, **increment_line_count** and **get_error_count,** to provide access to them.

Code management maintains the data structure which holds the assembled code and provides a link with the interpreter.

8.12 The interpreter

The interpreter models the machine described at the beginning of this chapter. In the absence of real hardware it allows us to simulate the execution of machine code programs. Main memory is modelled as the array **mem**. The eight registers are modelled as the array **regs**. Both these arrays have elements of type **unsigned long**

int, as does a further array, **return_address_stack**, used to hold return addresses. This is needed to simulate the instructions JSR and RTS. Associated with it is a variable, **top,** which indexes the position that the next JSR instruction should use for the subroutine return address. All machines have a register which gives the address of the next instruction to be executed. Here the variable **p_c** models this register.

The interpreter is implemented by the following functions of which the first two constitute its interface:

- **load_program,** which loads a program into **mem** setting **p_c** to the program start address. It takes as arguments the address of an array containing the assembled code, the program size and the program start address.
- **interpret,** which executes the instructions held in **mem** starting at the instruction addressed by the initial value of **p_c**. It stops executing on encountering an **end** instruction. It uses the functions below to extract the operation code and operands from the machine code instruction before simulating the effect of the instruction.
- **decode,** which takes an instruction held as an **unsigned long int** and creates a structure which is essentially a collection of integers, each corresponding to one of the bit patterns that make up the instruction. It makes use of the function **get_bit_field**.
- **get_bit_field,** which returns as an integer value the bit pattern of a given size at a given position in an **unsigned long int** argument.
- **get_value,** which takes a decoded instruction as its argument and which returns the current value of one of its operands. For example if the operand is a register it will return the value held in the element of **regs** that corresponds to that register and if it is a memory location it will return the value held in the corresponding element of **mem**. It takes a second argument which indicates which of the operands is to be used (the operand coded in bits **24 ... 22** or that coded in bits **21 ... 0**).
- **store_value,** which takes a decoded instruction and a value and stores the value at the operand address found in the decoded argument. A third argument is used to indicate whether it is the first (source) or second (destination) operand that gives the required address. Normally this would be the second operand (for

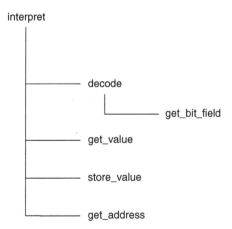

Figure 8.12 *The functions used by interpret*

ADD,SUB and MOVE), but because the READ instruction takes a single operand the possibility that it is the first operand exists and must be catered for.

- **get_address** which takes a decoded instruction and returns the memory address associated with its first (and only) operand. This is made use of in simulating branching instructions.

8.13 The switch statement

So far the only statement we have available to select alternative actions is the if statement. C provides a second method of selecting alternatives, which we use heavily particularly in the interpreter.

An expression, normally of integer type, is used to select a statement for execution from a list of possible alternatives. Each alternative is labelled with one or more constants of the same type as the expression. Again these are normally of integer type. The switch statement is executed by first evaluating the expression and then transferring control to the statement labelled by a constant value equal to that of the expression.

If the expression has a value not covered by any of the constant labels, no alternative is executed unless a default label is included in which case control transfers to the statement labelled by it.

The general form of a switch statement is

```
switch ( <expression> )
{
    case <constant_expression₁> : <statement₁>;
    case <constant_expression₂> : <statement₂>;
            .
            .
            .
            .
    case <constant_expressionₙ> : <statementₙ>;
}
```

with the possible inclusion of

```
default: <statement>;
```

as one of the alternatives.

Thus the selecting expression is preceded by the keyword **switch** and each constant expression is preceded by **case :**.

The switch statement transfers control. Thus for example in

```
switch (d)
{
    case 0: printf("zero");
    case 1: printf("one");
            .
            .
            .
            .
```

```
        case 9: printf("nine");
    }
```

if d has the value 3, say, then the effect of the switch statement would be to output

threefour ... nine

That is, all the **printf** statements from **printf("three")** would be executed.

In using the switch statement we normally only want to execute the labelled statement. To achieve this effect we need to use the C break statement. This can be used within the body of while, do, for and switch statements and its effect is to terminate their execution, taking control to the following statement.

Using it, our example becomes

```
    switch (d)
    {
        case 0: printf("zero");
        break;
        case 1: printf("one");
        break;

              .
              .
              .

        case 9: printf("nine");
    }
```

and its execution with **b** taking a value in the range **0 ... 9** would cause execution of just the print statement associated with the number.

The code for the assembler/interpreter is given in Appendix 2.

Exercises

1. Add instructions **AND** and **OR** to the instruction set. Each instruction takes two operands. The first logically **AND**'s the two operand values placing the result in the destination operand with the second logically **OR**ing the two operand values, again placing the result in the destination operand.

2. Assemblers normally provide a directive (EQU) which allows the programmer to associate names with values in a similar way to C's **#define**. Such directives normally take the form

   <identifier> EQU <constant expression>

   as for example in

   SIZE EQU 1000

   Add this facility to the assembler.

3. Extend the assembler to allow constant expressions involving numbers, labels, identifiers introduced using EQU and the arithmetic operators '+'.'−','*' and '/'.

Appendix I

The C language
– an outline

This outline covers most of the features supported by C.

In attempting to get an overview of a programming language a number of questions should be considered.

- What types of scalar value (integers,decimals, pointers, etc.) does the language provide?
- How are variables declared?
- What operations on values (arithmetic, comparison, etc.) does the language support?
- What mechanisms are provided for describing and accessing structured values(arrays, etc.)?
- What statements does the language provide to allow the programmer to direct the execution of the program?
- How are statements and declarations packaged together as units (blocks, functions, .c files, etc.) and how is communication between such units provided for (parameter passing, top level declarations, external objects, etc.)?
- What support is there for input an output and other system functions?

This outline answers some of these questions for C. It is neither a language tutor nor a definitive description of C.

In describing the written form taken by the various language features the following notation is sometimes (but not always) used:

- The angle brackets **< ... >** are used to indicate a form that is described elsewhere. For example **<expression>** is used to indicate that an expression may appear at this point in the construct being described, but the forms that expressions themselves can take are dealt with elsewhere.
- Any sequence of characters not enclosed in angle brackets can appear directly in the text of the program. For example **return <expression>;** describes a form consisting of the keyword **return** followed by an expression, followed by a semicolon.
- If a component is followed by a sequence of dots (**...**) this indicates that the component can be repeated **0, 1** or more times. For example **<component_declaration>;...** indicates possible repetitions of **<component_declaration>;**

- A component with the subscript $_{opt}$ is optional. For example in

  struct <type_name>$_{opt}$ {<component_declaration>; ... }
  <variable_name>$_{opt}$
  both <type_name> and <variable_name> are optional.

- It is sometimes necessary to distinguish between two occurences of the same type of component in describing the effect of a given construct. Numeric suffices are used to do this as for example in:
  Conditional statements take the form

  if (<expression>) <statement$_1$>

  optionally followed by

  else <statement$_2$>

1. Identifiers

Identifiers are used to give names to objects (variables,functions etc.) declared within a C program. An identifier can start with a letter or underscore and can be followed by one or more letters, digits or underscores.

Letters may be upper or lower case and for a given letter its upper and lower case forms are treated as different.

2. Declarations

Two classes of objects can be introduced and given names through declarations, namely **functions** and **variables**. Objects have memory associated with them and are created when the program in which they are declared is executed.

The memory associated with functions is used to hold function code. The memory associated with variables is used to hold values. Variables may have values assigned to them on declaration. A variable's value may be changed through assignment as the program executes.

Values are classified into **types**. C provides a set of built in types based on integers, reals and addresses and ways of constructing 'user defined types' from these.

The built in types have type names associated with them (**int, char** etc.) which are used in a variable declaration to indicate the type of a variable.

User defined types can also be given names which can then be used in declarations in the same way as built in type names. (How this can be done is covered later in Sections 12 and 13. Declarations involving the keyword **struct** can be used to introduce a variable of a new type, a type name for a new type or both. The new type is that of a structured object, with components drawn from built in types or named types already created by the user. Declarations involving the key word **typedef** can be used to give names to new or existing types).

A program consists of a collection of declarations, which must include the declaration of a function with the name **main**. Declarations other than those that appear within functions are called top level declarations

Program execution always starts at **main.**

Declarations of variables and functions may be either **defining** declarations or **referencing** declarations. A defining declaration introduces an object. A referencing declaration introduces the name and attributes of an object that has a defining declaration associated with it elsewhere in the program. The need for the two types of declaration arises from the fact that a program may appear in several files. Because these files contain the code of a single program there will be cross file references. For example a function declared in one file may be called in a second. Such files are compiled separately. Given a cross file reference a referencing declaration may be necessary to ensure that the compiler treats the reference in a way consistent with its defining declaration. This referencing declaration appears in the file making the reference, with a defining declaration appearing in the second file.

A defining function declaration consists of a function **header** and a function **body**. The function header describes the result type, provides a function name and gives parameter names and their types. A function definition that gives only the function name, the result type and the parameter types is a referencing declaration, for which a corresponding defining declaration should exist. A referencing declaration may give names for the parameters but it need not.

The function body may start with a sequence of declarations followed by a sequence of statements describing actions to be carried out by the function. Both declarations and statements are optional.

A referencing declaration for a function is called a **function prototype**.

Given that the same variable is declared in different files, a number of factors need to be taken into account in deciding which is the defining declaration and which are referencing declarations. Such declarations may include the key word **extern** and may have an initial values associated with them as part of the declaration. A sensible approach is to use the keyword **extern** only with declarations intended as referencing declarations. Such declarations should not include any initial values. The defining declaration should be without the key word **extern** and optionally with an initial value.

If a variable 'owned' by one **.c** file is to be accessed from a second file the first file should contain a defining declaration, with the second containing a referencing declaration.

A **struct** declaration can introduce a type name, a variable or both. It is often the case that the same structure type is made use of in several different **.c** files. In this case it is sensible to introduce a type name for the structure in a declaration that does not also introduce variables which is repeated in the **.c** files that use the structure type. Variables should then be declared using the type name.

typedef declarations introduce names for new or existing types. Again, where a user defined type is used in several **.c** files, the **typedef** declaration should be repeated in the files that make use of the type.

Files containing declarations have names with either the suffix **.c** or the suffix **.h**. Although there are no constraints on what declarations can be put in **.h** files they are normally used for referencing declarations and declarations of structure type names.

Variable declarations (defining or referencing) should always textually precede any reference to the declared variable. For functions, a reference may precede the function declaration but it is good practice to avoid this using function prototypes if necessary.

It is almost always possible to ensure that, within a given **.c** file, a defining declaration for a function appears before any calls to the function and where this is the case the text of the program is best organised in this way. A function **f** may call a function **g** which itself calls **f**. In this case a call before a defining declaration cannot be avoided.Since C allows both defining and referencing declarations for the same function to appear in the same **.c** file in this case a referencing declaration should precede the call to the function.

A group of statements preceded by a group of declarations appearing between '{' and '}' is called a **block**.

The body of a defining function declaration is a block.

During the execution of a program objects have a period of existence called their **extent**. There are three types of extent: **static, local** and **dynamic**. Objects with static extent are created at the start of the program's execution and remain in existence until the program terminates. Objects with local extent are created on entry to the block in which they are declared (with a defining declaration) and cease to exist on exit from the block. Objects with dynamic extent are created using **malloc**.

Top level objects have static extent, with objects declared within a block normally having local extent. Within a block the use of the keyword **static** as part of a declaration causes the creation of an object with static extent.

Objects declared within a block are not accessible outside the block. Top level objects are accessible from the point of their declaration within a **.c** file and from other **.c** files, although it may be necessary to provide referencing declarations for them in the other files.

To hide a top level object from other **.c** files its (defining) declaration should be preceded by the keyword **static**. An attempt to use the identifier used in this defining declaration in a top level referencing declaration in a different **.c** file is illegal and will cause an error. (The identifier can however be used in a defining declaration, but this is almost certainly undesirable.)

The **scope** of an object determines from where in the **.c** file in which it is declared it can be referenced. Within the same **.c** file the scope of a variable declared at the top level is the code that follows the declaration of the variable, unless the variable's identifier is used to declare a different object within a block, in which case the original variable is hidden within this block. Blocks can be nested within blocks. If if the same identifier appears in an inner and outer block declaration then references to the identifier in the inner block relate to the inner declaration.

3. The basic types of values used within C programs

The values variables may take are grouped into **types**. A type is characterised by a collection of values and operations that can be applied to these values. For example type **int** normally corresponds to the values –32768 ... **32767** together with arithmetic operations, comparison operations and so forth. A variable declaration will include a type **specifier** which gives the type of value that the variable can take.

C types are based on three classes of value, namely integers, decimal numbers and addresses.

Six different C types can be used for integers, the differences between these types being to do with the range of integer values associated with the type and whether or not negative values are included in the range.

Two different C types are used for decimal numbers, with the difference between the two being to do with the range of values associated with the type.

C integers may take one of three sizes short, normal and long. Normally short integers occupy single bytes, normal integers two bytes and long integers four bytes but this can be different on different C implementations. Integers may be signed or unsigned. If an integer variable is signed then it is interpreted as holding a range of values from some negative value (e.g. **–32768**) to some positive value (e.g. **32767**). If it is unsigned then it is interpreted as holding only positive values (e.g. **0 ... 65535**).

Variables introduced using **char** and character constants can be treated as integers, although their interpretation is implementation dependent. Normally they are interpreted either as signed or unsigned short integers.

Integers are also used in C to model conditional values (true and false). Expressions that would normally be considered as yielding a true or false value (for example a comparison) yield either **1** or **0** (an **int** value) instead. In the contexts where a condition is made use of any non-zero value is interpreted as true with zero interpreted a false

Addresses form the basis for pointer values. A pointer value gives the address of an object. (Pointer variables can be created and these as objects also have addresses associated with them. Thus for example the addresses of pointer variables can themselves be treated as values.) The type of the object addressed by a pointer value is considered part of the value although this is not represented as part of the value at run-time. The address of an **int** object is not for example treated as being of the same type as the address of a char object. The compiler checks that pointer values are used in a way consistent with their types.

We write 'pointer to **int**', 'pointer to **char**' etc. to describe the type of values based on addresses.

C allows values of different types to be mixed in expressions. Where necessary type conversions are carried out. For example, given that **i** is declared as a normal integer and **r** is declared as a real in the assignment

   i = r;

the integer part of the real value associated with **r** is assigned to **i**. There is not the space here to deal with the way C handles the many possible combinations of values of different types that can arise in expressions.

If the keyword **short** or **long** precedes the keyword **int** in a declaration a short or long integer is declared.

If the keyword **unsigned** precedes the keyword **int** in a declaration then an unsigned integer is declared. Otherwise the integer is signed.

The keyword **float** is used to declare a single precision floating point variable with **double** used for double precision declarations.

4. Dynamic objects

Objects introduced through declarations will have names associated with them through the declaration. The library function **malloc** allows the programmer to create objects dynamically. **malloc** takes as its argument the size of an object, allocating sufficient memory for the object. It returns a pointer to the object. Objects created in this way are unnamed unlike normal variables and are usually accessed using pointers.

5. Constants

C allows values to be expressed as constants. Integer constants appear as sequences of digits, characters as single characters within '' characters and strings as sequences of characters within "" characters.

Integer constants are normally given in decimal form. That is as a sequence of decimal digits of which the left-most digit is not '0'. Where it is necessary to describe a value in the form of a bit pattern what is called the hexadecimal form for constants may be used. Four bits may take 16 different values **0 ... 15,** corresponding to the bit patterns **0000, 0001, 0010, 0011, ... , 1111**. In the hexadecimal form the values **0 ... 9** are coded using the corresponding digits '0' ... '9'. The values **10 ... 15** are coded using the letters **A ... F** (or **a ... f**). In the context of hexadecimal representations the characters '0' ... 'F' (or '0' ... 'f') are called hexadecimal digits. Thus byte values may be represented using two hexadecimal digits, two bytes four and so forth. A hexadecimal representation makes it easier to see how a value is held as a bit pattern. If a sequence of characters '0' ... 'F' (or '0' ... 'f') is preceded by '0x' or '0X' then the sequence is treated as a hexadecimal constant.

The constant **0x00FF** for example gives the hexadecimal representation of the integer **255**.

Character sets such as ASCII provide codes for both visible characters (for example the letters and digits) and characters that have an effect when sent to a device but no visible form (for example new line and back space).

Because the characters '' and "" are used to delineate character and string constants there is a problem where they are needed as character constants or within strings.

To allow the programmer to construct constants involving both these and invisible characters C provides what are called **escape sequences**. An escape sequence consists of the character '\' followed by an escape **code**. The set of allowable escape codes includes **n, b, ', "** and \ with the first of these standing for new line, the second back space and the remaining three the characters themselves.

Thus for example the character constant '' would be written '\'' with a string of four "" characters written "\"\"\"\"".

Note that the ASCII code **0** is written '\0' in character and string constants.

6. The declaration of scalar variables

Values based on integers, decimals or addresses are called scalar values. A scalar variable declaration consists of a type specifier (**int**, **char**, **float** or **double**), followed by a sequence of identifiers for variable names separated by commas and terminated by a semi-colon.

The declarations

> **int i,j;**
> **char ch1,ch2;**
> **float f1;**
> **double f2;**

introduce four variables based on integers (**i** and **j** of type **int** and **ch1** and **ch2** of type **char**) and two variables based on decimals **f1** of type **float** and **f2** of type **double**).

The keyword **int** may be preceded by either the keyword **short** or the keyword **long** for the declaration of short or long integers.

If the keyword or keywords forming part of an integer declaration are preceded by the keyword **unsigned** then an unsigned integer is declared. **unsigned** may also precede **char**.

Defining declarations may include initial values. In this case the variable name is followed by the symbol '=' and an expression which is evaluated to give an initial value.

Pointer variables are declared in exactly the same way, except that the variable identifier is immediately preceded by the character '*'.

The declaration

> **double * d_ptr;**

introduces a variable **d_ptr** of type pointer to **double** which takes as its value an **address** of a value of type **double**. As with all variable declarations, space for the variable is created as a consequence of the declaration but no value is assigned unless an initialisation appears with the declaration.

Note that initialising expressions for pointer values can be included as part of a pointer declaration. These normally involve either arrays or the address operator, both of which are dealt with later.

A common error is to assume that space for any value pointed at by a pointer variable is also created as a result of its declaration. This is not the case. It is the programmer's responsibility to ensure that such variables are given pointer values before they are used.

Referencing declarations should be preceded by the keyword **extern**.

7. Expressions

Expressions describe values in terms of operators (for example arithmetic operators) and operands which may be given in terms of constants, variables or function calls. C provides a wide range of unary and binary operators. (Unary operators take a single operand with the operator immediately preceding or immediately following the operand. Binary operators take two operands with the operator between the two operands.)

Unary operators which precede their operands are called **prefix** operators and those that follow their operands are called **postfix** operators.

Note that expressions need not involve operators. For example a constant by itself is an expression as is a variable name or function call.

8. Lvalues and and Rvalues

Since objects have both addresses and values they really have two values associated with them. For example an **int** variable has both a value of type **int** and a value of type pointer to **int** associated with it. An expression may describe either of these values, depending on its context. In one case it is describing an object to be altered as in assignment. In the other it is describing the value held by that object. An expression describing an object to be altered is sometimes called an lvalue. Otherwise it is called an rvalue. For example, given **i** and **j** as **int** variables in the assignment

   i = j;

i stands for an lvalue whereas **j** stands for a rvalue. Here the context in which the identifiers **i** and **j** appear determine how they should be interpreted.

Not all objects can appear as lvalues in expressions. For example a constant cannot appear to the left of an assignment. The assignment

   3 = 4;

makes no sense because constant **3** can never be interpreted as an lvalue.

9. Precedence and associativity

In expressions involving more than one operator precedence and associativity rules are provided to determine which operands are associated with which operators.

For example in the expression

   i + j + k

Is the operand **j** the second operand for the first '+' operator or is it the first operand for the second '+' operator?

Operators are assigned precedence levels and each precedence level is assigned an associativity. If an operand is between two operators at different levels of precedence then the operand is associated with the higher precedence operator.

For example, multiplication has a higher precedence than addition. Thus in the expression

i + j ∗ k

'∗' takes **j** and **k** as its operands with '+' taking **i** and the result from **j ∗ k**.

Where operators have the same precedence, operands are either associated with the operator on their left (**left associativity**) or on their right (**right associativity**).

Addition and subtraction have the same precedence and are left associative. Thus in

i + j − k

the operand **j** is the second operand for the '+' operator with the result from **i + j** being the first operand of '−'.

If it is necessary to force a different association of operands with operators than that determined by the precedence and associativity of the operators involved then brackets can be used. The operands of bracketted expressions always associate with operators that appear within the same brackets. Thus in

i + (j − k)

the operand **j** associates with the '−' operator.

Precedence and associativity determine to some extent **but not completely** the order in which expressions are evaluated. For a binary operator the operands may be evaluated in any order.

Given that the functions **f** and **g** return integer results in the expression

f() − g()

the compiler may organise the executable code in such a way that **g** is called before **f** or vice versa.

For the operators '+', '∗','&' and 'I' it does not matter which way round the operands are written (**i + j** has the same value as **j + i**). Because of this the compiler may re-order expressions involving them for evaluation purposes.

For the expression

i + j + k

the compiler may permutate the operators and operands in generating code.

10. The operators

Table 1 gives most of the operators available in C. They fall into the following classes

- **The arithmetic operators '+','−','∗' and '/'.** In expressions involving these operators both integer and decimal values can be mixed fairly freely. Where necessary type conversions will be carried out automatically before the operator is applied following the principle that information is not lost. For example in the addition of a **char** value and a **float** value the first of these would be converted to a **float** value. The operators '+' and '−' have a special role in the context of pointer values. A value may be added to or subtracted from a pointer value to generate a new value. However the addition or subtraction takes into account the number of bytes needed to hold values of the type pointed at by the pointer value.

For example, if **i_ptr** is a variable of type pointer to **int** and **ints** are held in two byte fields then **i_ptr+1** would be a pointer value two bytes on from that of **i_ptr** itself.

- **The unary post-fix and pre-fix Increment and Decrement operators '++'
and '– –'.** '++' and '– –' each denote two different operators. Which operator they denote will depend on whether they precede or follow the operand. Operands should be lvalues. An expression involving either of these operators has a value in the normal way. However the operators also cause the value of the operand the be changed as if an assignment to it had been carried out. This change takes place either before or after the operand is used to provide a value for the expression in which it occurs depending on whether the operator is prefix or postfix. In the case of integers and decimals the operand is incremented or decremented by **1**. For pointers the increment or decrement takes into account the number of bytes needed to hold values of the type pointed at by the pointer value.
- **The comparison operators '<', '<=', '>', '>=', '==' and '!='.** These provide for the comparison of integer, decimal and pointer values. Such comparisons always generate an **int** result, being either **0** or **1,** with **0** corresponding to false and **1** to true. For example if **i** and **j** are integers then **i<j** has the value **1** if **i** is less than **j** and **0** otherwise. If the operands are of different types automatic conversions will take place before the comparison is carried out. The operators give the comparisons **less than, less than or equal to, greater than, greater than or equal to, equal to** and **not equal to.** (The first operand is less than the second, less than or equal to the second and so forth.)
- **The logical operators '&&', '||' and '!'.** These operators take integer, real or pointer values as operands, producing an **int** result that is either **0** or **1** (again corresponding to true and false). For **'&&'** and **'||'** the left operand is evaluated first. The second operand may or may not be evaluated as indicated in Table A.1 below. '!' produces the value **0** if its operand is non-zero and **1** otherwise.

Table A.1 *Evaluation of logical operators*

left Operand	right Operand	Result from **&&**
zero value	not evaluated	0
non-zero value	zero value	0
non-zero value	non-zero value	1

left Operand	right Operand	Result from ||
non-zero value	not evaluated	1
zero value	zero value	0
zero value	non-zero value	1

- **The bit-wise operators '&' and '|'.** These operators take integer valued operands and produce a result obtained by bit-wise ANDing or ORing corresponding bits. If the operands are of different sizes a conversion of the smaller sized operand will take place before the operator is applied.

- **The assignment operators '=', '+=', '−=', '*=', '/=', '<<=', '>>=', '&=' and '|='.** The assignment operator '=' assigns the value of the right operand to the left operand (which should be an lvalue). If the operands are of different types then the type of the left operand value determines how the value of the right operand is converted. Conversions between integers and decimals are allowed. A conversion may lose information. For example, if a floating point value is assigned to an integer variable then only the integer part of the real value is assigned.

  If the left operand is a pointer type the right operand value can be an integer. However it only makes sense for this to be the value **0,** which is treated as the null pointer value.

  For compound assignments the operation (addition, subtraction etc.) associated with the compond assignment is carried out using the assignment's left and right operands with the result assigned to the left operand.

  Because assignment is an operation and operations generate results it too has a result, this being the value associated with the left operand after the assignment has been carried out.

    Again because assignment is an operator, expressions involving assignment can appear anywhere where an expression is allowed. For example, the expression for an actual argument to a function may include the assignment operator. This freedom of use for assignment should be taken advantage of with great care. If assignment is used in an argument it is almost certainly ill chosen. A further property of expressions is that they can appear in contexts where their value is not used. For example the sequence of expressions

$$i = 0;$$
$$j = 1;$$
$$i + j;$$

  is allowable but in no case are the values of the expressions used. The first two have the values **0** and **1** respectively, with the third having the value **1**. Because the first two involve the assignment operator they also cause the values **0** and **1** to be assigned to the variables **i** and **j**. The third expression, although allowable, is pointless since the result, **1**, is not made use of and the expression has no other effect. It is given here simply to illustrate a parallel between expressions involving assignment and those that do not.

  Note that the right associativity of assignment means that assignments such as

$$i = j = 0;$$

  assign from the right. The value **0** first assigned to **j**. The value of this assignment as an expression is **0** which is then assigned to **i**.

- **The address operators '&' and '*'.** The operator '&' generates a pointer to its operand which must be an lvalue. Given

$$int\ i\ ,\ *\ i\_ptr;$$

  the assignment

$$i\_ptr = \&\ i;$$

  assigns the address associated with the variable **i** to the variable **i_ptr**. Note that

&i is an example of a constant expression producing a value of type pointer to **int**. We cannot change the address associated with the variable **i**, only its contents. It therefore does not make sense for **&i** to appear to the left of an assignment.

The operator '*' returns the object referenced by a pointer variable. Its operand should have a pointer value as its value. Using the declarations above in the sequence

  i = 10;
  i_ptr = & i;

Table A.2 Operator precedence table

Operator		Associativity	Brief description
[]	b	left	array indexing
.	b	to	structure component selection
->	b	right	structure component selection via pointer
++ [post-fix]	u	left	post increment
− − [post-fix]	u	to right	post decrement
++ [pre-fix]	u		pre increment
− − [pre-fix]	u		pre decrement
sizeof	u		object size in bytes
!	u	right	logical not
&	u	to	address operator
*	u	left	indirection operator
−	u		unary minus
*	b	left	multiplication
/	b	to right	division
+	b	left	addition
−	b	to right	subtraction
<<	b	left	left shift values of left operand by value of right operand
>>	b	to right	right shift value of left operand by value of right operand
<	b		comparison-is left operand value less than right?
<=	b	left	less than or equal to
>	b	to right	greater than
>=	b		greater than or equal to
==	b	left	comparison-are the two operand values equal?
!=	b	to right	not equal?
&	b	left to right	bitwise AND
|	b	left to right	bitwise OR
&&	b	left to right	logical AND
||	b	left to right	logical OR
=	b	right	assignment
+=, −=, etc	b	to left	combined assignment

$$i = * i\_ptr + 10;$$

the first assignment assigns the value **10** to the variable **i**, the second the address of **i** to **i_ptr** and the final assignment the value **20** to **i**. The dereferencing operator '*****' dereferences the pointer variable **i_ptr** to obtain the value pointed at by it.

- **sizeof** gives the size of an object or type. It takes as its operand either an expression. in which case its result is the size of the value of the expression. or a type enclosed in brackets, in which case it returns the size of objects of that type.

The operators '**[ ]**', '**.**' and '**->**' are used to break into structured values to gain access to a component of the object in order to use or change the value of the component. These are dealt with later.

Note that a number of symbols are used for several operators. For example the symbol '*****' is used both for the binary multiplication operator and the unary dereferencing operator. Such symbols are described as overloaded to indicate that they mean different things in different contexts. In reading a program there is normally no difficulty in determining which operator is intended. Where confusion might arise, the use of brackets is recommended.

For example with **i** and **i_ptr** above **i * (*i_ptr)** is easier on the eye than **i ** i_ptr**.

Table A.2 gives the associativity and precedence of each operator. Operators with the same precedence are grouped together between heavy lines. Each operator symbol is tagged with either '**b**' or '**u**', indicating whether it is a binary or unary operator. Operators appearing first in the table have the highest precedence.

I I. Conditional expressions

Conditional expressions take the form

$$<expression_1> \ ? \ <expression_2> \ : \ <expression_3>$$

expression_1 is evaluated. If its result is equal to zero then **expression_2** is evaluated and its value is the value of the conditional expression. Otherwise **expression_3** is evaluated with this value taken as the value of the conditional expression.

For example the conditional expression

$$i > j \ ? \ i : j$$

has as its value the larger of the two values in **i** and **j**.

Care should be taken to ensure that the types of **<expression_2>** and **<expression_3>** are consistent.

12. Structured values

Two classes of structured values are supported, namely **arrays,** which are collections of values called **elements** all of the same type and **structs,** which are collections of values called **components** which may be of different types.

Both the elements of arrays and the components of **structs** may themselves be either arrays or structures.

Both arrays and **structs** may be given initial values as part of their defining declarations.

The values associated with array elements may be accessed through the use of indexing operations. The values associated with **struct** components can be accessed through the use of component selection operations. For array and **struct** variables these operations may be used to index elements or select components either as lvalues or rvalues.

No whole array operations are provided in C. Whole array assignment is not supported and only the addresses of arrays are used in giving an array as an argument to a function or returning it as a result.

structs can be treated as single values in assignment, as function arguments and as function results. Pre ANSI standard C did not allow such values to be treated in these ways.

If an array is included as a component of a **struct** then its elements (not its address) are used in whole **struct** operations. Thus if whole array operations are required these can be achieved (rather clumsily) by declaring a **struct** with the array as its one component.

Since any object introduced through a variable declaration will have a type associated with it this will be true also for array and **struct** variables. This type is base on the element or component types but is nevertheless a type in its own right. Types introduced in this way are effectively user defined and can be given names which can then be used in the same way as built-in types.

13. Array declarations

Array declarations take the form of scalar declarations, with the variable identifier followed by an optional array size in square brackets.

For example

    int scores[10];

declares an array of **10 int** values. The brackets must appear. If a size is present then it must be given as a constant expression indicating the number of elements in the array. A size is not needed if the array is initialised as part of the declaration, is a referencing declaration or is a parameter declaration.

Array elements are labelled from **0**. The indexing operation which gives access to array elements takes the form of an expression enclosed in square brackets immediately following the array name. The indexing expression should evaluate to an integer value in the range **0 ... n – 1** where the number of array elements is **n**. The values **0** and **n – 1** are called the bounds of the array.

The expression

    scores[i + 3] = scores[j + 1]

assigns the value of element **j + 1** to element **i + 3**

C allows indexing expressions to evaluate to values outside the indexed array's bounds with unpredictable results. Since this is normally a programming error the programmer should check very carefully that indexing expressions evaluate to sensible subscripts.

It is in any case good practice to program explicit bounds checks before array accesses with appropriate action if the index falls outside the array bounds unless there is no possibility that it can.

An array may be referenced without indexes, in which case the reference is to the address of the first element of the array. The value associated with such a reference is 'pointer to ...'. Thus a reference to scores would yield a value of type pointer to **int**.

The declaration

> **int * i_ptr, arr[10];**

introduces a variable **i_ptr** of type pointer to **int** and an array of **10** integers.

The assignment

> **i_ptr = arr;**

assigns the address of **arr** as a value of type **pointer to int** to the pointer variable **i_ptr**.

An initial value may be included with a declaration. The element values should be given as constant expressions separated by commas within the brackets '{' and '}'. For example the declaration

> **int arr[] = {0,1,2};**

introduces a three element array with elements **arr[0]**, **arr[1]** and **arr[2]** initialised to **0, 1** and **2**.

The declaration

> **int arr[10] = {1,2,3};**

introduces a ten element array with the first three elements initialised to **1, 2** and **3**.

Arrays such as **scores** and **arr** above are called **one-dimensional** arrays. Arrays can be declared with more than one dimension. For example

> **int mat[10][5];**

introduces an array of ten arrays each consisting of five elements.

Multi-dimensional arrays are arrays with elements that are themselves arrays. These arrays can in turn have arrays as elements. Each array level is called a **dimension**. **mat** is a two dimensional array.

Indexing can be applied to such arrays in the way described above and because the indexed elements are themselves arrays these too can be indexed. As many indexes as there are dimensions can be given.

mat[1] references the second element (itself an array of five integers) of the array **mat**. **mat[1][2]** references the third element of this second element.

Array declarations may be defining or referencing declarations. A referencing declaration should specify all the dimensions apart from the first. If **mat** was declared in two different **.c** files the referencing declaration would take the form

> **int mat[][5];**

The second and subsequent dimensions are needed in order that indexing can be dealt with correctly by the compiler. The size of array elements has to be taken into account in generating code for indexing operations.

A defining declaration for a multidimensional array may include an initial value. The declaration

matrix[2][3] = {{1,2,3},{4,5,6}};

introduces a two dimensional array with the elements **matrix[0][0]**, **matrix[0][1]**, ..., **matrix[1][2]** initialised to **1**, **2**, ... , **6** respectively.

Although the nested brackets make clear the association between array elements and initial values they can be left out.

The declaration

matrix[2][3] = {1,2,3,4,5,6};

would achieve the same initialisation.

Where there is an initial value the expression for the first dimension can be left out. The declaration

matrix[][3] = {1,2,3,4,5,6};

has the same effect as the earlier declaration. The second and subsequent dimensions are needed here for the same reason they appear in referencing declarations.

Where an array reference has fewer indexes than the number of dimensions of that array the reference yields a pointer value. Recall that for a one dimensional array an array reference without a subscript evaluates to the address of the first element of the array. The reference **scores** for example has a value of type pointer to **int**.

The type of any pointer value produced in this way will take into account the array element size. Again this is because the element size is needed to ensure that indexing works correctly. For **scores** the element type is **int**. There will be a specific size associated with **int** values and hence the type associated with **scores** does carry information about the array element size. The elements of **matrix** are themselves arrays, each with three **int** elements. Thus the type of value generated by a reference to **matrix** is pointer to 3 element array of **int**.

Such types may be given names using **typedef**. A declaration of the form

typedef <declaration>

associates a name with a type. **<declaration>** looks like a normal variable declaration. However the name used in the position of the variable name is treated as a type name for the type introduced in the declaration.

typedef int integer;

introduces **integer** as a synonym for **int**.

typedef is rarely needed. However it is useful if names for array types such as 3 element array of **int** are required.

We have seen that

int ∗ i_ptr, arr[10];

and

i_ptr = arr;

are allowed.

If we needed a variable to take the value associated with **matrix** we would first need to introduce a type name for its element type as in

> **typedef int three_mls [3];**

which then allows

> **three_ints * m_ptr;**
> **int matrix [2][3];**

and

> **m_ptr = matrix;**

14. Struct declarations

struct declarations may be used to introduce structured objects where the object's components take different types and also to introduce names for new types. Such declarations take the form

struct <type_name>$_{opt}$ **{<component_declaration>; ...} <variable_name>**$_{opt}$

where both **<type_name>** and **<variable_name>** are optional identifiers. **<component_declaration>** looks like a normal variable declaration but it actually describes the type and names of **struct** components.

If **<variable_name>** appears then a variable with the given structure is created. If **<type_name>** appears it names the type introduced by the **struct** declaration.

In either case a new type is introduced by the declaration which is characterised by the sequence of components that appear in the declaration. If this type is needed in several places within the same **.c** file then it should be given a type name within a **struct** declaration.

The type name preceded by the keyword **struct** can then be used in declarations to denote this type, appearing where type normally appears. For example, the declaration

> **struct complex {int r,i;};**

introduces a new type that might be used to deal with complex numbers.

The declarations

> **struct complex arr[10];**
> **struct {struct complex c;char s[10];} s;**

use this type to create an array of ten complex numbers and a variable **s** which is itself a structured object with two components the first of which has type **struct complex** with the second an array.

Note that within the same **.c** file **struct** values will only be treated as having the same type if they have been declared together under a single use of **struct** or in declarations using the same type name. Even if two declarations use the same component names with the same types they will not be treated as the same type. In

> **struct {int i,j;} c1;**

struct {int i,j;} c2;

c1 and **c2** are treated as being of different type.

Where a structured type is needed in different **.c** files it is necessary to make type declarations in each of the files. This is best done by placing the **struct** declaration with a type name but no variable name in a **.h** file which is then included in any **.c** files that need the type.

The selector operator '**.**' is used to select component values. This is a binary operation with the left operand referencing a structure and the right operand giving a component name.

Using the declarations above,

c1.i = c2.i;

assigns the value associated with the first component of **c2** to the first component of **c1**. Note that, although **struct** values may be of different types, they may have component values with the same types. **c1** and **c2** have different types but their components are all of the same type (**int**).

Indexing and component selection can be mixed in an expression as in

arr[0].i = s.c.i;

which assigns the value of the first component of the first component of **s** to the first component of the first element of **arr**.

Given a **struct** type, pointer values based on that type can be created. The declaration

struct complex ∗ c_ptr;

introduces a variable of type pointer to **struct complex**.

The address and indirection operators can be used with structured values. Given the declarations

struct complex c, ∗ c_ptr;

the sequence

c_ptr = &c;
(∗ c_ptr).i = 0;

first assigns the address of the **struct complex** variable **c** to **c_ptr** and then via that pointer initialises its first component to **0**. Because the selection operator '**.**' has higher precedence than the dereferencing operator '**∗**' brackets are needed here.

Because dereferencing followed by component selection is so common the operator '**−>**' is provided to do this.

c_ptr −> i has exactly the same effect as **(∗ c_ptr).i**.

struct declarations can include initialisations. An initial value will consist of a sequence of constant expressions separated by commas within the brackets '**{**' and '**}**'. They look exactly like array initalisations except that the constant expressions may have values of different types.

The declaration

struct {char name[6]; int number;} s = {"Smith",1927};

introduces a structure **s** of two components the first being an array of characters initialised to the string **"Smith"** with the second an integer initialised to **1927**.

Components and elements can themselves be structured. Here initial values will include bracketted values that give initial values for structured components or elements. Given

   struct entry {char first_name[6]; char second_name[6];};

then

   struct {struct entry name; int number;} s = {{"john","smith"},1927};

makes use of this to introduce and initialise a variable **s**.

15. Function declaration

Function declarations consist of a header declaration and optionally a function body. If the function body is included then the declaration is a defining declaration.

The header takes the form

   <result_type>$_{opt}$ **<result_name> (<parameter_list>**$_{opt}$ **)**

where **<parameter_list>** is a sequence of parameter declarations separated by commas.

These are similar in form to normal declarations except that

- each type specification must be followed by only one parameter name
- parameter declarations are separated by commas
- new structure types cannot be introduced as part of a parameter declaration, although existing structure types can be used.

A function **call** consists of the function name followed by a sequence of expressions (called function **arguments**), each corresponding to a parameter. The correspondence is positional.

The parameters are treated as variables declared within the called function and initialised to the values of the corresponding arguments. Type differences between parameters and argument values are treated in the same way as for normal assignments.

The order in which arguments are evaluated is undefined.   The result type takes the form of a type specifier (**int, int ∗, char, char ∗, struct complex, struct complex ∗**, etc.).

If no result type is specified **int** is assumed.

Since a function call is an expression and the results from expressions can be discarded the result returned from a function may be discarded. For example if **f** is a parameterless function returning an integer value then both

  i = f();

and

  f();

are valid. The first assigns the result from **f** to **i**. The second discards the result.

Sometimes functions that return no result are required in which case the result type given in the function's header is specified as **void**.

16. Statements

The following statement types are described here:

- blocks (compound statements.)
- expression statements
- conditional statements
- iterative statements
- the break statement
- the return statement
- switch statements
- the null statement.

16.1 Blocks

A block is made up of a sequence of declarations (other than function declarations) followed by a sequence of statements. The declarations are preceded by the bracket '{' and the statements are followed by the bracket '}'. Both the declarations and statements are optional.

A block is executed by first creating space for any non-static variables declared at the head of the block and then by sequencing through the statements contained in the block, executing them in order. Static variables have space allocated to them at the start of the program's execution.

Note that the body of a function is a block and also that blocks are statements and can appear wherever statements are allowed.

16.2 Expression statements

An expression may appear as a statement, in which case it will normally include the assignment operation or be a function call. The value of an expression used in this way is discarded.

16.3 Conditional statements

Conditional statements take the form

if (<expression>) <statement$_1$>

optionally followed by

else <statement$_2$>

Note that **<expression>** is enclosed in brackets and that both **<statement$_1$>** and **<statement$_2$>** should end with ';' unless they are blocks.
<expression> should yield a value that can be compared with **0**.
If the conditional statement includes an **else** then if the value of **<expression>** is not equal to **0** then **<statement$_1$>** is executed otherwise **<statement$_2$>** is executed.

If the conditional statement does not include an **else** then if the value of **<expression>** is not equal to **0** then **<statement$_1$>** is executed.

16.4 Iterative statements

Three different types of iterative statement are described here:

> **while** statements
> **do** statements
> **for** statements.

The **while** statement takes the form

> **while (<expression>) <statement>**

<expression> is evaluated and if its value is equal to **0** execution of the while statement terminates. If its value is not equal to **0** then **<statement>** is executed with **<expression>** then re-evaluated. Again if **<expression>** evaluates to a value equal to **0** the while statement terminates. Otherwise the cycle is repeated.

Note that as with the above conditional statement **<expression>** is enclosed in brackets and that **<statement>** should end with a ';' unless it is a block.

The do statement takes the form

> **do <statement> while (<expression>);**

<statement> is executed and **<expression>** is then evaluated. If this value is equal to **0** the do statement terminates. Otherwise the cycle is repeated.

Again note that **<expression>** is enclosed in brackets and that **<statement>** should end with a ';' unless it is a block.

The for statement takes the form

> **for (<expression$_1$>$_{opt}$;<expression$_2$>$_{opt}$;<expression$_3$>$_{opt}$) <statement>**

If **<expression$_1$>** is present it is evaluated and its value is discarded. Normally this expression will involve an assignment.

If **<expression$_2$>** is present it is evaluated. If its value is equal to **0** the for statement terminates. If **<expression$_2$>** is not present or its value is not equal to **0** **<statement>** is executed.

If **<expression$_3$>** is present it is evaluated and its value is discarded. Again an assignment of some form would normally take place here.

The cycle is then repeated from the stage where **<expression$_2$>** is evaluated if it is present.

All the expressions are optional and semicolons, which should always appear even if expressions are omitted, separate the three expressions.

16.5 The break statement

The statement

> **break;**

terminates the while, do, for or switch statement in which it occurs. Such statements can be nested in which case it is the innermost statement that is terminated. **break** cannot be used elsewhere.

break is normally used with the switch statement and any use elsewhere as for example in while statements should be carefully considered.

16.6 The return statement

The **return** statement takes the form

return <expression>$_{opt}$**;**

return takes control back from a function to the point after the function call was made. If **<expression>** is present then it is evaluated before exit from the function and its value is returned as the function's result. The function result type will determine any conversions on the value of the expression. If **<expression>** is not present and the function call is in a context where a result is required the effect is undefined.

16.7 Switch Statements

A switch statement normally takes the form

switch (<expression>)

followed by a sequence of statements enclosed by '{' and '}' where some of the statements are labelled.

Labels take the either the form

case <constant_expression>:

where **<constant_expression>** is a constant expression, or the form

default:

A statement may have more than one label associated with it.

The values of the constant expressions should all be different and only one **default** label should appear. A **default** label is optional.

For a given switch statement the types of the constant expressions following **case** and the expression following **switch** should be consistent.

Although C does not require the use of labels with **switch** it is of very little value without them.

<expression> is evaluated and, if a label with a constant value equal to the value of the expression occurs in the switch statement, control is transferred to the statement associated with that label. If no such label exists but **default** does then control is transferred to the statement associated with the **default** label. Otherwise control is transferred to what follows the switch statement.

If control is transferred to a statement within the **switch** statement then statements are executed in order from that point.

In practice, each label apart from the last will normally label a group of statements the last of which is a **break** statement. The effect of executing a switch statement organised in this way is to execute only the group of statements associated with a particular label.

For example **ch** could contain a value of type **char**:

```
switch (ch)
{
    case 'a':
    case 'e':
    case 'i':
```

```
            case 'o':
            case 'u':  printf("Lower case vowel");
                          break;
            case 'A':
            case 'E':
            case 'I':
            case 'O':
            case 'U':  printf("Upper case vowel");
                          break;
            default:  printff("Not a vowel");
    }
```

This will output 'Lower case vowel' if **ch** contains a lower case vowel, 'Upper case vowel' if it contains an upper case vowel and 'Not a vowel' for any other character.

16.6 The null statement

The **null** statement consists simply of the semicolon. It has no effect.

It is sometimes useful in iterations where the expression controlling the iteration is also being used for its side effect.

For example suppose we have an array **name** with elements of type **char** and we know that a string is stored in the array. Suppose also that the variable **i** has been initialised to **0**. We want the position of the end of the string. Since strings are sequences of characters terminated by the character value '\0' (which is the same value as **0**) the while statement

while (name[i ++]);

will terminate when **i** subscripts the first element after the string. The expression controlling the iteration has the side effect of incrementing **i**. Since this is all we want of the while statement we use the null statement as its body.

17 The C library

C systems normally provide a rich set of functions that the programmer uses. These have been standardised and those described here should be common across most systems.

The library is split up into groups of functions and each group has a **.h** file associated with it that contains function prototypes for the group. Often the **.h** file will contain other components such as type declarations. Whenever functions in a given group are used the group's **.h** file should be **#include**'d.

17.1 File names

Backing storage is usually organised as a hierarchy of directories where directories can contain further directories or files, although this organisation will differ in detail from operating system to operating system. Both directories and files will have names. Since any given file will be held in a directory which itself may also be held in a directory, a file can be located by specifying a sequence of directory names followed by a file name.

Most operating systems employ the notion of a working directory. A system user can position himself in one of his directories, as his working directory and file name and directory name references are assumed to be to files and directories in this working directory. This means that it is not necessary to give the full sequence of directory names to identify a file or directory held in the working directory.

If **#include** (at the start of a line) followed by a file name in the form of a string appears in a program the contents of the file (which normally contains program text) will be added to the program at the line containing the **#include**. If the file name is a reference to a file in the current working directory only the file name is required. Otherwise the directory sequence locating the position of the file in the file store is needed. However with library files that hold among other things library function prototypes only the file name enclosed in angle brackets ('<' ,'>') is required.

To access a file from a C program the file must first be opened. Given a file name the process of opening a file entails locating the file within the file store and setting up a link between the file and the executing program. This link is call a **stream** in C. The stream associated with the file on open is then used to access the file.

Streams are accessed through values of type **FILE** * .

Two streams are created when the execution of a program is started, namely **stdin** and **stdout**. The first is used to obtain input from the keyboard and the second is used to generate output to the screen. Viewing the keyboard and screen as files the system automatically opens them at the start of program execution, linking them to **stdin** and **stdout**.

The **.h** file associated with input/output is **stdio.h**. This includes the declaration of type **FILE**.

17.1.1 Opening and closing files
The two functions described here are

> **FILE * fopen(const char * filename,const char * mode)**

and

> **int fclose(FILE * stream)**

For **fopen filename** given the name of the file to be opened. Its form depends on the naming conventions of the operating system under which the C system operates.

Note the way the type associated with **filename** is described. If the keyword **const** appears with a type specification the object created as a result of the declaration cannot be modified, although with a parameter it will get initialised to the argument value and if it is used with a normal declaration by any initalisation in the declaration.

mode gives the type of file access required and is expressed as a string of at least one character. The possible types include

> **"r"**   Open an existing file for input.
> **"w"**   Open a file for output. If the file already exists then it will be overwritten.
> **"a"**   Open a file for output. If the file already exists then it will be appended.

If the open fails then a null pointer is returned. Otherwise a stream is established for access to the file and its address is returned as the function's result.

For **fclose stream** is an expression with a value of type **FILE** * which identifies an open stream. The file on that stream is closed and the stream itself is lost.

17.1.2 File access

There are over 20 file access functions provided in the library of which seven are described here. (Strictly one of these is normally not implemented as a function but this does not affect the way it is used.)

stdio.h contains a **#define** for the identifier **EOF**. This value is returned from a number of the file access functions if a problem occurred in carrying out the operation.

The functions fall into two subgroups, a subgroup dedicated to the streams **stdin** and **stdout** and general functions that apply to any stream. It is always the case that effect of any function in this first subgroup can be achieved by use of a corresponding function in the second subgroup.

Access via stdin and stdout
The functions

> **int printf(const char * format , ...)**
> **int scanf(const char * format , ...)**
> **int getchar()**

can be used to write to the screen (**printf**) or read from the keyboard (**scanf** and **getchar**).

format is a string which directs the input or output of a value, specifying such things as what type should be assumed for the value and for output the field size to be used. It can contain input or output directives for more than one input or output operation. For **printf** these will all be output operations and for **scanf** these will all be input operations. Format strings can contain normal character sequences as well. In **printf** the character sequence will be output. A subset of the formatting directives available is given below.

, ... indicates a possibly empty list of expressions separated by commas. The number of expressions should correspond with the number of input or output directives that appear in the format string.

For **scanf** the expressions should yield values of type 'pointer to ... '. **scanf** requires a destination address for the input. This is often achieved through the use of the address operator '**&**'.

printf returns **EOF** if an error occurred on output.

scanf returns the number of successful input operations carried out or EOF if no further input is possible from the file. This result can be used to check for any input errors, since the number of input directives in the format string will be known.

getchar() reads the next character from **stdin** returning it as a value of type **int**.
Format directives used in **printf** format strings take the form

$$\% \text{ <flags>}_{opt}\text{<field\_width>}_{opt}\text{<precision>}_{opt}\text{<conversion\_type>}$$

where **<flags>** is a character sequence; **<field_width>** is an unsigned integer constant; **<precision>** is an unsigned integer constant preceded by the character '.'; and **<conversion_type>** is a one or two character sequence indicating the type the output value should be converted to, and, with integers, whether the output is in decimal or hexadecimal form.

A number of characters may appear in **<flags>**. Here we give just one of these ,'–', which when present causes the output to be left justified in its output field. Without it output is right justified.

<field_width> specifies the number of character positions in the output field. If the output value is smaller than this then the field is space filled. The output value may be larger, in which case as many character positions as are needed are used.

<precision> can (among other things) be used to specify the number of digit positions following the decimal point on the output of real numbers. This number is given by the integer constant specified with **<precision>**.

<conversion_type> indicates the type of the associated output value. Care should be taken to ensure that the specified conversion type and the expression giving the output value are consistent. **printf** will treat the result of any expression in its argument list as being of the type indicated by its corresponding **<conversion_type>**. If the types are different, no actual conversion takes place, the result being assumed to be of the indicated type. If for example the expression generates a value of type **int** but **<conversion_type>** specifies the output of a floating point a floating point value will be assumed. Because floating points take more memory than **int**s the actual output will certainly not be as expected. The **int** value is not converted to a floating point in the way it would be under assignment. A floating point value is assumed.

The conversion characters include

- 'd'   output an **int** value in decimal
- 'x'   output an **int** value in hexadecimal
- 'u'   output an **insigned int** value
- 'c'   output a **char** value
- 's'   output a string – the associated expression should have a value of type **char** ∗
- 'f'   output a real number.

If the conversion character is preceded by the character 'l' or by 'h' the output type is interpreted as **long** or **short**.

The following examples illustrate the use of output directives.

> **printf("The square of %d is %d",i,i∗i);**

If **i** has the value **10** this would generate the output '**The square of 10 is 100**'

> **for (i = 0;i<number_of_entries,i ++)**
>   **printf("%–10s %–10d\n",**
>   **telephone_directory[i].name,telephone_directory[i].number);**

If **telephone_directory** is an array of structures with the structure components **name** and **number** being of type **char** ∗ and **int**, respectively, the for statement outputs names and numbers left justified in columns provided that no name is longer than ten characters.

For **scanf** '%' followed by one of the above conversion characters can be used to control input. Characters will be read in and used to construct a value of the type indicated by the conversion character. (**scanf** discards initial spaces or '\n's for 'd', 'x', 'u' and 'f'.) This value is then placed at the address pointed at by the corresponding expression. Again care should be taken to ensure that the type of the object addressed by the expression and the type associated with the conversion character are consistent. No check is made to ensure that the object is large enough to take the input value.

The functions

int fprintf(FILE ∗ stream, const char ∗ format , ...)
int fscanf(FILE ∗ stream, const char ∗ format , ...)

behave much as **printf** and **scanf** do, except that the stream given by **stream** is used. For **fscanf** the file is read sequentially. If the file has already been completely read on a call to **scanf scanf** will return **EOF**.

The functions

int getc(FILE ∗ stream)
int ungetc(int c, FILE ∗ stream)

are used with streams that are open for input. The first returns the next character in the stream or **EOF**. The second pushes the value **c** out to the stream in such a way that it is the next character for input.

17.2 Dynamic allocation of memory

There are a number of functions that allow the programmer to obtain and release memory. Two of these are described here

void ∗ malloc (size_t size);

and

void free(void ∗ ptr);

The function prototypes are held in **stdlib.h**.

malloc allocates a block of **size** bytes and returns a pointer to the first byte of the block. If the block cannot be allocated for any reason the null pointer is returned. There are two points to note about the way **malloc** is specified. First its result type is given as **void ∗**. If a pointer variable is assigned a pointer value they should normally have the same type and if they do not the compiler will issue a warning message. The one case where this will not happen is where one of the types is **void ∗**. Thus **void ∗** can stand for any pointer type. Second the type of **size** is given as **size_t**. It will of course be an unsigned integer. Since there are three types associated with unsigned integers, corresponding to **unsigned long int, unsigned int** and **unsigned short int** any of these could be used as the type of **size**. The actual type chosen is system dependent and is given by **size_t** which is defined as one of these in **stddef.h**. However, in using **malloc** (and **sizeof** which also has a result of type **size_t**), the programmer almost certainly need not worry about this issue.

The operator **sizeof** is often useful here to compute the size of an object for which space is required.

free releases the memory addressed by **ptr**. The type of the argument will determine how much memory is released. For example if the argument is of type pointer to **int** the space occupied by a value of type **int** is released.

17.3 Exiting from a program

Exit from a function takes place either on a return or when control reaches the end of the block that forms the function's body. Exit from **main** in this way will lead to the termination of the program. It is sometimes convenient to terminate a program elsewhere. The function

> **void exit(int status)**

is provided for this. **status** will normally be **0**.

stdlib.h contains the function's prototype.

17.4 String handling functions

The four functions (among at least 18)

> **char * strcpy(char * s1, const char * s2)**
> **char * strcat(char * s1, const char * s2)**
> **int strcmp(const char * s1, const char * s2);**
> **size_t strlen(const char * s);**

are available via **string.h**. Unlike the functions described in Sections 17.1 – 17.3 these would be quite easy for the programmer to write for himself. However the system supplied functions are likely to be more efficient.

strcpy copies the string **s2** to **s1**. **s1** is returned. The programmer must ensure that the area of memory addressed via **s1** is large enough to hold the string.

strcat appends a copy of **s2** at the end of **s1**, overwriting the string terminator in **s1**. **s1** is returned.

strcmp compares **s1** and **s2** lexicographically. The function result is less than zero if **s1** is lexicographically less than **s2**, zero if the strings match and greater than zero otherwise.

strlen returns the length of the string **s**. (This length does not include the string terminator.)

17.5 Character classes

A number of functions are available which test if a character belongs to a particular class (a digit, a letter, etc.). These include

> **int isalnum(int c)** – is **c** a letter or a digit
> **int isalpha(int c)** – is **c** a letter
> **int isdigit(int c)** – is **c** a digit.

In each case a non-zero value is returned if the character is in the class and zero otherwise.

The file **ctype.h** contains the relevant header files.

Appendix **2**

The assembler/ interpreter described in Chapter 8

```c
#include <stdio.h>
#include <string.h>
#include <stdlib.h>
#include <ctype.h>


#define ID_ERROR        0
#define LAB_CLASH       1
#define ILLEGAL_REG     2
#define BRACKET         3
#define LIT_EXPECTED    4
#define ILLEGAL_MNEMONIC  5
#define OPAND_ERROR     6
#define COMMA_EXPECTED    7
#define REG_REQUIRED    8
#define ILLEGAL_OPERAND  9
#define PROG_TOO_LARGE  10
#define MEM_SIZE        4096
#define O_K             1
#define NOT_O_K         0
#define NO_OF_MNEMONICS  18
#define TRUE            1
#define FALSE           0

char * read_id(char next_char);
unsigned long int build_code(struct instruction i);

enum op_code { add,cmp,sub,bra,beq,bne,blt,ble,bgt,
      bge,jsr,rts,move,wri,read,end,ds,dc};

enum address_mode {gen_reg,literal,absolute,
```

```
        indirect,offset};

struct operand { enum address_mode a_m;int reg,lit_val;};

struct instruction {enum op_code o_c;
            int no_of_opands;
            struct operand opand1, opand2;};

/* Interpreter */


struct decoded_instruction {int opcode,s_d_bit,reg,a_m,a_m_reg,lit_val;};
unsigned long int mem[MEM_SIZE],regs[8];

int p_c;


void load_program(unsigned long int * assembled_program,int program_size,int
start_address)
{
   for (p_c = 0;p_c < program_size;p_c ++)
     mem[p_c] = assembled_program[p_c];
   p_c = start_address;
}



int get_bit_field(unsigned long int code,int pos,int size)
{
   code<<=(31–pos);
   return code>>=(31–size + 1);
}

struct decoded_instruction decode(unsigned long int code)
{
   struct decoded_instruction d_i;
   d_i.opcode = get_bit_field(code,31,6);
   d_i.s_d_bit = get_bit_field(code,25,1);
   d_i.reg = get_bit_field(code,24,3);
   d_i.a_m = get_bit_field(code,21,3);
   d_i.a_m_reg = get_bit_field(code,18,3);
   d_i.lit_val = get_bit_field(code,15,16);
   return d_i;
}


/* get_mem_val returns the value of an operand. It is used for
   both source and destination operands. The first argument holds the
```

decoded instruction with the second indicating which operand –
source or destination – is being accessed */

```c
unsigned long int get_value(struct decoded_instruction d_i,int s_d)
{
  if (d_i.s_d_bit == s_d) return regs[d_i.reg];
  switch (d_i.a_m)
    {
      case gen_reg:  return regs[d_i.a_m_reg];
         case literal:  return (unsigned long int) d_i.lit_val;
         case absolute: return mem[d_i.lit_val];
         case indirect: return mem[regs[d_i.a_m_reg]];
         case offset:   return mem[regs[d_i.a_m_reg]+d_i.lit_val];
    }

}
```

/* If s_d == 1 the first operand (source) specifies where the value is to
  be stored. Otherwise the second (destination) operand specifies this. */

```c
void store_value(struct decoded_instruction d_i,unsigned long int val,int s_d)
{
  if (d_i.s_d_bit == s_d) regs[d_i.reg] = val;
  else
  switch (d_i.a_m)
    {
    case gen_reg:  regs[d_i.a_m_reg] = val;
              break;
    case absolute: mem[d_i.lit_val] = val;
              break;
    case indirect: mem[regs[d_i.a_m_reg]] = val;
              break;
    case offset:   mem[regs[d_i.a_m_reg] + d_i.lit_val] = val;
    }
}

int get_address(struct decoded_instruction d_i)
{
  switch (d_i.a_m)
    {
    case absolute: return d_i.lit_val;
    case indirect: return regs[d_i.a_m_reg];
    case offset:   return regs[d_i.a_m_reg] + d_i.lit_val;
    }
}
```

```
void interpret()
{

    unsigned long int return_address_stack[1024];
    int top = 0;
    struct decoded_instruction d_i = decode(mem[p_c]);
    char cc_eq,cc_lt;
    unsigned long int input;

    while (d_i.opcode != end)
    {

    unsigned long int source_val = get_value(d_i,1),
        dest_val = get_value(d_i,0);

    p_c ++;
        switch(d_i.opcode)
        {
        case  add: store_value(d_i,source_val + dest_val,0);
            break;
        case  cmp: cc_eq = source_val == dest_val;
            cc_lt = dest_val < source_val;
            break;
        case  sub: store_value(d_i,dest_val–source_val,0);
            break;
        case  bra: p_c = get_address(d_i);;
                break;
        case  beq: if (cc_eq) p_c = get_address(d_i);;
            break;
        case  bne: if (!cc_eq)p_c = get_address(d_i);
            break;
        case  blt: if (cc_lt) p_c = get_address(d_i);
            break;
        case  ble: if (cc_lt || cc_eq) p_c = get_address(d_i);
            break;
        case  bgt: if (!cc_lt && !cc_eq) p_c = get_address(d_i);
            break;
        case  bge: if (!cc_lt) p_c = get_address(d_i);
            break;
        case  jsr: return_address_stack[top ++] = p_c;
                p_c = get_address(d_i);
            break;
        case  rts: p_c = return_address_stack[—top];
            break;
          case move: store_value(d_i,source_val,0);
            break;
```

```
        case wri:  printf("\n%lu\n",source_val);
              break;
        case read: scanf("%lu",&input);
              store_value(d_i,input,1);


     }
     d_i = decode(mem[p_c]);
     }
}
```

/* Error Management */

```
int error_count = 0;
int line_count = 1;

void error(int err)
{
   char * err_msg[] =
        {"Identifier more than 19 characters.",
         "This label already labels eleswhere.",
         "Register required here.",
         "Closing bracket required.",
         "Literal value required",
         "Unknown mnemonic",
         "Illegal operand specification",
         "Comma required",
         "At least one operand must be a register."};

   printf("%s at line %d\n",err_msg[err],line_count);
   error_count ++;
}

void increment_line_count()
{
   line_count ++;
}

int get_error_count()
{
   return error_count;
}
```

/* Instruction store used by assembler */

```c
unsigned long int assembled_program[MEM_SIZE];
int code_addr = 0;

void save_code(unsigned long int code)
{
   if (code_addr == MEM_SIZE) error(PROG_TOO_LARGE);
   else assembled_program[code_addr ++] = code;
}

void update_code(int location)
{
   assembled_program[location] += code_addr;
}

int get_code_address()
{
   return code_addr;
}

void call_load(int start_address)
{
   load_program(assembled_program,code_addr,start_address);
}

void update_code_address(int increment)
{
   code_addr += increment;
}


/* Label Table Management */


struct addr_list_entry {int addr; struct addr_list_entry * next;};

struct labtab_entry {char * label;
         int lab_addr;
             struct addr_list_entry * forward_refs;
         struct labtab_entry * next;};

struct labtab_entry * label_table = 0;



struct labtab_entry * find_label_entry(char * label)
{
   struct labtab_entry * table = label_table;
```

```c
        while (table)
        {
        if (!strcmp(label,table -> label))
            return table;
            else table = table -> next;
        }
        return 0;
}

struct labtab_entry * add_label(char * label)
{
        struct labtab_entry ** t = &label_table;
```

/* move to the end of the table, allocate space for a table entry
and for the name component and add name and value*/

```c
        while (*t) t = &((*t) -> next);
        * t = malloc(sizeof(struct labtab_entry));
        (* t) -> label = malloc(sizeof(char) * (strlen(label) + 1));
        strcpy(( * t) -> label,label);
        (* t) -> lab_addr = get_code_address();
        (* t) -> next = 0;
        (* t) -> forward_refs = 0;
        return * t;
}

void process_label(char next_char)
{


        struct labtab_entry * entry;
        char * label = read_id(next_char);
        if (entry = find_label_entry(label))
        {
        struct addr_list_entry * forward_refs = entry -> forward_refs;
        entry -> lab_addr = get_code_address();
            entry -> forward_refs = 0;

        if (!forward_refs) error(LAB_CLASH);

        while (forward_refs)
        {
            update_code(forward_refs -> addr);
            forward_refs = forward_refs -> next;
        }
        }
        else add_label(label);
}
```

```
void add_forward_reference(struct labtab_entry * entry)
{
    struct addr_list_entry ** e = &(entry -> forward_refs);
    while (* e) e = &((*e) -> next);
    * e = malloc(sizeof(struct addr_list_entry));
    (* e) - >addr = get_code_address();
    (* e) -> next = 0;
}

int look_up_label(char * label)
{
    struct labtab_entry * entry = find_label_entry(label);
    if (entry)
    {
    if (entry -> forward_refs == 0) return entry -> lab_addr;
    }
    else entry = add_label(label);
    add_forward_reference(entry);
    return 0;
}



void display_table(struct labtab_entry * table)
{

    while (table)
    {
    printf("%s    %d\n",table -> label,table -> lab_addr);
    table = table -> next;
    }
}



/* Lexical Analysis */

struct instr_properties {enum op_code o_c;
            int no_of_opands;
            enum operand_class opand1_class,opand2_class;};

enum operand_class {reg,memory,mem_or_reg,any,lit,none};

/* class_table is an address_mode by operand_class matrix.
   For each instruction the allowable address modes are given by
   an operand class associated with the instruction's operand(s).
```

Where an instruction appears in a program the address mode(s)
of its operand(s) need to be identified. Once this is done
class_table is used to check that the address mode is allowable
for that operand. */

```
int class_table [5][6]
          =
          {{O_K,NOT_O_K,O_K,O_K,NOT_O_K,NOT_O_K},
           {NOT_O_K,NOT_O_K,NOT_O_K,O_K,O_K,NOT_O_K},
           {NOT_O_K,O_K,O_K,O_K,NOT_O_K,NOT_O_K},
          {NOT_O_K,O_K,O_K,O_K,NOT_O_K,NOT_O_K},
          {NOT_O_K,O_K,O_K,O_K,NOT_O_K,NOT_O_K}};


void check_class_ok(enum address_mode a_m,enum operand_class o_c)
{
   if (class_table[a_m][o_c]) return;
   error(OPAND_ERROR);
}
```

/* the mnemonics table associates the operation code, the number of operands
   and the allowable operand class for each operand with each mnemonic. */

```
struct {char  mnemonic[5];
        struct instr_properties i_props;
        } mnemonics_table[NO_OF_MNEMONICS]

           =

          {{"ADD",{add,2,any,mem_or_reg}},
           {"CMP",{cmp,2,any,any}},
           {"SUB",{sub,2,any,mem_or_reg}},
           {"BRA",{bra,1,memory,none}},
           {"BEQ",{beq,1,memory,none}},
           {"BNE",{bne,1,memory,none}},
           {"BLT",{blt,1,memory,none}},
           {"BLE",{ble,1,memory,none}},
           {"BGT",{bgt,1,memory,none}},
           {"BGE",{bge,1,memory,none}},
           {"JSR",{jsr,1,memory,none}},
                {"RTS",{rts,0,none,none}},
           {"MOVE",{move,2,any,mem_or_reg}},
           {"WRI",{wri,1,any,none}},
                {"READ",{read,1,mem_or_reg,none}},
           {"END", {end,1,memory,none}},
           {"DS",{ds,1,lit,none}},
```

```
                {"DC",{dc,1,lit,none}}};
```

```
/* instruction_properties uses the instruction mnemonic to locate
   the instruction's properties in the mnemonic table
   which are then returned as the function's result.
*/

struct instr_properties  instruction_properties(char * name)
{
    int i = – 1;
    while (i ++< NO_OF_MNEMONICS)
    if (!strcmp(name,mnemonics_table[i].mnemonic))
       return mnemonics_table[i].i_props;
    error(ILLEGAL_MNEMONIC);
}
```

```
FILE * source;
```

```
void open_source()
{
   source=fopen("APROG","r");
}
```

```
/* read a sequence of digits returning the corresponding integer */

int read_int(char next_char)
{
   int i = 0;
   while ((next_char >= '0') && (next_char <= '9'))
   {
      i = i * 10 + next_char–'0';
   next_char = getc(source);
   }
   ungetc(next_char,source);
   return i;
}
```

```
/* read a sequence of letters,digits or '_' characters, create
   a corresponding string and return a pointer to it */

char * read_id(char next_char)
{
   static char id[20];int in = 0;
   while (isalnum(next_char)||next_cha == '_')
   {
   if (in < 20) id[in ++] = next_char;
   else error(ID_ERROR);
```

```
    next_char = getc(source);
    }
    id[in] = '\0';
    ungetc(next_char,source);
    return id;
}
```

/* obtain the next non-space character from the source file */

```
char get_next_char()
{
    char next_char = getc(source);
    while (next_char == ' ') next_char = getc(source);
    return next_char;
}
```

/* move to the next source line discarding comments and blank lines */
```
void move_to_next_line()
{

    char next_char = getc(source);
    while (next_char != '\n') next_char = getc(source);
    increment_line_count();
}
```

```
char next_instruction()
{
    char next_char = getc(source);
    while(TRUE)
    {
        if (next_char == '*')
        {
            move_to_next_line();
            next_char = getc(source);
        }
        else
        if (next_char == '\n')
        {
            next_char = getc(source);
            increment_line_count();
        }
        else break;
    }
    return next_char;
}
```

```c
void offset_or_abs(struct operand * opand)
{
   char next_char = get_next_char();
   if (next_char == '(')
   {
      (* opand).a_m = offset;
      if (((*opand).reg = a_reg(get_next_char())) == - 1) error(ILLEGAL_REG);
      if (get_next_char() !=')') error(BRACKET);
   }
   else
   {
      (* opand).a_m = absolute;
      ungetc(next_char,source);
   }
}

int a_reg(char next_char)
{
   char ch = getc(source);
   if (((ch >= '0') && (ch <= '7')) && (next_char == 'R')) return ch-'0';
   else return - 1;
}

struct operand analyse_operand(char next_char)
{
   struct operand opand;
   if (isdigit(next_char))
   {
      opand.lit_val = read_int(next_char);
      offset_or_abs(&opand);
   }
   else
   if (next_char == '#')
   {
      opand.a_m = literal;
      next_char = get_next_char();
   if (isdigit(next_char)) opand.lit_val = read_int(next_char);
   else
   if (isalpha(next_char))
   {
      char * id = read_id(next_char);
      opand.lit_val = look_up_label(id);
      }
      else error(LIT_EXPECTED);
   }
   else
   if (next_char == '(')
```

```
    {
        opand.a_m = indirect;
        if ((opand.reg = a_reg(get_next_char())) == - 1) error(ILLEGAL_REG);
        if (get_next_char() != ')') error(ILLEGAL_REG);
    }
    else
    if (isalpha(next_char))
    {
    char * id = read_id(next_char);
        if ((strlen(id) == 2) && (id[0] == 'R') && (id[1] >= '0') && (id[1] <= '7'))
    {
        opand.reg = id[1] - '0';
            opand.a_m = id[0] == gen_reg;
        }
    else
    {
        opand.lit_val = look_up_label(id);
            offset_or_abs(&opand);
    }
    }
    else error(ILLEGAL_OPERAND);
    return opand;
}


/* This function deals with a line of assembler code
   checking for errors and returning the instruction in
   an intermediate form as a value of type instruction
   which build_code uses to generate its machine
   code equivalent.
*/


struct instruction analyse_instruction()
{
    int operand_count = 0;
    struct instruction i;
    struct instr_properties i_props;
    char next_char = next_instruction();

/* Read and analyse the assembler instruction.

   Start with a possible label */

    i_props.no_of_opands = 0;

    if (next_char != ' ') process_label(next_char);
    next_char = get_next_char();
```

```
/* followed by a possible instruction mnemonic */

    if (next_char != '\n' && next_char != '*')
    {
        i_props = instruction_properties(read_id(next_char));
    next_char = get_next_char();
    }

/* and a possible source operand */

    if (next_char != '\n' && next_char != '*')
    {
    i.opand1 = analyse_operand(next_char);
    operand_count ++;
    next_char = get_next_char();
    }


/* and second operand. */

    if (next_char != '\n' && next_char != '*')
    {
        if (next_char != ',') error(COMMA_EXPECTED);
        else next_char = get_next_char();
    }

    if (next_char != '\n' && next_char != '*')
    {
    i.opand2 = analyse_operand(next_char);
        operand_count ++;
    }

/* Build the internal form of the instruction in i,
   checking that the operands make sense.

   First set up the operation code */

    i.o_c = i_props.o_c;

/* followed by operand details. */

    i.no_of_opands = i_props.no_of_opands;

    if (i_props.no_of_opands != operand_count)
        error(OPAND_ERROR);
    else
    {
```

```
        if (operand_count != 0)
           check_class_ok(i.opand1.a_m,i_props.opand1_class);
        if (operand_count == 2)
        {
        check_class_ok(i.opand2.a_m,i_props.opand2_class);
        if ( (i.opand1.a_m != gen_reg) && (i.opand2.a_m != gen_reg))
           error(REG_REQUIRED);
        }
     }
     if (next_char !='\n') move_to_next_line();
     return i;
}
```

/* Directives */

```
int directive(enum op_code o_c)
{
    enum op_code dirs[3] = {end,ds,dc}; int i;
    for (i = 0;i < 3;i ++) if (dirs[i] ==o_c) return TRUE;
    return FALSE;
}

void process_directive(struct instruction i)
{
    switch (i.o_c)
    {
    case end: if (i.opand1.a_m != absolute) error(ILLEGAL_OPERAND);
            save_code(build_code(i));
         break;
    case ds:  update_code_address(i.opand1.lit_val);
         break;
    case dc:  save_code(i.opand1.lit_val);
    }
}
```

/* Code Generation */

/* This module generates code from the output from the
   lexical analysis module (lex.c). lex.c generates a description
   of each instructon as a value of type instruction (defined in
   instrs.h) Type instruction makes use of a further type
   operand (again defined in instr.h). The coded instruction is
   built in an unsigned long int. The assumption is that long ints
   are 32 bits long. */

/* set_bit_field assumes long ints are 32 bits. It takes the address
   of a long int (code) in which an instruction is being built and inserts
   a bit pattern. The position in code and the size of the bit field
   to be used are given in pos and size. The pattern to be inserted is
   held as a long integer. The most significant bit position
   in code is numbered 31, the least 0. */

```
void set_bit_field(unsigned long int * code,int pos,int size,unsigned long int
setting)
{
    setting <<= (pos-size + 1);
    (*code)|=setting;
}
```

/* This function inserts the operation code. */

```
void set_op_code(unsigned long int * code,struct instruction i)
{
    set_bit_field(code,31,6,i.o_c);
}
```

/* In the 32 bit coded instruction bits 21 .. 0 are used to code an
   operand address. (Operands may also be coded as registers in
   bits 24 .. 22). This function builds this part of the coded
   instruction
*/

```
void build_effective_address(unsigned long int * code,
                    enum address_mode a_m,
                    int reg,int lit_val)
{
    set_bit_field(code,21,3,a_m);
    if ((a_m == gen_reg) || (a_m == indirect) || (a_m == offset))
        set_bit_field(code,18,3,reg);
    if ((a_m == literal) || (a_m == absolute) || (a_m == offset))
        set_bit_field(code,15,16,lit_val);
}
```

/* Operands may either be coded as registers in bits 24 .. 22 or
   as registers of other types of operand references in bits
   21 .. 0. Operands are classified as source or destination operands.
   Bit 25 is used to indicate where source and destination operands
   are coded. If it is set then the destination operand is coded in
   bits 21 .. 0. This function builds the operand codes
*/

```c
void set_operands(unsigned long int * code,struct instruction i)
{
    if (i.opand1.a_m == gen_reg)
    {
        (*code)|=0x02000000; /* set bit 25 if source is register*/
        set_bit_field(code,24,3,i.opand1.reg);
    }
    else
        build_effective_address(code,i.opand1.a_m,i.opand1.reg,
                     i.opand1.lit_val);

    if (i.no_of_opands == 2)
        if (i.opand1.a_m == gen_reg)
            build_effective_address(code,i.opand2.a_m,i.opand2.reg,
                         i.opand2.lit_val);
        else
            set_bit_field(code,24,3,i.opand2.reg);
}

/* This function provides the interface to this module. It takes as
   its argument a value of type instruction and returns the instruction
   coded as a 32 bit unsigned long int. */

unsigned long int build_code(struct instruction i)
{
    unsigned long int code = 0;
    set_op_code(&code,i);
    if (i.no_of_opands) set_operands(&code,i);
    return code;
}

/*
void display_instruction(FILE * f,unsigned long int code)
{
    fprintf(f,"op_code             = %d\n",get_bit_field(code,31,6));
    fprintf(f,"source-destination bit = %d\n",get_bit_field(code,25,1));
    fprintf(f,"register            = %d\n",get_bit_field(code,24,3));
    fprintf(f,"address mode        = %d\n",get_bit_field(code,21,3));
    fprintf(f,"address register    = %d\n",get_bit_field(code,18,3));
    fprintf(f,"absolute addr/literal = %d\n",get_bit_field(code,15,16));
}

void display_code()
{
    int i;
    FILE * code_file = fopen("MCODE","w");
```

```
        for (i = 0;i < p_c;i ++) display_instruction (code_file,mem[i]);
} */


main()
{
    struct instruction i;
    unsigned long int code;
    open_source();
    do
        {
        i=analyse_instruction();
        if (directive(i.o_c)) process_directive(i);
        else save_code(build_code(i));
        }
    while (i.o_c!=end);

    if (!get_error_count())
        {
            call_load(i.opand1.lit_val);
            interpret();
        }
    printf("\nexecution complete\n");
}
```

Appendix 3

ASCII Character Codes

The codes 0 ... 31 and 127 are associated with non-printable characters. These are not included in the list below. Among them is the code for '\n' which has the value 10.

Character	ASCII code in decimal	Character	ASCII code in decimal	Character	ASCII code in decimal
space	32	@	64	`	96
!	33	A	65	a	97
"	34	B	66	b	98
#	35	C	67	c	99
$	36	D	68	d	100
%	37	E	69	e	101
&	38	F	70	f	102
'	39	G	71	g	103
(	40	H	72	h	104
)	41	I	73	i	105
*	42	J	74	j	106
+	43	K	75	k	107
,	44	L	76	l	108
-	45	M	77	m	109
.	46	N	78	n	110
/	47	O	79	o	111
0	48	P	80	p	112
1	49	Q	81	q	113
2	50	R	82	r	114
3	51	S	83	s	115
4	52	T	84	t	116
5	53	U	85	u	117
6	54	V	86	v	118
7	55	W	87	w	119
8	56	X	88	x	120
9	57	Y	89	y	121
:	58	Z	90	z	122
;	59	[	91	{	123
<	60	\	92			124
=	61	]	93	}	125
>	62	^	94	~	126
?	63	_	95		

Index